Enjoy!
You have been a
good friend,

Robert M. Alvey

ROBERT ALVEY

THE RULEBOOK FOR PERFECT DADDYHOOD

Copyright © 2021 by Robert Alvey

THE RULEBOOK FOR PERFECT DADDYHOOD

All rights reserved.
No part of this publication may be reproduced or transmitted
in any form or by any means electronic or mechanical, including photocopy,
recording, or any information storage and retrieval system now known
or invented, without permission in writing from the publisher, except by a reviewer
who wishes to quote brief passages in connection with a review written
for inclusion in a magazine, newspaper, or broadcast.

Print ISBN: 978-1-66780-353-1
eBook ISBN: 978-1-66780-354-8

Printed in the United States of America

INTRODUCTION BY ROB ALVEY

I want to start off this introduction by simply thanking you for buying this book. I am confident that you will enjoy reading the humorous stories of the many experiences I have had during my unexpected and unplanned life as a "Daddy"- a role I am fully aware I have been unsuited for. I wrote these incidents down as potential lessons for all couples who are either anticipating a new baby or are already exhausted by trying to raise their children. My empathy to all those who are wondering whether it would have been better to just get a puppy instead. I keep wondering about that myself.

Based on my personal experience, I am a firm believer in the 'Afterlife'. Why do I conclude that? It was only a few weeks after the birth of my first child, Alexis Aileen, when the epiphany sunk into my exhausted and quickly shrinking brain that "MY LIFE", as I knew it, has ended and I was now on the journey of my "AFTERLIFE"! I was now assigned a role which was completely foreign and scary, and one that I had no interest or experience in doing. My previous life as part of a "couple" had ended. My nights of accompanying my lovely and sexy wife into Manhattan and Long Island discos, bars, and partying until dawn had ended. Our quiet romantic nights alone in our house were over. My long-term wife, the love of my life (and my high school sweetheart), was no longer the same person I had been with for over 14 years. We had both been suddenly and mysteriously replaced simply because of a small 7-pound newcomer who had arrived.

We had now been assigned the strange and unexpected roles as "Mommy" and "Daddy". I had no experience in this role whatsoever. My wife, in contrast, had regularly assumed the "Mommy" duties in her own household while growing up. She was the oldest of the 5 children in her family and readily accepted the role as necessary to help her younger siblings survive in a rather dysfunctional family. She did her best even though this was purely a volunteer job, and she never received any financial compensation for her efforts. She did earn good money from her early childcare skills through babysitting neighborhood children.

On the opposite side of the spectrum, I was the youngest of 2 children in a very quiet and stable family and had no experience with children, other than observing the 4 boys my older, and only, sister was struggling to raise. I had always been glad to quickly return to my quiet home after visiting with them with my parents…and so were my parents. The boys were just being typical boys, and maybe a wee bit rambunctious. The main conclusion I came to was that I'd try to avoid having any children until I was about 50 and, after reaching that age, might decide to simply die rather than face life trying to raise a child.

The stories in this book are all true. Each and every one of them. It is also my personal biography of the decades I have had in my life since accepting this assigned role and became a Daddy. I'm glad I have a sense of humor. Each of my 3 daughters has enjoyed my writing and have let me know they love reading my stories about their experiences growing up with me. Many of them were published in a local community newspaper, "*The Garden City News*" and I even received letters from readers thanking me for my entertaining stories and enquiring how the girls were doing. I'd write them back telling the reader that I had submitted the stories because I was simply desperate and needed the $35.00 payment I received for each article to financially survive trying to raise the girls.

THE RULEBOOK FOR PERFECT DADDYHOOD

TABLE OF CONTENTS

CHAPTER 1.	THE ART AND SCIENCE OF DADDYING	1
CHAPTER 2.	QUEST OF THE PRINCESS PONY TOYS	5
CHAPTER 3.	DADDY'S WOODSHOP	10
CHAPTER 4.	POLITENESS RULES AND DADDYHOOD	13
CHAPTER 5.	FOUND MONEY	17
CHAPTER 6.	THE CHICKEN POX BLUES AND DADDYHOOD	21
CHAPTER 7.	DADDY'S GARDEN PLOT	26
CHAPTER 8.	DIAPERS AND DADDYHOOD	35
CHAPTER 9.	BRING YOUR DAUGHTER TO WORK DAY	40
CHAPTER 10.	DADDY'S DREAM CATCHER NIGHTMARE	46
CHAPTER 11.	DOCUMENTING DADDYHOOD	53
CHAPTER 12.	THE LAUNDRY DAY DEMON	60
CHAPTER 13.	DADDYHOOD AND THE HARD TRUTHS	65
CHAPTER 14.	BIRTHDAYS AND DADDYDUMB	74
CHAPTER 15.	DADDY AND THE SANTAHOODS	81
CHAPTER 16.	THE CAREER GAME AND DADDYHOOD	88
CHAPTER 17.	DADDY GETS VOLUNTEERED	94
CHAPTER 18.	SOCCER DAD	98
CHAPTER 19.	SWAMP STOMPING WITH DADDY	105
CHAPTER 20.	DADDY GETS COOKED	112
CHAPTER 21.	CONVERSING ON DADDYHOOD	119
CHAPTER 22.	DADDY'S SHOCKING SHOPPING SAGA	126
CHAPTER 23.	DADDY GETS PLAYED OUT	131
CHAPTER 24.	DADDY GETS TREED	137
CHAPTER 25.	BIG SISTER AND DADDYHOOD	143
CHAPTER 26.	SANTADAD.COM	149
CHAPTER 27.	DRESSING UP DADDYHOOD	157
CHAPTER 28.	POKEYDAD 2000	165
CHAPTER 29.	DADDYHOOD AND PETS	171
CHAPTER 30.	ENCORE FOR DADDY	179
CHAPTER 31.	THE ITALIAN TRIP AND DADDYHOOD	185
CHAPTER 32.	DADDY'S CHRISTMAS TRADITIONS	192
CHAPTER 33.	THE BIG '50" AND DADDYHOOD	200
CHAPTER 34.	DADDYHOOD AND THE ENERGY SUCKING SOFA	207
CHAPTER 35.	PROFESSOR DADDY AND THE STARS	214
CHAPTER 36.	DRIVING AND DADDYHOOD	221
CHAPTER 37.	A DIFFERENT YEAR FOR DADDYHOOD	228
CHAPTER 38.	THE MASTER OF DADDYHOOD	233

CHAPTER 39. DADDY'S NOT DONE AT 21 240
CHAPTER 40. DADDYHOOD AND THE CURSE OF THE FIVE BUCKS 245
CHAPTER 41. INSIGHT AND DADDYHOOD 250
CHAPTER 42. DADDYHOOD AND THE MIDDLE CHILD 257
CHAPTER 43. A DISTRACTING YEAR FOR DADDYHOOD 265
CHAPTER 44. PENGUINS AND DADDYHOOD 273
CHAPTER 45. DADDYHOOD AND THE OFFICIAL NASSAU
          COUNTY BIRD 278
CHAPTER 46. FLIGHT PLAN FOR DADDYHOOD 287
CHAPTER 47. THANKSGIVING AND DADDYHOOD 293
CHAPTER 48. HAIR-RAISING TIMES FOR DADDYHOOD 301
CHAPTER 49. BOXES AND DADDYHOOD 309
CHAPTER 50. DADDYHOOD GETS SET-UP, A CHRISTMAS STORY 314
CHAPTER 51. A MINOR DETAIL AND DADDYHOOD 321
CHAPTER 52. KERMIT THE FROG AND DADDYHOOD 328
CHAPTER 53. DADDYHOOD, THE CAR, AND THE CAT 334
CHAPTER 54. THE ENDING OF DADDYHOOD 340
CHAPTER 55. WEATHERING THE STORM AND DADDYHOOD 347
CHAPTER 56. FURLOUGHED AND DADDYHOOD 356
CHAPTER 57. LUCKY PENNY AND ME 361
CHAPTER 58. THE LAST OF MONGAUP POND AND DADDYHOOD 370

DEDICATION

This book is dedicated to a very special woman in my life. Her name is Suzanne Beth Los Kamp Alvey. She has shared and been a part of my life for many years. She is truly a wonderful person with a great smile, a great work ethic, and a deep love of family. She has also been able, somehow, to put up with me for decades. I correctly refer to her in this book as "The Mommygoddess" or "The Advice Queen" and am truly thankful that she did her best with all her talent to love to our children and for the tremendous efforts she put in raising each of them. And trying to raise me. Suzie defines the meaning of family.

This book is also dedicated to my three individual daughters, Alexis Aileen, Erin Claire, and Kathleen Carolyn (K.C.) each of whom has been individually told many times in private, "You are my favorite child. Just don't let your sisters know." My nickname for each of them is Princess, and not merely because I kept mixing up their names. They know who their Dad(dy) is… and put up with me anyway.

An additional dedication is to Meg Morgan, the long-time editor of "*The Garden City News*" – weekly community newspaper. She understands "family" and has been a gracious supporter of my writing.

PUBLIC NOTICE:

The characters in this compendium are based on actual people (or dogs) who have been part of Robert Maurice Alvey's "family" and are a source of some of the influences on his unique personality quirks. Much of the rest is self-inflicted. My sincere sympathies are extended to my daughters Alexis, Erin, and K.C. for not confessing I had misplaced my assigned copy of '*The Rulebook for Perfect Daddyhood*' instructions which forced me in desperation to try to simply "wing it" for many years. The stories- sadly, are absolutely all true.

CHAPTER 1

THE ART AND SCIENCE OF DADDYING

According to my wife, I flunked the Adult Education course, Fatherhood Planning 101. Actually, I don't know whether taking a course or classes on "Daddying" would have done much good. I'm not afraid to admit I didn't really want to be a "Daddy". Before becoming a father, I could think of no rational answer to why any man would want to have a baby. I was quite sure that if men and women were somehow suddenly biologically reversed by a malevolent God, the entire population of the world would die out in one generation. My idea of "sharing the birth process" was that if my wife went into labor, I would immediately fly to Florida to wait for a postcard that she was done, and it was finally safe to come home.

These feelings were carefully nurtured for the first 30 years of my life. I did not have much experience around babies or little kids. I usually refer to myself as an only child, which really gets my sister upset. What I mean by the words "only child" was that I was the youngest child and that my older sister got married and moved out just as I became a teenager. I had just reached the height and weight where I could finally knock her down, but she knew it and left. During the few years we lived in the same house, my sister's favorite name for me was "Pest", followed by her equally favorite expression "Vamoose!"

I loved my parents and had an enjoyable and happy childhood. Still, it did not adequately prepare me for eventual fatherhood. Our house was quiet. Both of my parents were only children, so I had no cousins to grow up with. I have no recollection of diapers, spit-up, or major sibling fights. The only "baby" was me, and I was raised to "please grow up quick".

My father was almost 50 when I was born, and I think he would have preferred it if I was born as a 20-year-old. In this "traditional household", raising children was the primary responsibility of my mother. My father's life philosophy was "If you have a problem, go see your mother. If you want to play poker, come see me." I remember how my dad dutifully volunteered to be an umpire the one year I was in Little League, and how relieved he was when other fathers volunteered in his place for overnight camping during my Boy Scout years.

When I was fourteen, he carefully told me the "facts of life" and offered to give me $1,000 if I waited until I was 30 to get married. "Wow," I thought, "this is the same guy who only charged me $50 bucks when he found out I started to smoke cigarettes. I guess marriage might wait..." I was 16 when my father retired. He and my mother promptly relocated to Florida leaving me in New York with a part time job and orders to "Finish school - and do good!"

Even though I grew up in the turbulent 1960's, I managed to successfully court and marry my steady high school sweetheart, Suzie. Suzie and I dated for almost seven years before we married. Our relationship has always been a good one and I consider her my best friend. The aspect of having children was frequently discussed but was actively avoided both during our courtship and for the first eight years of our marriage.

Suzie and I were very happy as a "couple", each pursuing our careers and shared interests, vacation trips, and our lives as equals. Children were something we knew we were expected to have, but we kept putting off that commitment for "maybe five years in the future." I hoped I could stall long enough so that my eventual child would be born when I was fifty. Suzie reminded me, however, that she would also be fifty and she was not seriously going to wait that long before having a baby.

Suzie was the oldest of five children and was designated as "Mommy II" in a very raucous and somewhat dysfunctional family. By necessity, she had lots of experience and training in organizing, nurturing, caring, healing, and other "Mommy Arts and Sciences". She was constantly surrounded by younger brothers and sister with at least one sniffling nose or diaper that needed changing.

In spite of her vast experience and expertise as Mommy II, when my wife became pregnant after 8 years of marriage, our house suddenly overflowed with books on "*How to Be a Mother*". Suzie bought every book and magazine on prenatal instruction, infant care, childcare, and parenting. She devoured each book and even had her girlfriends give her written tests. I felt as if she were gearing up for her doctoral dissertation in Mommyology.

She continually tried to force feed me information which she felt I would surely need to be a successful Daddy. I was resistant. I did skim through one book I recommend, "*The Art of Fathering*" - the book has cartoon illustrations showing a safe way to flip your child up into the air without breaking their neck. That seemed practical, but I had not had too much success with the previous book I'd read, "*Juggling for the Complete Klutz*". My personal view was that no amount of "Fatherhood Planning" would ever be enough to address all of the countless variables of life. I preferred to rely on my own self confidence and "wing it".

3

Ten years and three babies later, I realized I was wrong. I should have waited until I was 60. It's Grandparents who have the most fun with children. If the children cry or start to fight, Grandparents can just get up and leave the mess to the Mommy and Daddy.

There is no "Rulebook for Perfect Daddyhood", but there sure is a need for one. I even checked the local library myself, but the reference librarian gave me back my reserve card request. "Sorry, we don't have any book by that title, why don't you check the Science Fiction and Fantasy section?" (I did, but no luck there either...) I love being "Daddy" to our three girls and I honestly do my best to be a "Good Daddy". Still, I know I need lessons from the missing "Rulebook for Perfect Daddyhood". Other Daddies I've talked with have the same hopeless look in their eyes. We all need help, and none of us has a copy of the Rulebook. As a desperate gesture, I've put together this book as a guide. It's full of mistakes, and examples of Daddyhood deeds where things don't quite work out. Before I throw up a white flag, give up being Daddy, and decide to just go bowling with the guys the rest of my life, I'm going to try to write enough "stuff" I've learned to help other new Dads out. I'm cramming for a lifetime of tests on being a dad, but as each month ends, I seem to come to the same conclusion - "Mommy's PERFECT, and Daddy's learned another lesson."

CHAPTER 2

QUEST OF THE PRINCESS PONY TOYS

An important duty outlined in the "Rulebook for Perfect Daddyhood" is for Daddy to play with his children. I'm sure that even cavemen followed this rule and spent time playing "pick-up-sticks" with their cave-kids. At least those sticks were free, and a cave-urchin could collect as many sticks as he wanted without Daddy having to get a second mortgage on the cave.

Times have changed. So have toys. I'm a Daddy to three lovely daughters. Before our first daughter was born, our house was comfortable and amply sized for my wife and my use. The house had closets with close-able doors. I could walk barefoot through the rooms without fear of impaling my sole on a Lilliputian plastic spiked shoe or two-inch pony bridle. I never had to empty a zillion boxes or look under every piece of furniture in the universe on a search and rescue mission for a "lost" doll so my daughter could stop crying and go to bed.

The American advertising industry has instilled a subliminal message deep into the reptilian brain of each child - "**BUY THIS TOY**". From the day the child is born, an eternal quest is begun to own every toy in the universe. Boys and girls across the nation spend their entire childhood trying to fulfill this cranially "etch-a-sketched" goal. A child's status is

5

apparently determined by how extensive and costly the toy collection is. Daddies, however, spend their time trying to avoid bankruptcy without permanently damaging their child's social status and psyche.

A decade ago, as a new Daddy, I had good intentions and plans to play as much as possible with my new child. I remembered my own childhood adventures with countless toy army men, Tinker toys, cowboys and Indians, model trains, and especially the Little Wizard Deluxe Chemistry Set. The chemistry set was given to me by my Uncle Edgar who was subsequently prohibited from giving me any "non-Mommy-approved" gifts after I used the chemistry set to melt our family dog while playing The Wizard of Oz. (Hey, what did I know? I was a boy!)

My nostalgic reveries of playing with toys as a boy did not, unfortunately, prepare me for three daughters, Barbie dolls, or My Little Pony. When my first daughter, Alexis, was two, one of her cousins gave her a My Little Pony - a soft plastic, horse shaped toy about six inches high. The toy looked innocent enough. It was pink bodied with blue nylon mane and tail "hairs" and a small design imprinted on its hindquarters which represented its name, "Windy", in some language only a two-year-old could decipher. Windy also came with a short, silky ribbon and a plastic comb. At cost of five bucks, I thought it was fairly priced. In retrospect, I probably would have saved money if Alexis had received the actual Budweiser Clydesdales instead. At least that way I could see what was eating my money.

Alexis was delighted by Windy, and she spent hours braiding and combing its hair. Alexis and I played with Windy together, although I could never manage to tie the frustratingly short ribbon into a bow for Windy's tail. I did manage to teach Alexis how to neigh like a horse and we had fun playing. A few weeks later, however, Alexis and I were at a toy store when I happened to pass an aisle with a My Little Pony display. Alexis saw the display and immediately stopped and gasped. The racks were filled with all sorts of My Little Ponies in a variety of colors and names.

"I want that!" Alexis proclaimed with a determined look in her eyes. "OK, Princess," I naively replied, and I stupidly purchased her second My Little Pony, "Ribbon". I didn't know that the two My Little Ponies would breed. A few months later, I noticed that Alexis had eight My Little Ponies, including eight frustratingly short ribbons and eight brushes. Alexis knew all of the ponies' names and she spent countless hours brushing pony hair and tying pony ribbons. Since I flunked ribbon tying and couldn't get their names straight, my assigned task during "pony playtime" was as designated "Monster" whereby I would kidnap and imprison stray ponies until Alexis and her fearless pony herd could sneak over and free them.

The manufacturing gremlins continued to introduce endless new versions of the My Little Pony horde. Alexis continued to buy each one. Christmas brought an endless parade of My Little Ponies and Pony paraphernalia to our home. Alexis "wanted it all". Her insatiable pony appetite was fed with Big Sister ponies, Princess ponies, Newborn ponies, Dance and Prance ponies, Mother and Daughter ponies, and Baby Twin ponies - each costing "a mere five dollars".

The marketing demons showed no mercy. The following year "Pony Clothes" were introduced, and I was doomed. I still couldn't correctly tie any of the microscopic lengths of pony ribbons, so I was hopelessly inept at trying to button a two-inch jacket over a three-inch pony chest. In compromise, I bought Alexis the prohibitively extravagant Paradise Pony Estate - a five-foot-wide pink plastic pony "dollhouse", complete with pool and pony furniture.

Alexis soon was on a quest to own the entire My Little Pony City. The My Little Pony Castle, My Little Pony Nursery, My Little Pony Ice Cream Parlor, and My Little Pony Beauty Parlor avalanched into our house. Each plastic building cost more than my first car. My daughter became founding member of the Long Island My Little Pony Fan Club and I secretly began to scour toy stores for another Little Wizard Deluxe

Chemistry Set. I was tempted to play The Wizard of Oz again and melt the My Little Ponies to try and stop the onslaught.

My Little Ponyitis lasted for eight long years. Alexis's two younger sisters also succumbed to the disease and have their own collections of My Little Ponies. It took awhile, but I finally found a way to tolerate playing 'My Little Pony' with my girls. I made a large racetrack, and we have My Little Pony races using dice to count how many spaces each pony runs. Parimutuel betting is allowed, and so far, Daddy's up 260 My Little Pony dollars for the season.

The 1993 Christmas season was nearly a disaster. When I went to the local toy store, the usual mile wide My Little Pony display was ominously gone!!! The 15,000 varieties of pink and blue plastic My Little Ponies were no longer for sale!! Alexis was heartbroken, but not yet defeated. She wrote a letter of protest to Hasbro Company's President. "I like My Little Ponies! Make more ponies! My sisters and I will buy them all! signed -- Alexis."

Alexis insisted that other stores might still have My Little Ponies. During one dinner, she politely asked me if we could drive to Missouri since she had heard that a store there was selling My Little Ponies. She seemed to think I wasn't being reasonable when I politely declined to drive 2,000 miles that very night. Meanwhile, I scoured every toy store, department store, discount store, and pet shop on Long Island for the last remaining supply of My Little Ponies. I finally found four dusty My Little Pony refugees in the back shelf of Ahkmed's Cheep Discount shop in Brooklyn and rescued them.... I mean I bought them, bent and faded boxes and all.

Hasbro, perhaps recognizing that Alexis was a super loyal customer, and personally responsible for a ten-point swing in their stock price, sent her two letters apologizing for canceling the My Little Pony line. They also sent her two samples of their new line, "Magic Meadow Ponies". AAARRRGGGHHH!!!!!!! I thought, here we go again! Alexis, however, was not impressed with Magic Meadow Ponies--- they did not hold the same fixation as My Little Ponies. Still, she finally accepted the fact that there would be no more new My Little Ponies. I thought she would be depressed for a month or so, then go on to something new.

I was wrong, (again). A few weeks later I noticed the following advertisement in our local newspaper: "WANTED - MY LITTLE PONIES. TO BUT OR ADOPT. CONTACT ALEXIS." Oh, good grief, I thought, she's finally gone off the deep end. I was about to scold her for wasting her time and money on a classified ad for used My Little Ponies when the phone rang. The caller was another 11-year-old with several My Little Ponies of her own!!!! Alexis and Jennifer made plans to get together and share pony tales.

Later that evening, Alexis got another phone call - this time from a woman who had been planning on selling a box full of My Little Ponies at a garage sale, and would Alexis be interested in adopting them instead? The calls and responses continued. Within a few weeks time, Alexis had met three other girls with the same My Little Ponyitis addiction, and had bought 35 more My Little Ponies as a result of the ad. I'm taking lessons from Alexis's success. Next month I'm having my own classified ad printed, "Wanted - Electric Trains or the Little Wizard Deluxe Chemistry Set -- To adopt or buy. Contact Robert."

CHAPTER 3

DADDY'S WOODSHOP

I've been a Daddy for ten years and I still can't find the guidebook that explains what a Daddy is supposed to do. One of the unwritten rules in the "Rulebook for Perfect Daddyhood" is that Daddy is supposed to have a woodworking shop. Daddy is also supposed to have a vast array of tools that he proudly displays on a peg board mounted in the garage or basement. Daddy is also required to spend evenings and weekends in his woodshop building perfect soapbox cars or doll houses with his children. These precious mementos are then supposed to be passed lovingly from generation to generation as a testament of "Daddy's love."

My list of hobbies and interests has never included wood shop. My own dad had a small woodworking shop in the basement, but I have no fond memories of working with him on any project. I do remember the strings of curses and expletives that echoed through the house whenever he happened to hit his finger with a hammer or cut himself with a saw or screwdriver. Dad could not be considered an "expert craftsman" and these accidents seemed to occur whenever he was sentenced by mom to the basement workshop dungeon to fix something.

It never dawned on me that the "Rulebook for Perfect Daddyhood" included mandatory woodshop. I was, however, warned that someday it would be my turn to take over this role as "Daddy fix it". At the time my wife and I bought our first house, we had no children. The house came with an elaborate woodshop in the basement including the obligatory peg board. I distinctly remember the former owner proudly showing me his woodshop area. He cautioned me that he was planning to remove his "vise" from the workbench and take it with him when he moved out. "Vise?" I replied, "Sure, go ahead and take it, I'm trying to cut down on my vices anyway."

The woodshop remained unused for the first eight years we lived in the house. We used the area to store countless boxes of used boy's clothing that my sister kept giving my wife and me. My sister had four boys (which, incidentally, was a major factor in my own efforts postpone having children). As the youngest boy outgrew a hand-me-down pair of pants or jacket, my sister would put it in a box and pass it on to me with a note, "You will need these someday, won't you?" …….. God sort of heard my prayers against having children and my wife and I eventually had three daughters. (I think I was tricked!)

With the birth of our first daughter, Alexis, I was given the new title "Daddy". Shortly thereafter, my wife donated the boxes of boy's clothes to charity and, upon rediscovering the woodshop, reminded me that my duty as a father included woodworking. She began to plan elaborate rocking horses and dollhouses for me to construct. I began plans to sell the house.

Eventually, we compromised. "Mommy" and "Daddy" worked together to construct "BIG LAMBY". My wife's artistic talents were put to creative use. She designed an intricate, large, wheeled, wooden, lamb-shaped wagon, covered in sheepskin. The goal was to build Big Lamby strong and sturdy enough for Alexis to ride. Daddy was to then pull Big Lamby along the sidewalks so that all of our neighbors could see our beautiful child atop Daddy's masterpiece of expertise woodworking.

11

I was sentenced to the woodshop dungeon and began to construct Big Lamby after wiping out my savings account to purchase various sizes and quantities of lumber. Weeks passed and the sound of sawing and hammering mixed with the echoes of the painkiller curses I had learned from my father. Instead of spending "quality time" with my daughter, I was doomed to pass what seemed like eternity in the basement, bloodying my fingers so I could earn the Daddy Woodworker Merit Badge.

Finally, the day came when I finished this Herculean task and was released from woodshop prison. I dragged Big Lamby outside and placed my darling daughter, Alexis, on the beast's back. My wife carried the trusty video camera and filmed me as I dutifully and proudly pulled Big Lamby and Alexis along the sidewalk. Alexis, however, did not joyfully smile for the camera. She was too busy hanging on for dear life. She held tight, even as Big Lamby's wheels hit a bump in the sidewalk and tipped over. She held tight, even as she cried for Mommy to rescue her. All of these "precious moments" were captured forever on video.

At least I was done with woodshop. Our present home has no garage, no woodworking area in the basement, and no sidewalk. Alexis, her sisters, and I spend our "quality time" outside gardening, while Big Lamby roams the basement in search of new victims.

CHAPTER 4

POLITENESS RULES AND DADDYHOOD

The "Rulebook for Perfect Daddyhood" was originally intended to be a guide to help Daddies rear their children without resorting to spanking their rears or threatening to quit the Daddy career. Spanking or fleeing the scene are not appropriate courses of action for Daddies. Society has certain rules that should be followed. Some of these rules are written laws - "Thou shalt not kill", "Thou shalt not steal", etc. These types of written laws are fairly clear cut and help children and Daddies learn "right" from "wrong". In spite of a growing number of prison inmates, most people obey written laws and understand the penalties for breaking them.

There are other types of laws for "acceptable" social behavior that are much less clear. Some of these "laws" aren't even written down and the penalties for breaking these laws vary considerably. For lack of a better term, these laws are called "Politeness Rules". Politeness rules are laws of behavior that, while they make absolutely no sense, and may seem illogical, must be obeyed, and followed or you risk supreme but unspeci fied punishment. If a Daddy can get his children to accept politeness rules, he will be considered a success as a Daddy. That's one of the first politeness rules.

13

Having three growing daughters, I have firsthand experience in the importance of politeness rules. There are five people living in our house, and only two bathrooms. There was not much of a problem with sharing a bathroom when the girls were babies. As babies, they were not entitled too much privacy anyway. Any of us could heed nature's calling as necessary as long as a seat was available. While I don't frequently romp around the living room naked, if I happened to be in the bathroom "doing my thing" the girls could come and go as they pleased.

This "necessary bathroom politeness" rule with the babies ended immediately if I caught any of the girls staring or giggling. Our oldest daughter was either oblivious to our physical differences or very sneaky. She was allowed to share the bathroom with Daddy until she was seven. Our middle daughter, Erin, seemed innocent but confused. She kept trying to pee standing up until she was four. Apparently, Mommy had a long talk with her because one day she burst into the bathroom with a gale of laughter while I was "standing" and was immediately banished.

Erin broke the "politeness rule" and then compounded it. The next day, while I was again "draining the dragon", I heard a small scraping sound behind me. I turned my head around to find that K.C., my two-year-old and definitely last but not least daughter, had dragged her "potty stool" over, sat down right behind me, and was quietly but intently looking between my legs. This was the end of the shared bathroom privilege and the start of the new politeness rule "Knock Before You Open the Door".

It took awhile before this new rule sunk in. Little girls in particular still needed help getting dressed and buttoning up after going to the bathroom. Blame the sadistic fashion designers that place all the buttons on a dress or blouse on the back side where it's impossible to reach. Erin, still four years old and existing under a Daddy threat to never live to see her fifth birthday, quickly realized she could no longer be in the bathroom alone with Daddy. One Sunday, our family was at an after-church service coffee hour in the church parlor. Out of the corner of my eye, I vaguely noticed Erin disappear into the adjoining bathroom while wearing her Victorian style, buttons-up-the-back, formal dress with petticoat and tights. I continued to stand and talk with pastor's wife.

A few minutes later, I noticed that everyone in the parlor had suddenly stopped talking, and that pastor's wife seemed a bit oddly stiff. Then, I felt a polite small tapping on my back. I politely turned around, and there politely stood Erin... with her Victorian style, buttons-up-the-back formal dress, petticoat, and tights politely draped over her arm. Erin simply but politely handed me her panties and said, "I'm done". So was coffee hour. So was my term as a trustee.

We had an easier time with the politeness rule on picking one's nose. There's no written law against it, and it might seem an illogical rule if something's stuck up your nose. However, politeness rules say that it's wrong to pick your nose (except when you're along in your car driving at high speed). Picking your nose, sticking anything up your nose, and getting caught, are serious violations of politeness rules and the punishment is eternal social ostracism.

I prevented this nosey problem by telling my daughters about their Uncle Perry, my wife's younger brother. When he was in third grade, he thought he had been seen picking his nose in the school cafeteria and tried to conceal his actions. Unfortunately, Uncle Perry was never too bright. In a desperate but misguided attempt to distract the onlookers, he somehow stuffed a French fry up his nose. His classmates definitely noticed this. The French fry got stuck up there and finally sprouted until his whole head turned into a potato plant. I explained to the girls that this was very embarrassing for Mommy's whole family and twenty years later Uncle Perry was still referred to as Mr. Potato Head. His invitation to his class reunion was even addressed "Dear Spud".

A similar politeness rule is a ban on scratching your groin or rear in public. This ban is illogical - after all an itch is an itch, and Daddies commonly scratch their heads in wonder trying to figure out why and when they ever decided to be parents. Still, there is a formally imposed mandate against scratching or otherwise rubbing "private parts". The only ones exempt from this ban are professional baseball players. In fact, it's mentioned in their contracts and some even get a bonus if they are seen scratching themselves on television. This is probably why so many boys want to be ball players when they grow up.

Some politeness rules defy all logic. We raise our daughters to always tell the truth. Why then, did we insist that they tell Grandma "Thank-you for the Christmas Gift" when she actually gave them each a 1978 vintage plastic key chain which she probably got from 7-11 as a freebie when she stopped in the store to read a newspaper off the rack. Politeness rules dictate that you appreciate each gift and thank Grandma for all of the cheap junk. Hey, I didn't complain (to her anyway) when she gave me a sock... and promised to give me the matching one for my birthday.

Anyway, God bless Grandma. At least she follows the politeness rule of not visiting a friend or relative empty handed. My wife is also a strict adherent to this politeness rule. I couldn't understand my wife's insistence on bringing food or a gift when visiting until she explained that she learned this rule while growing up at home. Her family was more than a little disorganized. Unless the guest brought over food, her mother kept forgetting to cook dinner. I didn't believe this until I remembered when I had Thanksgiving dinner at my future in-law's house while I was still courting my fated wife. The only food we were served was macaroni and cheese and the individually wrapped Saltine crackers which my mom had picked up from the local diner three years earlier. Mom had told me it wasn't polite to go empty handed.

CHAPTER 5

FOUND MONEY

The "Rulebook for Perfect Daddyhood" stresses that one of the secrets to being a successful father is to have mutual interests with your children. If both Daddy and child share an interest in a hobby or activity, a lifelong bond can be established. The key to success in this endeavor is to persuade the child to have an interest in something Daddy actually likes to do. Mommy, however, will remind Daddy that smoking, drinking, gambling, and attending nude mud wrestling competitions are not interests to be shared with children no matter how much Daddy enjoys them.

In an effort to find a more practical and positive interest, my thoughts turned to money and time. Most hobbies cost money, and it seems the more time you invest in a hobby, the more money it costs. This Daddy doesn't have much money and I needed to think of a hobby or interest that wouldn't strain either my bankbook or back. I have three daughters, ages ten (going on 24), six (going on 16), and three (going on 2 again). The selected activity had to be simple enough for my three-year-old to do, interesting enough for my ten-year-old to want to do, as well as funky enough for my "teenaged" sixteen- year- old to admit to be doing. Tough choice.

The proposed interest came to me in a burst of creative inspiration. Why not have the girls help me get more money? This seemed like the perfectly logical solution. After all, I have an interest in money and I spend a lot of time trying to get more money. Furthermore, I could certainly support the girls' interest in earning money rather than spending it. I discussed this proposed "hobby" with the girls. Their reactions surprised me.

Alexis, my ten-year-old, was enthusiastic. She immediately made plans to order the Wall Street Journal and asked if we could subscribe to Forbes and Money Magazine. Erin, six and fast approaching her teens, suggested we raise money by selling her three-year-old sister for medical research testing purposes. K.C., the three-year-old potential research lab project, objected and flatly stated she already had money. What? "How did you get this money, K.C.?" we asked. With a devilishly proud gleam in her eyes, she replied, "It's mine 'cause I found it!" BINGO! Found Money!

Whether you are an adult or a child, "found money" has a mystique all of its own. Readers are always entranced by newspaper stories of crowds scrambling after bags of cold hard cash blown off the back of an armored bank truck. Television viewers love to see coverage of kids who find thousands of dollars in old bank notes while playing in a vacant lot. "Found Money". Found money makes us feel good. Ever find a $20 dollar bill? I did once, and almost was able to actually spend it myself until my psychic wife took one look at me when I came home and said, "My, aren't you happy today, what happened, did you find some money?" I had to hand it over. At least she bought me a small bag of Doritos as a reward.

The children and I readily agreed that finding money had merit as a mutual interest, and we established ground rules on how to play the "found money" game. Since it was close to January 1, we agreed to save all of our "findings" for an entire year and split the proceeds evenly the following New Year's Day. We set aside a special piggy bank to hold our accumulated "riches" and the girls made me promise not to borrow funds from the bank. (They know me very well!)

A few days later, it was New Year's Day, and I found a nickel while getting milk at the local 7-11. I proudly showed the coin to the girls and put it in the "found money" bank. The girls were suitably impressed and for the rest of the year, whenever Mommy or Daddy went to 7-11, the girls would beg to come. The act of buying milk became a commando raid as the girls literally would burst though the doors and dive beneath the counters in search of change. Shoppers standing near the newspaper rack were frequently elbowed in the knee by pint sized combat veterans on search and find missions for lost cash. The recovered pennies, dimes, and other 7-11 war booty were added to the "found bank" stockpile.

The girls and Daddy held weekly status meetings on our "found money" hobby. Since I walk several blocks during my daily train commute, I began to keep a lookout for lost coins. Surprisingly, Brooklyn streets seem to be a magnet for copper. Almost daily, I would find at least one penny, many times two or three. My daily "coin watch" became addictive. I began to take longer walks if my normal route didn't turn up at least one coin. At least once a month I would bend down to try to pick up the same shiny penny that was embedded in asphalt at the intersection of Flatbush and Fulton Avenues. (It's still there, dammit!)

During the entire year, the girls enjoyed going for walks with Daddy. The days following Halloween were a special treat as the sidewalks and streets around town were littered with pennies and coins - probably dropped by small trick-or-treaters greedily trying to munch down their candy corn and run to the next house for even more candy before it got dark. The girls became experts in "found money". Erin puzzled me by wanting to go for a car ride whenever I brought a company car home from work. It turned out that her special "found money" activity was to search under the government fleet car seats for lost coins - and, I might add, she was doing pretty well. I began to consciously rotate fleet cars for her.

19

Originally, I thought that by the end of the year we might have found barely enough change to be able to buy ice cream cones. By the end of the year, however, the "found bank" was pretty heavy. On New Year's Eve, we emptied the "found bank" onto the bed and spent over an hour counting and rolling pennies and assorted coins. It was a very educational experience. The girls became thoroughly proficient in how many pennies, nickels, dimes, or quarters equal a dollar. Even three-year-old K.C. could tell the difference between a dime and a quarter and she became adept at counting to ten (but kept skipping the number 6). I thought she might have a career future as a government contractor accountant.

Our "findings" for the year totaled $26.72 (after correcting for K.C.'s mishaps with the number 6). I was surprised that the total was so high, and the girls were absolutely ecstatic. Each of them took their fair share of the "found treasure-trove" and promptly high tailed it to the nearest toy store to help the "found money" get back into circulation as soon as possible. Daddy must have made a good suggestion with the "found money" game since the girls all agreed to start the game over again for the next year. However, one change has been made to the rules. This year, Daddy gets an equal share of the find!

CHAPTER 6

THE CHICKEN POX BLUES AND DADDYHOOD

A recent New York Times article discussed the development of a new vaccine for chicken pox. Several pros and cons to the merits of a chicken pox vaccine were presented. The article stressed that chicken pox is a relatively harmless childhood disease that causes no long-lasting health concerns. The primary problem in dealing with a chicken pox outbreak is the stress factor and inconvenience experienced by the parents trying to cope with afflicted children. The newspaper also attributed a significant economic loss to society from parents who had to miss work to stay home with their "pocked" children. This "parental inconvenience" was apparently the driving force to the development of the vaccine.

How true... in fact, this Daddy has just completed a firsthand intensive study on dealing with chicken pox. As an added attraction, this study was initiated on the day before the school year ended and was conducted on multiple subjects - all three of my daughters! The chicken pox plague at our household gave new meaning to the term "inconvenience" and made the words "summer plans" an oxymoron like "army intelligence".

My wife, bless her organized soul, starts making summer plans on February 2, Ground Hog's Day. She meticulously researches every potential summer activity known to Mankind and constructs a detailed schedule in five-minute increments. Our three daughters are "time managed" into swimming lessons, tennis lessons, library reading programs, arts and crafts, the annual four-day family trip to a dude ranch, math and English refresher courses, vacation Bible school, summer nursery school, a plethora of scheduled play dates, cultural enrichment programs, and day trips. Supercomputer Mommy designs a summer schedule that is guaranteed to provide a busy and productive upbringing with no more than five minutes free time allocated per child.

This scheduling instinct is an inherent Mommy art. Daddy is usually more content to just "wing it", relax, and watch the children, flowers, and vegetable grow. (Yes, vegetable. That's not a typo. I only managed to grow one cucumber this year, but gardening's another story...) This year, however, the fates decreed that neither Mommy nor Daddy could plan anything. Actually, it wasn't the "fates", but the working parents of our oldest daughter's classmate. "Doctor" John, a medical student, and "Ditzy" Dawn, a nurse, the parents of a fellow fourth grader, sent their daughter to school with chicken pox because neither of them was willing to take time off from work to stay home with her. Only after the school nurse noticed that the girl was a giant red spot with legs, were the parents forced to take the child elsewhere. I think "Ditzy" then sent the child to Oregon to infect the timberlands.

Meanwhile, the damage was done. On the day before school ended, our oldest daughter, Alexis, showed up at the breakfast table with a new visitor - the "dew drop on a rose petal" trademark signature of a chicken pox. My wife was distraught. I, however, was merely perplexed at her distress. "Honey, chicken pox is a harmless childhood disease. Why are you so upset?", I naively asked. I learned the hard way.

Alexis missed the last two days of school, including the end-of-the-year class party. As she changed from a ten-year-old girl to a pink, living pox factory, Alexis lost much of her appetite. She spent the next several days watching her body grow new appendages and quietly playing in her room. "This isn't so bad," I thought. Alexis liked the oatmeal baths and lotions we smeared on her to ease any itching. The main drawback was racing the clock to see if she could become well soon enough to start her already scheduled swimming lessons.

We had to postpone her summer gymnastics lessons due to the "pox", and several playdates and outings were canceled. Still, Alexis was coping nicely. Her friend Alison, however, also caught the pox and had to miss her dance recital - after a full year's worth of classes and an extra thousand dollars for the dress, invitations to 400 relatives, and a hired video camera technician to record her debut for the other 250 relatives and friends who couldn't make it to the recital. Alison's parents were more than a little upset that their precious daughter had been infected with chicken pox from Ditzy's daughter. They were livid and threatened to unleash a plague on Doctor John and Nurse Ditzy - who, by the way, were now spending their summer vacation leisurely relaxing at a resort in the Bahamas.

No such leisurely relaxing for this Mommy and Daddy, however. Ten days after Alexis's first pink blemish made its conspicuous appearance, both of our other daughters showed the symptoms of chicken pox. Erin, age 6, began her inevitable "Why Me? It's not fair!" routine. She conveniently forgot that I had scolded her the previous week when I noticed her licking Alexis's elbow to catch a stray drip of ice cream. K.C., age 3, also began to resemble either an overripe strawberry or a nuclear accident victim. So much for summer nursery school or tennis lessons.

The girls became prisoners in the house, and it was a psychological torture chamber for Mommy and Daddy. I had to order calamine lotion in 55-gallon drums and cotton balls by the bale. Mommy gave the girls so many oatmeal baths our house began to smell like a restaurant. When we ran out of oatmeal, in desperation we tried farina and Wheatena baths.

Two days later our plumbing backed up after I inadvertently used plaster of Paris in the bathtub.

Even though Alexis was recovering, neither Mommy nor I noticed. We were too tired from the no sleep nights, lotions, and potions. Everyone had cabin fever, made especially worse since during the early days of that July a heat wave visited Long Island and decided to stay. Each day was hot, long, hot, sunny, hot, humid, and hot. Our single window air conditioner became a magnet for everyone in the family and turf wars frequently broke out over cool air rights. K.C. decided that she was too itchy to sleep and spent the next 8 nights prowling around the house saying hello to everyone.

This midnight rambling fatigued both Mommy and Daddy. I finally solved the problem by putting on an 8-hour videotape of cartoons before I went to bed and managed to keep K.C. occupied. "It's Not Fair" Erin, however, also managed to sneak downstairs and watch TV throughout the night with K.C. When I went downstairs the next morning, I discovered that K.C. and Erin had not merely watched TV. K.C.'s body was literally covered and crisscrossed with green magic marker. Bored with the cartoon marathon, Erin had invented a new game to pass the time - "Connect the Pox", using a permanent marker pen and K.C.'s body as a game board.

"I itch" was a constant echoing cry from our household. The girls were continually telling us the strange new places where they had found another chicken pox. Erin couldn't eat for three days after she discovered a "pock" inside her mouth. I believed her at the time, but somehow, this particular chicken pox makes a regular return appearance inside Erin's mouth whenever she has a plate of vegetables to eat. Mysteriously, it seems to disappear if ice cream is served.

Mommy and Daddy were both strung out and worn out. Just when it seemed there was no hope, however, we got a call from my wife's sister. Her five-year-old had the chicken pox the previous year, and she found an excellent way to deal with it. Her secret? Antihistamine and screwdrivers. Give the children safe but generous doses of antihistamines. The drug slows down the itching and also makes the children tired, so they sleep constantly until the disease has run its course. The screwdrivers, also to be taken in generous portions, are so that Mommy and Daddy can relax and sleep until it's over. It sounded like practical advice to me!

Following my sister in law's advice, I don't remember much about the next week. Eventually new chicken pox eruptions ceased, and the girl's bodies began the slow but steady process of healing. The "pox prison" doors of our house were unlocked, and the girls were again allowed to venture outside to enjoy the remaining weeks of summer. The calamine lotion drum was sealed, the plumber rotorooted our bathroom drainpipes, and Mommy and Daddy began to try and restore our wearied psyches. Life was slowly returning to normal until we got a postcard, "Having a wonderful summer!' from Ditzy Dawn in the Bahamas." I plan on coating their doorknob with poison ivy sap before they return home!

CHAPTER 7

DADDY'S GARDEN PLOT

My wife and I have separate household maintenance duties. Inside, she is the General - the Supreme Commander. Being a Mommy to three daughters doesn't even slow this General down -- she just has three more Troopers drafted to follow her commands for a clean and orderly house. There's a designated place and scheduled time for everything. Are the clothes picked up and neatly folded? Yes, General Mommy. Have the toys been put back into the color-coded Tupperware storage boxes when you're done playing? Yes, General Mommy.

Surprisingly, General-Director Mommy's kingdom doesn't extend beyond the outside walls of our house. Outside, Daddy is the Field Marshall. It's my responsibility to keep the lawn semi-green and under three- feet high, commit various trees and shrubs to slow hideous deaths by planting them on our property, and to try and have at least the same amount of flowers as weeds. I am fairly successful with all these tasks, but my wife doesn't really notice. The only time she comments on my gardening prowess is when the neighbors call to complain about my compost heap or if I happen to track some evil dirt onto the rugs when I come inside.

Actually, I am perfectly suited to gardening. I don't mind getting dirty and I love being outdoors. (Especially with all three children in the house vacuuming and polishing.) Do you want me to take out the garbage? Sure, I'd be glad to. I'll be back inside in about four hours. I can't walk across the lawn without stooping over to pull out a stray crabgrass. I fantasize about having unlimited resources to create the Long Island Botanical Gardens in my yard. Having three growing girls, however, doesn't allow me the luxury of much free time or extra cash. I explained the consequences of this cash and time shortage to my lawn and garden. "It's a hard life," I told the shrubs, "If you don't flower or if you need constant watering, you're out-a-here! Fertilizer? Fagetaboudit! Don't think you have to just sit there and look pretty either. Each of you plants has to contribute something to my family or you're mulch!"

For some plants, it was a losing turf war. Each casualty became a resident of my compost heap. One area of lawn mysteriously turned brown and died each summer --- gone! The maple tree became blighted and died----gone! The privet hedge stopped growing and began to look moldy---- gone! The mums grew spindly and refused to flower until two days before the first snowstorm. Gone! The old pear tree only yielded small, green, misshapen balls of concrete. Gone. No mercy. Even the old green apple tree was chain sawed for refusing to stop growing suckers. It went down fighting, however. The squirrel that had been using the tree for its nest relocated to my chimney. I didn't notice until heating season began, and my basement filled with black smoke. I had to call my heating company, then spent a ton of money to get the nest removed. Score one for the plants...and the chief territorial squirrel, Smokey.

No, our property did not become a barren moonscape. I replaced the deadbeats with plants more willing to be helpful to my family. The privet hedge was replaced with a hedge of blueberries. The misshapen pear tree was replaced by dwarf cherry trees. The old sucker-laden apple tree was replaced by two dwarf top-of-the-line varieties. "Smokey" the squirrel was eventually caught and stuffed. The mums were replaced with

27

daffodils that needed no special care yet sent up a beautiful flower every Spring. I even replaced the blighted maples with saplings of larch trees I had dug out of a vacant lot. (As I said, it's hard to save money when raising children.)

The patch of dead lawn almost became my vegetable garden. I dug out all the dead sod from a strip about ten feet long and four feet wide. I spent three entire weekends lining the strip with cobble stones. I also dug out three tons of dirt from the strip to a depth of two feet and backfilled the entire area with my naturally cured, neighborhood famous, compost. I dug, I lifted, I pushed, and I beat the area into a mounded, carefully pre- pared bed in which to nestle a tender crop of tomatoes and cucumbers. My chiropractor was very appreciative of my efforts --- to the tune of $300 for six back treatments.

I was so proud of my work. I went inside the house for the first time in three weeks to get my tray of tenderly nurtured hybrid exotic super sweet Cherry tomato seedlings. I called to my wife and children, "It's Daddy! Girls! Come outside, I want to show you paradise!". I walked out- side and proudly showed them my wonderful, expertly designed, meticu- lously crafted, backbreaking, but glorious vegetable garden. "Ta Dah!", I pointed, and waited for their applause.

There was no applause. For a few minutes, General- Director Mommy and her troops just stood there at attention without saying any- thing. Finally, K.C. -- my youngest daughter, sadly looked up at me and quietly asked, "Daddy, who died?"

I was stunned. Then Mommy slowly asked, "What on earth did you do to the lawn? It looks like you buried someone here. This isn't a vegeta- ble garden - it's a burial plot!"

Well, in retrospect, it did sort of resemble a grave, but I told the girls that as soon as I planted the tomatoes, the vegetable garden would blossom into a thing of beauty. They were unimpressed. K.C. and her sisters fled back into the house to dust the silk flowers, leaving me alone at the mercy of the Mommygoddess's wrath. She inspected my tray of Hybrid Exotic Supersweet Cherry Tomato seedlings. "Don't even think about planting those 'things' in that spot. If you want a vegetable garden, move it over to the edge of the property."

I was crushed. "MOVE IT?!?!? How do I move it? Do you see a handle anywhere on the garden that says, 'LIFT HERE'? I spent a lot of time building this garden, it's not something that can be picked up under the arms and carried around. Where do I plant these spectacular Hybrid Exotic Supersweet Cherry tomato plants?"

The Mommy goddess of doomed plants glanced down and inspected my rare and prized hybrids. "Tomato plants? I thought they were alfalfa sprouts. Just stick your killer tomatoes in the back somewhere."

"JUST STICK THEM IN THE BACK??? Five weeks of work to start the perfect garden and you want me to just stick them in the back?" I pleaded- but it was a lost battle. Two hours later, a group of soon to be pale and spindly Hybrid Exotic Not-so-sweet Cherry tomato plants sadly peered up at me from the deep, dark, fenced back of our property. I felt like Vlad the Impaler as I staked them down-- extra deep to prevent them from crawling back into the light.

Now, what to do with the "family crypt"? I gazed longingly at my condemned vegetable garden. We'd been exiled. I knew how Adam felt when he was locked out of the Garden of Eden. I looked at the cobble-stones ringing the ten-foot by four-foot area. I suddenly got another brilliant idea, build a pond! A genuine backyard pond with a small fountain, filled with crystal clear water, a few lillypads, maybe a frog or two, some fish, and....my mind raced as images of owning waterfront property sailed through my brain. I figured that my daughters would love watching the birds come to the pond to drink and wash. I could create a miniature nature refuge in my own backyard! (Also, I wouldn't have to remove the ring of cobblestones, I'd use them to line the pond instead.)

I did a little research, and discovered a pond kit available, with "all you need" to create a backyard pond. Naively, I bought the kit which had a picture of a crystal clear, rock lined paradise of a lily-flowered pond with happy, healthy fish smiling as they played under the small fountain. I tore open the box to find only what appeared to be a gigantic black plastic garbage bag, a small sump pump, and an instruction book. Like a typical father, I tossed the instruction book back into the box with a promise to read it later if I needed it and went out into the yard with my garbage bag-pond liner and a shovel.

I began to dig, then stopped. Wait a minute, I thought, this can be a valuable educational experience. I went back inside and brought out my oldest daughter, eleven-year-old Alexis, and our video camera. After carefully filming the "family plot", Alexis and I began our urban excavation project. We dug. We filmed. We dug some more. We filmed some more. Slowly, a gaping hole grew in our backyard, each step recorded for posterity with the trusty video camera. We dug some more, steadily deeper, and wider. Alexis and I both got incredibly dirty. It was fun! Most importantly, we bonded, Daddy and Daughter, as the dirt and dust became glued to our skin. We spread the dirt around the backyard, leveling and filling in low spots, and even made a small Lilliputian Mountain bordering the future shoreline of "Lake Daddy". When Alexis could no longer reach up out of the crater to throw another shovel full of dirt over the top, she asked me a simple question, "Daddy, how big is the pond supposed to be?"

"Good question, Princess." I replied throwing her a rope so I could pull her out of the pit, "The pond should at least be big enough for fish to swim in without bumping their noses."

"Daddy, I think Monstro the Whale could swim in this hole. Maybe you should read the instruction book before we do any more digging."

"Mommy has gotten you well trained, Alexis." I said as I felt us unbonding rapidly. Reluctantly, I got out the instruction manual. She was right. The pond kit was designed to make a 4- foot by 9- foot pond, with a maximum depth of 2 feet. Our afternoon excavation measured roughly 10 feet by 7 feet by 5 feet. Oops. The rest of my afternoon was spent teaching Alexis the true meaning of the term "backfill". This part was not filmed.

At last, we finally had reduced the hole to a manageable size. Alexis and stretched the black plastic "garbage bag" liner over the hole and weighted the edges down with cobblestones. I dragged the garden hose over to the covered pit. As Alexis turned on the water to begin filling our new pool, I turned on the camera, only to film 30 cobblestones tumble into the pit as the weight of the water dragged the liner to the bottom. STOP THE CAMERA!

We fished out and reset the cobblestones, taking extra care this time to stake the corners of the liner. Finally, we carefully placed the hose on the center of the liner and began filling. As the water flowed from the hose, the liner slowly began to sag, eventually forming the shape of a 4 foot by 9 foot, 2-foot-deep inverted cow stomach. At least it held water. In our eyes it was as beautiful (almost- if you squint) as the Mediterranean Sea.

The rest of the yard, however, resembled the Dakota Bad Lands with piles of dirt spread everywhere. Mount Dirtmore, the pile of excavated dirt on the far side of the pond, lay barren and threatened to erode into our pond with the first rain. Something still didn't seem right. I looked again at the photograph on the empty pond kit box. Instead of the crystal-clear water, we had muddy brown ooze. Instead of flowering water lilies, we had a few floating grass clippings. Instead of happy, healthy, smiling fish, we had three drowning earthworms. I looked at the photo once more and finally noticed a small message in tiny, fine print: "CAUTION! ARTIST'S CONCEPTION OF NATURAL POND! MEN SHOULD OBTAIN WIVE'S PERMISSION BEFORE ATTEMPTING TO INSTALL POND

IN YARD". Still, we had taken our first step in recreating Eden. Daddy and Daughter were proud of their efforts. We would press on until our garden pond was a finished masterpiece. We planned to work on it again the next weekend. In the interim, Alexis and I were again "bonded" in secrecy. We both agreed with the same philosophy: Don't let Mommy see the pond until it looks decent!

In planning to hide the pond from General Mommy, neither Alexis nor I had taken one major, uncontrollable factor into consideration --- K.C., my youngest daughter. K.C. was four years old. When she went into the back yard the next day, she didn't realize that Alexis and I had installed a pond. She thought it was just a puddle-- conveniently next to a pile of dirt.

She climbed up Mount Dirtmore and decided to go mud sledding -- without a sled. Yelling her usual war cry, "SUPERDUPER!!!" she slid down the "novice slope"....... into the pond. With typical four-year-old mentality, she repeated this four times before realizing: 1) the water was deeper than a puddle, and 2) she was now pure chocolate brown colored and coated with mud. When I located her (two hours later) she was skinny dipping in the pond surrounded by her entire collection of Teenage Mutant Ninja Turtles having a naval battle. Mud-covered K.C. looked a bit like a mutant herself.

How I ever managed to get K.C. cleaned up and inside without being seen by General Mommy I'll never know. At least the pond secret remained safe for another day. And another day. And another day. Actually, what happened was my back was still sore from installing the pond, and I was resting until the next weekend. Meanwhile, the inside of the house was undergoing another mortar attack by the cleaning commandos. The midget dirt terminators had even initiated chemical warfare to polish the brass handrail on our stairs. This task is actually a suicide mission since the chemicals give off noxious fumes as they react to change the dull, pit-ted metal surface to a bright, shiny new fingerprint catcher. After getting

32

the stair rail completely blemish free, we usually spend the next two weeks tripping and falling down the stairs since everyone is too afraid to be the first to get their fingerprints on the handrail.

After cleaning the handrail, the house also was vented to eliminate the noxious chemical smell. All windows were thrown wide open, and the fans were set to purge speed. The house sort of resembled a nuclear plant emergency shutdown. After General Mommy's ACME Home Chemical Detector registered "0" on the "0 to 10" scale, we removed our gas masks, shut off the fans, closed all the windows (so we thought), and went to bed.

I woke up from a deep, sound, sleep at 2AM to find General Mommy standing on the bed swinging a rolled-up newspaper at my head. Before I could yell "I surrender!" the weapon sailed a millimeter over my ear and smashed into the wall by my head.

"That's six!" commented Mommy as she prepared another attack. "Six of them! Where the heck are they coming from?" They were mosquitoes. Our bedroom had been invaded as we slept by a swarm of mosquitoes. The entire house had been mysteriously infiltrated by hungry mosquitoes. General Mommy rallied her troops into action, handing each of the girls a full can of hair spray and a flyswatter. It was a massacre. Within twenty minutes, there were several little buggy smears on the walls. The carpets were littered with the bodies of hundreds of forever "permed" mosquitoes. Mommy General strolled through the battlefield, inspecting the carnage - then stopped in front of a window, an open window. The very window which was closest to my secret pond. A lone surviving mosquito fled through the window and made a hasty retreat to the pool of mosquito breeding stagnant muddy water in our backyard, my unfinished pond. Uh Oh..... Suzie slammed the window shut, then turned slowly around to glare at me.

I survived -- barely. Generalissimo Mommy commuted my death sentence with the understanding that I immediately complete all necessary work to finish the pond, including all control systems to prevent any mosquito from even thinking of trying to breed on our property. Three days later, the pond was completed. My natural pond now had fresh, clean, clear, highly chlorinated water, a circulating pump to keep the water from becoming stagnant, a half dozen smiling rubber fish, a plastic flowering lillypad, artificial turf landscaping, and a 3,000-kilowatt bug zapper in the remote case anything alive even tried to come near the pond. Ah, nature!

CHAPTER 8

DIAPERS AND DADDYHOOD

Daddies have different responsibilities and duties than Mommies. The "Rulebook for Perfect Daddyhood" says so and the text explains some of these differences. Some differences are biological. My wife breast fed our infant daughter, so I was temporarily relieved of "feeding patrol" until much later. My responsibility during breast season was limited to nudging my wife during the night if I happened to hear the baby cry. After all, I needed my sleep so I could go to work in the morning. Yes, in retrospect, I know that's a nasty thing to say. Back then, I was young and naive and said a lot of foolish things. I still do.

During the infant stage, there really isn't much for a Daddy to do except stand around and tell everyone how proud you are of Mommy and Baby. The main responsibility is to buy diapers, pay off the national debt sized hospital bill, buy diapers, photograph Mommy and Baby, buy diapers, try to limit relatives from "dropping over" to see the Baby, buy diapers, and of course, buy more diapers. Daddies are also called on to hold Baby while Mommy takes a nap. I originally interpreted the "hold the baby" command to mean keep Baby on my lap until three seconds after Mommy left the room whereupon I could then place Baby on the floor in front of the TV. I thought "quality time" meant that I wasn't supposed to let

35

beer or potato chip crumbs litter her nightie while I munched and watched the ball game.

Baby Alexis, however, had other ideas. She fully intended to use these visits with Daddy as a means to "bond". I quickly learned what "bonding" is. Bonding is when the baby uses its invisible Velcro fasteners to attach itself to Mommy or Daddy. Alexis was an expert with this technique - once she glued herself into position on my hip, and no mere industrial-strength solvent could remove her. I still have sucker marks on my side. Her favorite position was on the hip. She even managed to stay attached without using her hands-- she somehow perfected a technique of pressing my kidneys out of the way and stepping directly on my bones. Ten years of carrying three children has left me permanently bonded, to the kids as well as to my chiropractor.

Infants are wonderful for Daddies. Ours slept a lot and were especially prone to nap times whenever it was Daddy's turn to take care of them during the day. Unfortunately, it meant the little darlings would stay up late when it was Daddy's next shift that night. The "Rulebook for Perfect Daddyhood" explains that this is a no-win situation for Daddy. When it's Daddy's turn to watch the baby, just go with the flow and try not to doze off yourself.

"Flowing" is another frequent activity for infants. Babies leak constantly and from both ends. There was a perpetual freight train of clean diapers entering our house through the front door and a growing mountainous landfill of soiled diapers exiting the back door. Mommy did not appreciate my fatherly suggestion to stop using disposable diapers. As an alternative, I thought we could leave the baby naked in the shower and just hose it down every twenty minutes.

There is a continual debate about whether cloth or disposable diapers are "better" for the environment. Each variety has its merits and faults, but I have a strong hunch that what's actually best for the environment is to have no babies. Disposable diapers were more convenient for our use, and I was amazed at the endless variety of sizes, styles, colors, and absorbent materials. Parents should use caution in the type of diaper they put on their infants, especially when bringing baby to the beach or pool.

When our middle child, Erin, was about a year old, I came home with a box of "super duper dry absorbent" ultra-thick deluxe diapers, which promised to keep her bottom dry even in the event of a monsoon. She happened to be wearing one of these 'weather-beater' diapers on the hot, summer day we brought her to the community pool. She toddled into the kiddie wading pool with me and disaster struck. First, she couldn't sit down in the water. Her diaper's waterproof lining made her butt act like a cork, and she floated. It's not, however, a good idea to wear a life preserver around your bottom. Every time I turned around; Erin was floating upside down. She looked like a humongous marshmallow with feet.

Trying to make the best of the situation, I continued to play the game of "Bobbing for Erin". My fingernail must have torn a hole in the diaper lining, because it suddenly dawned on me that my daughter's staypuffed marshmallow butt was growing bigger. It was soon the size of a weather balloon and quickly approaching the Graf Zeppelin. I could feel a rip-tide current as the kiddie pool water was sucked into her "superduper dry absorbent" ultra-thick deluxe diaper. Erin sank like a white stone, but then her whale sized diaper hit the bottom of the pool and exploded.

The diaper explosion was like being at the creation of the universe and verified the Big Bang theory. Billions and billions of clear, jelly-like beads of absorbent blew in all directions. The absorbent mini planets formed growing galaxies and Milky Way patterns as they spread through-out the pool. I grabbed Erin, tore off the remains of her diaper, and dragged her out of the pool. We joined the crowd at the edge and watched in fas-cination as the kiddie pool slowly turned into a giant clear Lucite block.

Fortunately, there were no casualties and I have a new theory on how Moses parted the Red Sea. He merely threw in a box of diapers.

The destiny of all diapers is to become soiled. There is nothing "cute" about changing dirty diapers. The experience is often educational and full of surprises. I never could get used to the endless variety of exotic colors and smells which made their appearance. The used diaper odor was sometimes unbearable and inherently indestructible. My wife attempted to prevent permanent scent contamination of the house by placing each soiled diaper in a self-sealing plastic bag. The individual bags were then placed in a large twist-tie plastic bag, and finally in a heavy lead-lined metal garbage can outside. Even so, cats stayed out of our backyard. I have nightmares of a future mining expedition unearthing our landfilled diaper time bombs and accidentally destroying all life on the planet. My only hope is global warming kills us all first.

Still, baby regularly made her contributions to "Mount Diaper" and needed changing, on average, every nine minutes. So, since "a Man's got to do what a Man's got to do", I tried to pass the buck to Mommy as often as possible. Mommy, in turn, kept trying to pass the buck back to me. This game of "pass the poop" would continue until either my nose malfunctioned, or the baby's bottom was in danger of the dreaded red menace: "diaper rash."

The "Rulebook for Perfect Daddyhood" does not have to mention diaper rash. One major episode with this red plague is sufficient warning that fun and games are over, and baby's bottom should stay soft and dry. I learned this lesson quickly, and I became an expert in slathering numerous ointments over our baby's bottoms as a preventative. I still remember the sigh-of-relief expression on my daughter's face when the mysterious healing gook was spread on her bottom. This ointment, however, is totally waterproof and permanently bonded Daddy's fingers together.

Fortunately, almost all children, at some age become toilet trained and masters of their own fate. There was always a celebration as each of our daughters completed toilet training. After three children and many years and countless diapers, the changing table has at last been retired, and cats are slowly returning to our backyard.

CHAPTER 9

BRING YOUR DAUGHTER TO WORK DAY

In the business world, I am considered an endangered species-- a white male over 40. In scientific terms my species is called "homo executivus rex", He-Rex, a dinosaur who's power is fading fast. At one time, packs of He-Rexes ruled the business world, building empires, waging corporate battles, and protecting their turf. All corporate positions were filled by He-Rexes, and all decisions were made exclusively by the mighty He-Rex. Females of the species were only secretaries or were considered ornaments for He-Rex, much like a good cigar or country club membership.

The dinosaurs, however, have already become extinct. They didn't see the comet coming or realize the danger from the little furry mammals. He-Rex is also soon to be extinct, but this time there won't be any cute little plastic models of He-Rex for sale in the Museum of Natural History. Like the Piping Plover, Texas Toad, and the African Elephant, He-Rex is losing his habitat. No one, however, mourns the decline of He-Rex. He is simply being replaced by another stronger force --"She-Rexus".

Good riddance to He-Rex! No, I am not a traitor to my species, I'm just the father of three daughters. These girls are being raised by a very competent and shrewd "Mommy-Rexus" who is determined to overcompensate for her own business-stifled upbringing. Back in the Dark Ages (the 1950's) when Mommy Rexus was a little girl, her father -- a pseudo He-Rex, wouldn't let her join him in his business because "she was just a girl". Pseudo-Rex used the same reason to not support Mommy-Rexus's college education plans. "Girls don't belong in business, what do you need an education for?" proclaimed Dodo-Rex.

Time passed. Mommy-Rexus grew up, paid her own way through college, met and married me, and works as a professional, well-respected artist in addition to being Supermom for our daughters. My family responsibility is limited to bringing home enough money to pay 87% of the bills, and to act as the male role model on "what not to do" or the expert example of "this is why all men are stupid".

I don't talk about my work much when I'm home with my family. Since I used to work helping design and build nuclear power plants, I found that discussing my job was about as welcome a conversation topic as discussing the benefits of cigarettes. In addition, I'm a scientist and have never had much direct He-Rex business acumen. I prefer to teach my daughters about wildlife, the environment, and frogs rather than discussing corporate politics. My work is usually highly technical and complicated. For several years, I was the resident geotechnical engineer on a soil stabilization project for the New York City Transit Authority. Huh? At parties, when people asked me what I did for a living, I was never tempted to explain about slope protection methods, surcharging, inclinometers, or hydrogeologic principles. I merely told them I got paid to watch sand settle. After that, most people left me alone and talked with Mommy-Rexus instead.

In the 1990's daughters have more of an opportunity to have viable corporate careers than any previous generation. Still, there is a lot of room for improvement. The utility company I work for, Brooklyn Union, recently had a "bring your daughters to work day". This is an expanding national program to help nourish self-esteem among teenage girls and foster the notion that She-Rex is here to stay. Needless to say, the program was conceived by a women's organization, and heartily endorsed by Mommy-Rexus and her three daughters. Alexis, our oldest daughter at 11 years old, had the privilege of joining me for a typical day at work. She was always asking me what I did for a job and was one of the few people who realized I didn't just watch sand settle. "Bring your Daughter to Work Day" seemed to be a good opportunity for her to observe what I actually do when I'm actually at "work".

Alexis and I commuted by train and walked to my office in Brooklyn, me grabbing a cup of coffee on the way. As part of my "typical day", we first joined 300 other girls and their sponsors in our corporate auditorium where we were given an extra-large tee shirt, custom designed with the Brooklyn Union logo and "Bring Your Daughter to Work Day 1994" stenciled across the front. Next, we heard a series of lectures by several of our executives on what Brooklyn Union does, how natural gas is the best thing in the world, and how many different opportunities are available for women in the workforce. Alexis seemed very interested and was pleased to get a list of rooms and times where special activities for the day were scheduled.

First, however, I had another cup of coffee and spent time saying hello to many of my coworkers and their daughters. It seemed wherever Alexis and I went, we ran into someone I knew, and introductions were politely exchanged. Everyone politely gave a brief explanation of their part in the Brooklyn Union corporate family. Alexis got a bit tired of telling everyone over and over that she was going to be an artist, and occasionally nudged me if the introductions went on too long.

I had another cup of coffee, then we visited the Corporate Library where my good friend and Corporate Librarian Nancy B. gave a nice presentation on how research is conducted and the types of resources available.

About six minutes into the presentation, however, Alexis realized our particular high-tech Corporate Library had no books, just computer terminals. Since there weren't even any art magazines, she proceeded to gently nudge my side repeatedly. The nudges became increasingly strong. I then had two choices, either I could move on to the next presentation, or I could stand there until my rib broke. We left, and I had a quick cup of coffee.

Next, we went to the corporate photo and video studio, where I again exchanged introductions and had a cup of coffee. Alexis and I got a mini education on Brooklyn Union's photo resources and how the company uses video for communications. At least this was art related, and after a lengthy tour of the dark room, Alexis only nudged my sore ribs a few times before we left. We then went to the art department where Alexis's talent is geared. Alexis thoroughly enjoyed seeing the artwork and drafting tables, but suddenly yelled very loudly, "Look, Daddy, there's Paint!"

"Yes, Honey," I innocently replied, "art departments do tend to have paint."

"No, Daddy," Alexis clarified, "I don't mean just paint, but a photo of our pet frog, "Paint!" Sure enough, on the wall of the art department was a photo of our family pet frog, "Paint", which had been the subject of an article in our corporate newspaper. This bit of unexpected news obviously made Alexis's day! She was very pleased that her frog was famous. I, however, was wondering which staff artist had brought a genuine toad-skin pocketbook into the office to torment me. We spent the next hour in the art department, as I drank some more coffee and Alexis used crayons at one of the drafting tables to draw a picture of her and me on the train on our way to "work". So far, however, I'd been at "work" for three hours and hadn't actually gotten any "work" done.

We had lunch in the corporate cafeteria, sharing Brooklyn Union Gas Corporate hamburgers and French fries, coffee (for me) and milk (for her), then made more introductions. Our afternoon was just as busy. Alexis and I colored "Save the Harbor" posters, learned how to make origami fish, made more introductions, had more coffee, and continued to take mini tours of the Company building. As a special treat, we went up to the executive floor and took a self guided tour of the Executive Conference Room and Executive Lounge.

Alexis was suitably impressed with the Executive Conference Room plush chairs and spun around in one until she was dizzy. So did I, as this was probably the first, and last time I would ever see the hallowed halls of the Corporate Executive Conference Room where so many He-Rexes had made "Big Deals" throughout history. Alexis and I marveled that the Executive Lounge had solid brass sinks! Alexis was a bit puzzled on why there was a forty-foot, solid wood table in the middle of the conference room. I explained that the people who run Brooklyn Union meet there occasionally to make business decisions and use the table to play a giant game of knock hockey. She then asked me if I wanted to be a He-Rex when I grew up. "Time to go, Alexis!" I replied, not wanting to confess I had never been invited to the He-Rex brotherhood.

We went back to my office cubicle, where I still hadn't accomplished any real work on "Bring Your Daughter To Work Day." We made several more introductions, I had more coffee, and I received several more nudges to my ribs. As I read back the many messages accumulating on my desk, Alexis saw my personal computer. "Daddy, can I play a game?", she asked. I turned the computer on, and set it on a games program, "Solitaire", which comes with the software package. Alexis, a potential She-Rex cardsharp, discovered Corporate heaven! She played computer-solitaire for the next hour, while I hurried to try to catch up on my assignments. I only spilled a half a cup of coffee when Alexis nudged me to let me know she had won another game.

As five PM drew near, the "work" day ended, and my daughter and I headed home. We again took the train and walked hand in hand back to our house. I was perfectly content in my own mind holding her hand as we walked. Mommy-Rexus and Alexis's two sisters waited anxiously at the door for us to arrive. Alexis's career planning education was accomplished. She had seen Daddy in action and learned everything that corporate life has to offer. So naturally, when Mommy-Rexus asked Alexis if she had learned what Daddy does for a job, my former favorite daughter replied, "I don't think I'd want Daddy's job, all he does all day long is drink coffee and introduce people!"

CHAPTER 10

DADDY'S DREAM CATCHER NIGHTMARE

My wife, our three young daughters, and I share a cluttered four-bedroom house in a quiet, suburban neighborhood. Each child has her own windowed bedroom for sleeping. Every night the girls, Mommy, and Daddy go through the same routine. "Brush your teeth, go to the bathroom, get on your nighties, drink a glass of water, say your prayers, give Daddy a kiss, shut up, and go to sleep." Well, not exactly as simple as that. I also have to say prayers and good night with Doll-Doll, Froggy, Fluffy, Barbie, 600 My Little Ponies, and the other four thousand assorted stuffed animals and dolls that share bed space with the girls. I also have to sing soft lullabies, wind up 13 different music boxes, adjust night-lights and window shades, and try to quietly tiptoe out of the semi-darkened rooms without tripping or impaling myself on the toy debris on their floors.

This "routine" sometimes takes me over an hour. Then, to keep things equal, Mommy also has to do it. We scurry back and forth between the girls' rooms, giving them comfort, kisses, and hugs so they can sleep peacefully through the night. And they usually do, thank God. This routine might not be logical, but since the girls normally have a peaceful and rest filled night, we are all more apt to be a happier family during the day. Except for nightmares......

I almost never ever dream. I lay down, close my eyes, and sink into oblivion. My nighttime memories are a complete void. My wife, however, dreams constantly. She also doesn't like to waste any time just sleeping. Since she also remembers her dreams vividly, she somehow manages to use her "dream-self" to help her plan the next day's activities, do the housework, and help her prepare her postdoctoral thesis on Advanced Mommyhood. She even manages to "visit" with her ancestors during dreams to get background information and advice. I don't understand how this occurs. It's not really logical but I'm getting used to it. My wife is a tad bit unusual, if not actually psychic. Once, she woke me up at 4AM to tell me, "Grandma says 'hello', Robert, and wants to let you know that your missing work file is just stuck behind the filing cabinet in your office." Yeah, right! Grandma died in 1968! This was a completely illogical "message", until I found the file that next day -- stuck behind my filing cabinet. That night I told my wife to tell Grandma "Thanks!"

I guess the kids have some of Mommy's "dream gene". Each of them has occasionally told us an interesting or amusing story at the breakfast table about one of their dreams. Awhile ago, however, five-year-old Erin-- our middle child, began to frequently wake up crying in the middle of the night from nightmares. My wife would hear Erin's cry, politely excuse herself from her "visit with Grandma", wake up and run into Erin's room. After being comforted and reassured by Mommy that everything was "all right", Erin would drift off back to sleep. I only heard about this the next morning at breakfast --- I'm "night-dead", remember, but it bothered me too.

The nightmare episodes went on for a couple of weeks until my wife's sister, Claire, came over with a special gift for Erin, a "genuine dream catcher". The "dream catcher" was a circle shaped ring with a spider web like netting stretched across. Attached to the webbing were a couple of beads, bones, and a few small feathers. Still, I had never heard of a "dream catcher" before.

Aunt Claire gave the dream catcher to Erin and explained that it had been made by American Indians to help keep "bad" dreams from entering a room. Aunt Claire helped Erin hang the dream catcher on her bedroom window, said a short Indian prayer to ward off bad dreams, told my wife to say Hi to Grandma, and left. I was not amused. I now had a spider web with dead bird parts stuck to Erin's window. This seemed neither logical nor rational. Unfortunately, five-year-old girls are also not always logical or rational. According to Erin, the "dream catcher" worked! And, as fate would have it, Erin's nightmares abruptly ended.

A couple of nightmare free years passed. Last week, however, four-year-old K.C.--our youngest, woke me from the dead in the middle of the night with a blood curdling scream, "D A A A A A A A A D D D Y Y Y Y Y Y ! ! ! ! M O O O M M M M Y Y Y ! ! ! AAAAAARRRRRRRGGGGHH!"

I jumped out of bed and rushed into her room. "K.C., what's the matter?" I stammered.

"Bad dream! Bad dream! Bad dream! WAAAHHH!" K.C. cried.

"Oh great", I thought - then stumbled back into my bedroom, and shook my wife awake. "Sorry to interrupt your sleep, honey, but K.C. wants to talk with you.", I said, then I plopped back into bed and boarded the express train back to "Deadville, USA".

K.C. and Mommy, however, derailed my plans. A few minutes later, they walked into our bedroom where K.C. spent the rest of the night whimpering, dozing, fidgeting, and squeezing my belly button to make it smile. I am not used to having a four-year-old foot in my ear while I try to sleep. I finally gave up and slept on the couch -- sort of.

The next night, K.C.'s nightmares returned, and our sleep was interrupted again. This was not fun. The next day, everyone in the family was crabby and drained. We struggled through the day and made plans to go to bed early that night. Both Mommy and Daddy spent extra time with K.C., trying to logically explain that bad dreams do not mean dangerous things are really happening to her. We assured K.C. that we loved her, and that she was perfectly safe and fine. Except, maybe I shouldn't have hinted that I was tempted to sell her as a medical research specimen if she woke me up again. After all, I hadn't actually received any written offers.

K.C. woke up screaming at 11PM. Mommy (and "Grandma") and I all groaned. Suddenly, Erin walked into K.C.'s room. She calmly ambled over to K.C.'s window, raised the Venetian blind, and stuck her "dream catcher" onto the glass. Erin then turned towards K.C. and simply said, "There, K.C., you can borrow my dream catcher for tonight, now go back to sleep!", and left. K.C. looked at the dream catcher on her window, then quietly lay down and instantly fell asleep.

I was dumbfounded. I was awed! Actually, I don't know what surprised me more, whether the fact that the Indian magic was actually working, or the fact that it was Erin who solved K.C.'s nightmare problem. There had to be some reasonable explanation, but whatever the reason, we all slept soundly that night.

The real problem developed the next night at bedtime. K.C. wouldn't go to sleep without the dream catcher, and Erin wanted it back. "IT'S NOT FAIR!!!!", Erin yelled, "I ONLY LENT IT TO HER!!! IT'S MINE!!!!"

"Well," I thought, "at least Erin is acting like her usual self again." One puzzle was eliminated, but what to do about the dream catcher shortage?? I couldn't figure this one out until "Grandma" (through my wife's voice) suggested the two girls sleep together. Problem solved- at least temporarily.

The next day, my wife called me at work (using a telephone since I don't get "direct" messages like she does) and asked me to pick up another dream catcher on my way home from work. "Oh, really?" I replied, "Why, is 7-11 out of them today? Come on, honey, where in the world does one buy a dream catcher - I haven't noticed any at Sears lately." Perhaps I sounded a wee bit sarcastic, but at least I did suggest that my wife call Aunt Claire to find out where she got the original. I had no intention of scouring all around Brooklyn for a genuine American Indian dream catcher.

Wrong. Aunt Claire didn't remember where she's gotten the dream catcher, and I spent the next three evenings searching every store and boutique in Brooklyn, as well as Queens and Nassau Counties for a dream catcher. Countless store owners and salesclerks gave me only blank stares or raised eyebrows in reply to my question, "By any chance do you sell dream catchers?" I was becoming desperate. The word of my quest began to spread. Shop owners began to call me at work and home, leaving messages that No, they don't sell dream catchers, and would I please refrain from coming to their store as I seemed to be upsetting their other customers. K.C. and Erin, still shared a bedroom each night. Each morning they reminded me to get another dream catcher.

I was trying! The girls had made a reasonable request - under the circumstances. It wasn't a very logical request since I really didn't think chicken feathers and string on a window had any affect on dreaming, but if it worked for them, I wasn't going to argue. I needed my sleep too. After another two days of fruitless searching (Suffolk and Westchester Counties) I'll admit I was getting worn out. Finally, as I drove home late at night, I happened to pass a closed building where a flea market is usually held each weekend. As I drove past, out of the side of my eye, I suddenly thought I'd seen a rack of Indian jewelry and..... a dream catcher!

I raced around the block, stopped at the corner traffic light, turned again, and drove slowly by the window again. It was another dream catcher!

50

At long last! I yelled and cheered! My quest was nearly over! Yippee!! Then I looked at the dream catcher in the window again. Something about it was different. Mysteriously, it was glowing a flashing red. That's odd. I looked again. Then I realized it wasn't the dream catcher flashing red, it was the cop car behind me.

At first, the officer was only going to give me a warning for making an illegal right turn at the corner, but then he asked me what I was doing in front of the closed building at night. When I told him how happy I was to have at last found a dream catcher, the next thing I knew, I was taking a Breathalyzer test and holding an $80 traffic ticket in my hand. It was a long night.

Maybe the cop wasn't a father and couldn't appreciate the logic and effort in my dream catcher search. After the breath and urine tests came back negative, the police finally let me go home. I was exhausted, angry, and embarrassed, but at least slightly satisfied with the knowledge I could return to buy one of the cursed dream catchers next Saturday.

Exhausted, but with the nightmare problem seemingly solved, I stumbled back into bed and fell asleep only to have the first vivid and strange, but hopefully last dream of my life:

I dreamed I was at the very edge of a steep cliff, dressed for field work in my geologist's outfit. I had been caught tightly in a giant spider web, with a few scattered feathers entangled next to me. A large, angry crowd of people stood in front of me shouting and threatening, trying to decide whether to push me off the cliff or let the giant Spider eat me. The people were thoroughly mad, a frenzied mob of illogical hatred - all directed straight at me.

They were all there. They were going to Get Me!!!

It looked for certain I was in deep, deep, trouble. Suddenly, there was a brilliant light, and an angel appeared next to me. He talked and pleaded with the mob, but they kept shouting him down. Finally, the angel stepped aside, pulled out a cellular phone, punched in a few numbers, and I could hear him say:

"Dad? Hi, J.C. here, sorry to interrupt you again, but there's a real problem on Earth and I've had enough. I just can't deal with this Daddy anymore; he keeps making the same mistakes! Are you absolutely certain the mud you used to make Adam wasn't contaminated? Did you ever run a lab analysis? There has to be some logical reason for such irrational behavior! I bet you're sorry you rested on the seventh day; it looks like you never got all the bugs out of the system. The Hell with him! Thanks a bunch Dad, beam me up-- there's no intelligent life on this planet."

J.C. looked at me, shrugged, and beamed up as the angry mob surged forward to throw me over the cliff.....

I woke up suddenly, sweating profusely and breathing hard. I noticed a small feather on my heaving chest, and nearly screamed. My heart pounded furiously! "That was just a dream, just a dream, just a dream," I said to myself over and over again. "It's not logical to be scared of a dream." Then I got up, tiptoed into Erin's bedroom, stole her "dream catcher" and silently went back to my room, where I finally went back to sleep clutching the dream catcher tightly in my arms. Logic be damned, I'm buying a dozen dream catchers Saturday!

CHAPTER 11

DOCUMENTING DADDYHOOD

I have been a Daddy for over ten years so far without having had the advantage of completing a prerequisite university course in fatherhood. I'm becoming adept at "winging" it, but many things are a blur. Am I being a "good" Daddy? Where did I go wrong? How did I manage to have three girls when I used to be certain I didn't want any children at all??? Did I really threaten to sell my youngest daughter for medical research?

Actually, I don't worry too much about what this Daddy might be doing wrong, as much as trying to keep track of what everyone's been doing - period! If I'm going to have any chance of a passing grade in this Daddyhood experience course, I should at least remember what the girls and I have done together. This, however, presents a problem... I have a poor memory for life. It's difficult for me to remember the names, faces, and places I've gone to, particularly if it's a family event. When my mother recently heard me refer to myself as an only child, she threw up her arms and wailed, "Will you please stop saying that? Your sister is getting very upset!"

My wife, Suzie, is the polar opposite of me when it comes to recalling names, faces, and family facts. She is Webster's definition of the term

"TOTAL RECALL". She can remember and fully describe every person she's ever met in her entire life, including the doctor and nurses that delivered her. She still sends birthday cards to the other babies that shared the hospital nursery with her when she was born!

Suzie has a knack for accurately recalling the where and when of every family event in her lifetime. The oldest child in her family, she was relied on by her 4 own siblings to remember things for them too. When we once discussed the possibility of reincarnation, I thought Suzie was going to go into shock. She thought she'd have to remember every person she ever met in each of her lifetimes -- and was afraid she'd miss someone!

My wife recognized that I might have a bit of a problem trying to keep track of "all the wonderful things we've done together". Her first solution was for both of us to keep diaries. This idea was spawned in 1983 when our first daughter was born. We each got a small 6" high, 80-page, blank book which could be used to write down various experiences, events, and thoughts.

If we happened to go on a long drive or vacation, Suzie would bring her "diary" along and write copious notes about what we're doing, where we're going, how we feel, and so on. She would even have the girls dictate a few sentences so they could "share the experience." Suzie is already on her 16th diary book, which have now grown to 16", 200-page volumes. I'm still on my first book, which has about four pages of my thoughts from when: 1) my dad died, 2) my second daughter was born, 3) my third daughter was born, and 4) I grew a really neat looking zucchini. I also added a few notes like, "You have an older sister, her name is Maureen". I'm sure I'll remember, someday!

Actually, I have an excuse for not writing in my own diary on these drives. I'm supposed to be paying attention to the road and traffic rather than musing about my feelings as a Daddy. I cannot imagine a police officer tearing up a ticket he was about to hand me because I tell him, "Sorry about the stop sign, officer, I was jotting a few notes about how I was a great Daddy and the wonderful trip to the beach we just had, and I didn't notice the group of nuns crossing the street."

It became evident that neither I nor future historians could never conclude from reading my diary whether I was a "good" Daddy. (Obviously, if the historians have time to read my wife's encyclopedia, they'll posthumously give her the Mother of the Decade award.) Suzie then hit upon a documentation plan more suitable to my capabilities - photographs!

Suzie and I sometimes feel as if our lives began when we got married. Our best, and most utilized wedding gift was a good 35mm camera. The first few rolls of film were of our wedding and honeymoon. The camera has gone everywhere with us carefully and quietly recording our lives. Vacations, holidays, relatives, and landscapes have been lovingly preserved in glossy 4" x 6" images, mounted, and labeled in an entire bookshelf of photo albums. Only one thin album, however, contains any record of our separate lives before we got married - a few Kodak brownie black and white shots and genuine "official school grade" portraits.

We have eight full albums of photos of our first-born daughter, Alexis, with shots of her "firsts" - first diaper change, first bath, first sit-up, first car ride, first stand-up, first Oreo cookie, etc. Everything Alexis did was new and precious for us. As per most families, however, we eventually got worn out.

When our second child, Erin, was born, changing a diaper was no longer a wonderfully interesting experience to preserve FOREVER. Neither was her first car ride, and I was out of film when she first stood up. There are maybe three photo albums of Erin, and probably at least one album's quantity of pictures of KC - our third and last child. The photos continue to breed and multiply on their own.

These photos are not lovingly mounted and carefully labeled but are stuffed into a drawer in our den waiting for when we can finally organize them. I estimate over six months of work will be needed to organize and finish the photo album collection - if my wife lets me. I recall her stern warning: "Touch those photos and you're a eunuch, buster. I am not going to let you merely staple them into the album and label them all 'Kids - 20th Century.'"

At least I'll have one project lined up for after I retire. Why have we become lax? I felt all three of the bald headed chubby cheeked blue-eyed babies looked the same, especially when Erin and KC both wore clothes and sleepers handed down from their older sister. Besides, technology has changed, and we've gone video!

We bought a video camera when KC was born and during the next 3-1/2 years, I've filmed 43 separate video cassettes with over 80 hours of family home videos. Holidays, birthdays, home tours, bath times, play-times, sledding, eating, school concerts, and every conceivable family event is on tape. I've managed to keep up with a computerized filing system, so I know exactly which tape has what event, who's in it, and when it took place. I need a computer to keep track. By the time the girls are married and on their own, I'll need six full years to watch each tape to determine whether I was a good Daddy.

Photo and video documentation of our lives as Mommy, Daddy, and Daughters is a big part of our lives. At almost all family gatherings, one or more video cameras is present. I have videos of my sister-in-law videotaping me videotaping her. The ultimate in our video documentation obsession was even stranger. Last year, my wife discovered a box of old 8mm films which her father had made of the family during the 1960's. Incredibly, one of the old films was of 8-year-old Suzie taking a photograph of her sisters with a Kodak Brownie camera. Little did they know......

Eager to preserve this newly discovered treasure trove of familiabilia, she had the grainy films converted to videotape, made five copies, and gave a copy to each of her siblings as Christmas presents. We then were told to all sit down in front of the TV and watch all six complete copies while I videotaped the family watching the videos -six times. (I think her brother, Perry kept expecting to see something different in one of the copies. Perry is not exactly known as an intellectual.)

I have seen entire school concerts with one eye closed and one eye behind a lens. We religiously rush home after videotaping a family event to watch it all over again on the TV. I can't quite understand this déjà vu addiction. I was just there, why am I watching what I just did? On the bright side, my family regularly watches America's Funniest Home Videos together and are always tempted to submit our own foibles.

There is a drawback to photography and videotaping that is frustrating; someone has to take the picture - and it's usually me. With photos, at least my wife and I would pass the camera back and forth. Some pictures are of me, some are of my wife, but very few are of us together. With video taping, it's a bit more complicated - my wife cannot use this mechanical instrument. Although she is a wiz at people and places, "point and shoot" is a difficult mystery to her. Maybe she used up all of her available brain storage cells to remember the dates each of our daughters lost each of their baby teeth.

My wife has bad "gadget karma". If it's mechanical, it's something she can't get to work or remember how to operate. Once, after I explained for the twelfth time how to operate the video camera, she innocently looked at me and asked, "Honey, what does 'on' mean?" So, I do almost all of the video taping. My face rarely shows up on tape. My daughters may only remember me as that disembodied voice that kept yelling, "stop blocking the camera" or "turn around and face me you idiot - the camera's on!"

In spite of 28 photo albums and a drawer full of loose photos, 16-1/2 diaries, and 43 video tapes, my wife still does not trust me to remember every detail of Daddyhood. She introduced yet another means of recording all important family events -- and without resorting to a mechanical gadget. She discovered the "Official Nursery School Fill-in Personalized Calendar"! When our oldest girl, Alexis, entered nursery school as a three-year-old, my wife bought our first Nursery School calendar.

The "Official Nursery School" calendar has large fill-in spaces, a blank monthly color-in section, and 3,000 small decorative squares you can cut out and glue onto the appropriate days. These squares include "happy teeth" cutouts to document each lost baby tooth, "birthday cake" cutouts to note family birthdays, "ruler" cutouts to record height and weight of your child, and "dollar" cutouts to remind you when nursery school tuition is due. What a joy! Seriously, where do these people get the idea for this "stuff"?

The top half of each calendar month's page contains a blank "framed" area where the child can either draw a picture or write a paragraph on a "big or important" event during the month. My wife has each of the girls take monthly turns creating a special picture to be permanently mounted on the calendar page. Alexis and Erin fight over who has the special privilege of being "calendar artist of the month". KC, presently 3-1/2, was just as creative and earnest in her attempt to preserve a "big or important" event when it was her turn. Last March 1, our pet frog, "Sticky" died suddenly. KC was the first one to notice. Without asking us, all by her little three-year-old self, KC took Sticky out of the tank and glued him to the calendar. It definitely was a "big" event!

We buy a new "Official Nursery School" calendar every year. My wife saves each of the previous years' completed calendars in a steamer trunk along with the actual baby teeth, Doctor's check up results, and the children's various crayon drawings and crafts projects. It is hard for my wife to say goodbye to these "precious" memories of our children's developing years. A few weeks ago, Suzie sat on the sofa with all three girls and actually read the entire previous year's calendar square by square and note by note. I overheard Alexis finally try and stop her by saying," Golly, Mommy, it's almost February. Can't we start living this year now???"

Although I plan on waiting until after my last daughter has grown up and moved out on her own before I start reviewing the entire "Daddy collection"-- videos, photos, diary, artwork, and calendars, I think I'll probably be able to use some of the data when my girls are teenagers. If they start to complain they were deprived or never did anything good as a family, I'll grab them by the arms and tug them into the den with a firm but gentle, "Oh yeah? Well, let's go to the video and see!"

CHAPTER 12

THE LAUNDRY DAY DEMON

My wife, Suzie, and I each have our own assigned chores and responsibilities in maintaining our home. Suzie is the designated boss and superintendent inside of the house. She rules her kingdom with a firm hand, keeping the rugs moderately lint and stain free, the pile of dishes no more than two feet high, and the washing machine continually fed lest it rampage through the basement and eat one of the kids.

In addition to professionally orchestrating her household duties, Suzie is Supermom - nurturing her three little girls and one little-at-heart husband. She also works part-time as an artist and full-time giving advice. How does this maven of motherhood accomplish so much? To start with, she always sends me outside to work in the garden. I'm not allowed to "help" her.

I don't consider this punishment. At one time, I did like to help her out when I could but have now come to realize how dangerous this can be. Anyway, I can stay in the garden as long as I want. My daughters can even come out and visit me or bring me an iced tea. But, never, ever, am I to try and "help" do the housework inside.

The reason for this is a sad tale of good intentions gone wrought. I was exiled from our house after trying to surprise Suzie by washing the clothes for her while she was out for the day. I didn't realize I had limited laundry intelligence. I certainly never expected the full consequences of my good intentions.

Although I had spent five full years at college, I did not have any practical laundry experience. I remember that my own mother had fully prepared me for my sleep-away collegiate years. She carefully wrapped 12 pairs of new socks in separate plastic bags. She had sewn my name in all 5 sets of underwear and wrapped each brief and tee-shirt in individual baggies. Six new shirts and pants were also tagged and lovingly wrapped and folded into my new steamer trunk. Off to college I went with a box of Tide and a roll of quarters.

Five years later, Mom welcomed me back home and she began to unpack my steamer trunk. Out popped 11 pairs of new socks, 4 sets of new underwear, and 5 new shirts and pants - all still fresh but mummified in their plastic wrappings. Oh yes, there was also an unopened box of Tide. "Robert," Mom commented, "You never did any laundry?!? Whatever did you wear?" She was unimpressed with my response that I saved money by wearing the same socks for five full years. She really didn't want to know that I spent the quarters on video games. Please don't ask why it took me 5 full years to complete my college education. My college transcript is still framed and posted in the Dean's office as an example of a person who was simply not even smart enough to give up.

That was long ago. Although I still hadn't actually washed any clothes myself, I had at least occasionally seen my wife washing clothes. It looked easy. I figured it must also have been fun. After all, Suzie was always down in the basement washing clothes, (especially after out third daughter was born).

One early autumn Sunday afternoon, Suzie announced that she was going out to visit her sister for awhile. I kissed her goodbye and told her to say Hi for me -- and begged her to take our daughters with her for the visit. Surprisingly, she did. A short time later, I happened to go into the basement and noticed a very large pile of clothes on the floor next to the washer. Some evil demon suddenly possessed me and made me try something I'll always regret. I decided to wash the clothes myself and surprise my wife when she returned home. What a good guy I was going to be!

I stood at the edge of the pile of laundry trying to figure out how to begin. I opened the washer lid, then leaned down over the pile and said, "O.K. clothes, jump in!" Nothing... not one sock moved an inch. This was going to be harder than I thought. Still undaunted, I tried really hard to figure out how to proceed next. I vaguely remembered something about "separating the dirty clothes", so I made separate piles for: 1) all of the "underwear", 2) all of the "regular wear" clothes, and 3) all of the "overwear" -sweaters and my wife's suede jacket with a small mustard stain. Needless to say, it was her favorite jacket, and the mustard stain was my fault.

After washing both loads of under wear and regular wear, it had taken me over fifteen minutes to stuff all of my wife's 38 sweaters and her designer suede jacket into the washer. I then added a few cups of the laundry powder, some bleach, and a bar of lava soap. I figured the lava soap would find its way to the exclusive designer suede jacket and scrub off the mustard stain.

I started the washer and for the next half hour listened to it swish, churn, and grind its way through its wash cycle. I didn't quite understand that the 80-pound motherlode of wet sweaters was causing the washing machine to have a heart attack from stress. I just thought, "Wow, those sweaters must really be dirty," and I added another half gallon of bleach. The washing machine's cries gradually subsided until the spin cycle clicked on.

At first, the machine just sat quietly as a gear began to groan louder and louder. I began to feel sorry for the washer, wondering if it was trying to call for its lost mate or was suffering from a hernia. The strained, pleading noise grew increasingly louder until at last I could hear the wash begin to turn. Concerned with "Mr. Washer", I watched the machine rumble to life as the speed slowly began to pick up.

Still, all was not well -- the washer started to bounce up and down frantically. A strange thumping sound began to echo throughout the neighborhood. Inky black liquid began to squirt out of a hose from behind the washer. "Beam me up, Scotty!", I shouted, "She's going to blow!!!"

The mad machine rumbled and snorted across the basement, swinging back and forth, straining against its hoses and electric cord. Inky water sprayed wildly from the discharge hose. The incessant thumping and slamming warned me that the machine would explode. I started to run to the stairs, but Mad Max the Washer cut me off. Desperate, I leapt onto the charging monster. I held tight and said my prayers as the berserk machine continued to rampage, spit and thump. Then, with a simple click of the cycle timer, the washer dropped dead.

I slowly got off the washer, carefully opened the lid, and peeked in. A dark, damp, mass peeked back. On top of the soggy load of sweaters was half of a bar of lava soap. All was quiet. "It must have not liked the bar of soap", I mused, and emptied the clothes from the washer. I pulled out a giant doughnut shaped single knot of wet clothes. I was perplexed that I could not separate any of the sweaters from each other. A single suede jacket arm pointed at me from the middle of the giant sweater doughnut.

Rather than waste more time, I stuffed the bundle of washed sweaters directly into the dryer, figuring they'd sort themselves out as they dried. I set the dryer to broil for three hours, figuring "10 minutes to a pound - just like turkey" and went upstairs to watch a football game.

I returned to the basement after the game to empty the dryer. As I descended the stairs, however, I detected the faint odor of fried lamb and pork. "Hmm, someone's barbecuing", I thought, as I reached down to pop open the dryer door. The door opened without a hitch, but a steamy cloud wafted out of the dryer. What appeared to be a giant crisp scorched pork rind was welded onto the door. My wife's exclusive designer, one-of-a-kind deluxe suede jacket was fried! "OHMYGOD!!" I stammered and tried to pry the jacket off the dryer. No use. I reached in to rescue the sweaters and instead pulled out an immense ball of yarn. The sweaters had unraveled and been remade into a giant rainbow-colored bird's-nest. I screamed, "GIVE ME THE SWEATERS BACK, YOU BEAST!!! WHAT DID YOU DO WITH THEM????" The dryer merely burped up a zipper.

"Nooooo," I moaned clutching the huge multicolor furball. Suzie's entire wardrobe of 38 sweaters was destroyed. I had killed them all. Goodbye Liz Clairborne pullover, goodbye wool fisherman knit, goodbye blue fuzzy mohair crewneck, goodbye. Even the indestructible red polyester V-neck was a mere gray lifeless fuzzball. Murdered by me, the laundry room slasher. My only hope was maybe my wife wouldn't notice......(and by now you intelligent readers have already concluded that hope was both futile and stupid.)

I tried to hide the evidence of my destructive deed. I spent the next hour cleaning and venting the basement and buried the remains of the sweaters in my backyard compost pile. Later, when I heard my wife's car pull into the driveway, I met her at the front door with a long stem rose from my garden. "Hi, honey," I greeted her, "I missed you! How would you and the children like to move to Florida with me? Let's leave now! We can send for our stuff."

"Aren't you the dreamer," she replied smiling what was to be her last smile for the decade, "but let's at least go out to dinner. First, let me come inside and get my suede jacket."

P.S. from the garden: She noticed... As I said, I now spend a lot of time out in the garden.

CHAPTER 13

DADDYHOOD AND THE HARD TRUTHS

Sometimes Daddies have trouble explaining hard truths to their young children The understanding of such concepts as divorce, death, violent crime, and similar but common tragedies are things we'd prefer to shelter our children from. Still, we realize that these are things they will have to know about if they are to be prepared for adulthood. There is no easy way to explain some things and no handy reference chapter in the "Rule Book for Perfect Daddyhood". It takes a long time before it even dawns on some children that Daddy can't always give them everything they want. Even if we really wanted to, sometimes our prayers are answered a little differently than we expect. Recently, an unexpected visitor to our home gave our entire family a lesson. As usual, this Daddy wasn't prepared for it.

Our family was having an unusually stressful time. It started on a Saturday when we entirely emptied out my oldest daughter's bedroom to paint, add new carpeting, and redecorate. Alexis, 11 years old, had decided that she had outgrown the lavender walls and The Little Mermaid mural of her childhood. She camped out in the den as I started to convert her room into a more mature teenage apartment. Meanwhile, her furniture and boxes were scattered everywhere around the house. We were constantly tripping over boxes every time we took a step.

On Sunday, as I was scraping her bedroom molding, I accidentally cut the telephone line. Oops. No phones. Unfortunately, the oven must have gotten jealous of my neglect of the kitchen and that night we noticed a gas leak. The local utility was very helpful, but we still lost a lot of sleep until the repairs were completed.

On Monday, there were still no phones, and I was up and out of the house before breakfast for a day long series of important meetings. I staggered home about 10:30 at night to find my wife, Suzie, on crutches. She had fallen in the street in front of our house while making sure the kids were safe as they ran down the block on their way home from school. Suzie had badly hurt her foot and knee. Her foot was very painful and somewhat swollen, but she thought it might only be a bad sprain. She borrowed the crutches from a neighbor but declined to go to the hospital.

Starting Tuesday, I was drafted to be Mr. Mom, Mrs. Doubtfire, Mr. Handyman, as well as Daddy and Mr. Businessman. While Suzie tried to rest her foot, I got up extra early to make the breakfast and school lunches, get the kids dressed and off to school, do the laundry, take out the garbage and still have enough energy to do my job at work. Alexis continued to camp in the den as her empty bedroom gathered dust. And oh yeah, the phone was still out of order. Late in the evening, I realized our refrigerator was nearly empty, and one of my newly acquired responsibilities was food shopping. I dashed to the supermarket without a shopping list but I somehow managed to come home with the five basic food groups: Doritos, potato chips, coffee, vitamin C, and a video tape of Jurassic Park.

The children were all upset because of Mommy's injury and the sudden upheaval within the house. As much as I tried to do things to keep their routine normal, each of them took turns telling me that I wasn't doing "it" the way Mommy did it. They were unusually uncooperative when I asked them to pick up their toys and dirty clothes. I finally grabbed the three girls and sat them down to give them a straight talk.

"Listen carefully girls because I'm only going to say this once. You're right, I'm not doing things the way Mommy does. I'm not Mommy, I'm simply the Daddy. Mommy's absolutely perfect. I'm just a dumb geologist. I can't do everything as good as or as fast as Mommy. Even God would have trouble keeping up with her. Unfortunately, you're stuck with me in charge for awhile. That's life! From now on each of you is chipping in an extra 15 minutes a day to help clean up!", and I turned to leave the room.

Erin, my seven-year-old middle daughter, angrily yelled after me, "That's not fair!!!"

I turned my head and merely asked her, " Erin, here's Hard Truth Number 1: Who ever told you life is always fair?", and I kept walking.

Wednesday, with the phone still out, was another day bordering on the edge of a nervous breakdown. After making breakfast and sending the children off to school, I realized I had packed dirty socks in their lunch boxes. Actually, I only realized this when I opened the washing machine and discovered three soggy tuna sandwiches. "Oh well," I thought, "they'll survive without lunch for one day." Little did I know that 5-year-old K.C. actually would eat her socks for lunch.

I was at work when I got a phone call from the school nurse. No, it wasn't a K.C. tummy sock- ache, it was Erin. She had fallen in the school playground and banged up her face in addition to chipping some teeth. The nurse also told me she had tried to call my wife first, but she couldn't get through on the phone. (Thanks for the reminder!) That day, Erin got another hard lesson. Chipped adult teeth don't grow back. The dentist did a good job filing them even, and Erin was a pretty good trooper through the process. She was a bit sore and uncomfortable, so that night I played

Doctor Daddy in addition to my other roles -- and had maybe 26 total minutes of sleep.

I struggled through work on Thursday praying for the weekend to come so I could finally get some sleep, finish painting Alexis's bedroom, and try to make our home stop looking as if it had been sacked by Visigoths. It rained most of the day, and I was drenched by the time I got home. Suzie's foot was still very sore, and I planned to bring her to the clinic to get an x-ray. At least the phones were sort of working-- we could now get calls, but still couldn't make calls.

When I got in the door, the girls all ran to meet me. "Great," I innocently thought, "they still love simply seeing their Daddy come home!" Wrong! The first words out of their mouths were "Can we keep it?"

"Keep what?"

"The kitten!! Erin found a kitten! Can we keep it?" they pleaded in unison.

"Where is the cat now?" I asked.

"It's still in the back yard. Mommy won't let us bring it inside."

"Well, let me check with Mommy before we make any decisions, girls. You know Mommy is allergic to cat fur."

"Please Daddy, can we keep it?"

"DIDN'T YOU HEAR WHAT I JUST SAID?"

I went upstairs to talk with Suzie. t seems Erin had noticed a little kitten lying in the rain in the back yard. It was drenched and crying. Suzie had no idea how it got there, but she was hoping its mother would come back for it. I told her the girls were pestering and pleading with me to keep it, but Suzie said I'd better take a good look at it before I said anything else.

Puzzled, I went back downstairs and looked out the den window into the backyard. It was getting dark out, and the rain was still coming down. I saw the large clear Tupperware container laying sideways on the lawn, with one of my Kermit the Frog towels crumpled inside of it. No cat in sight. "Good", I thought, "that problem solved itself." I walked outside to retrieve the towel and container. When I bent down to pick up the container, I saw a small, wet fur ball stuck in the towel, then I realized this tiny wet clump of hair was actually a live kitten. It was barely alive.

I gingerly picked up the entire container and brought it into the house, thinking "what in the world do I do now?" Cradling the tiny kitten in my hands, I inspected it as best I could. It was very small, completely wet, and limp. The girls surrounded me quickly, but at least stayed quiet while Dr. Daddy did his work. Careful inspection revealed no broken bones or cuts, but the kitten gave out an occasional cry as if in pain. Its front legs stayed ominously straight, and it would turn its head in a queer manner, as if it was seeing something we weren't. Not good.

Whatever was wrong, I knew two things for certain -- it needed milk and to get dry. Throwing away my plans to finally paint Alexis's bedroom, I sat K.C. and Erin on the sofa, and gave them the kitten to hold. Unfortunately, this was a mistake. In the short time it took to hand the kitten to them while I ran to get a hair dryer, the girls completely "bonded" with it. I returned within 30 seconds to discover they were already fighting over what to name it and whose room it would sleep in.

"NO! NO! NO!", I said. "Girls, I did not say we could keep it. I brought it in only try to help it. I don't even know what's wrong with it. Now, I will not allow you to even name it at this point. I don't even know if it's going to live or die. Hard Truth Number 2: Daddy doesn't know everything."

"We know that Daddy," K.C. replied, "but Mommy does."

Mommy and the girls used the hair dryer to dry off and warm up the kitten while I made a run to the local pet store where I asked as many questions as I could and came home with a can of kitten formula, an infant pet feeder bottle, and the phone number of a recommended veterinarian. Suzie was already sneezing from handling the kitten, which was now cradled and held lovingly in K.C.'s arms. Suzie looked at me imploringly, but I just shrugged my shoulders and told her "I know your allergies are bothering you, but I don't think I had any choice in this. It seems as if this kitten was dropped out of the sky or abandoned. Her mother's not coming to pick her up."

Alexis, Erin, K.C., and I each took turns holding the kitten and trying to feed it with the doll sized baby bottle. This was a tedious, slow, and frustrating process. No matter how long we kept the nipple in the kitten's moth, the milk level in the bottle never declined. It took a long time before I realized that there was not actually anything wrong with the bottle itself. The bottle was fine. The kitten wasn't. For some reason, the kitten didn't even have a nursing reflex and wasn't drinking. K.C. didn't really seem to notice that the kitten drank the same amount of fluid as her dolls, namely nothing. She continued to hug and hold the poor animal and offer it her instant love.

Alexis slept in my bed that night with Suzie while I stayed on the couch with the kitten. The instructions on the can of formula indicated that feeding was required every two to four hours. I spent the entire night with the kitty on my chest, trying to coax it to drink, or merely watching it sleep. I observed how its dark grey fur had subtle streaks of brown. It had blue eyes that barely moved. Was it blind as well? Despite my wife's allergies and my own reservations, I offered to give it a loving home for the next fifteen years if God would only make it get well.

K.C. and Erin both came downstairs early Friday morning to see if the kitty was all right. (Needless to say, they didn't bother to ask if I was all right.) I handed the kitty off to Erin and told the girls I was surprised the kitty had even survived through the night. "But Daddy," K.C. cried, "I don't want the kitty to die!!"

"I know, Princess, but here's Hard Truth Number 3: Everything dies. Everything that ever lives has to die sometime. It's Nature's way, and it's been happening ever since there's been Life. The nice part about Heaven is that no one has to die any more."

Again, I cautioned the girls not to name the kitty, put ribbons in its hair, or plan on adopting it. It was a very sick kitten, and the girls should be prepared for the worst. As I left for work, still promising myself to take Suzie to the clinic to get her foot x-rayed, I also instructed the girls on how to take care of the kitty until I could get home from work. I would take it to a veterinarian as soon as I got home. Erin hugged the kitty on her shoulder as she kissed me goodbye.

I rushed through the day and was able to come home a bit early. The girls were in the den, watching the kitty sleep on my Kermit the Frog towel in the Tupperware container. "Did it eat anything while I was gone?" I asked Suzie.

"No, not much, but K.C. held her almost all day. If there was any way that child could make that kitten get well through shear willpower, K.C. would have done it. I think we've done everything we could. Are you going to take it to the Doctor now?"

I went into the den and told the girls it was best if I took "Kitty" to the veterinarian. I told them the truth. I thought the kitty was going to die, and if that was true, I'd ask the vet to put it to sleep. The girls sadly said goodbye to the kitty. Alexis asked if she could take a picture of it. I fumbled for an answer, but finally told her I wouldn't need a photo to remember this cat.

At the animal hospital, my worst fears were confirmed. The kitty was beyond saving. It was brain damaged and blind besides having pneumonia. The nurse told me we obviously had done the best we could, but it was useless. Choking back tears (Hard Truth Number 4: Daddies aren't allowed to cry in public), I agreed to let the vet put the kitty to sleep.

When I returned home, the girls first thought I had miraculously "saved" the kitty but were crushed when they saw that the Tupperware container was empty. All the girls cried, particularly K.C. I gave them revised Hard Truth Number 4: It's O.K. to be sad once in awhile. However, also be happy that God knew we were a nice enough family to be given the opportunity to provide comfort and care to one of His creatures. No matter how mixed up our house has been during the last week, or how much we think things aren't fair, this was just a way of showing us how lucky we are to have each other.

I tried not to think about the kitty during the next two weeks. Things sort of got back to "normal". Suzie did have a fractured foot, (and needed a cast for the next two months). Alexis did eventually get her room painted and redecorated. No, we did not go out and buy a new kitten, but we did get a new phone. I wondered if the girls might have forgotten about the kitty. After all, they were still very young.

Two weeks later, as I was driving Erin to a soccer game, she and I began to play our favorite car game, "Jeopardy". The rules are simple, one person establishes three categories, and then asks appropriate questions in the same format as the popular TV show. Erin's selected categories were "school", "family", and "Precious Moments". I asked for "family" for $10.

Erin's question was, "What was the name of the kitten that Erin found, but died?"

I was stumped and surprised. "Erin, I don't know. I thought I told you girls not to name the kitty. I thought we were going to wait to see if it would live...... O.K., what was its name?"

"Its name was Kitty. Daddy, you were the one who named it that!", and Erin smiled.

Erin was right. Hard Truth Number 5: Sometimes the kids are smarter than you think!

CHAPTER 14

BIRTHDAYS AND DADDYDUMB

My older sister had four boys. Being "Uncle Ribbit" to this diverse variety of male genetic traits should have warned me not to have any children, particularly boys. Even though I did not see `I think I've had my fill of watching them devour 48 "Fudgy the Whale" Carvel ice cream cakes. I watched as the excited birthday boys tore open countless gift boxes of sports equipment, superhero underwear, and killer toys. I remember them shuddering when they opened the inevitable new pair of pajamas from Grandma. I remember the noise and screams of pleasure from the boys when they got a drum set, and the quick exit I made from the house when they started to play it.

It used to amuse me to observe that my sister's hair turned grayer with each year of mommyhood. Somehow, God heard my prayers when I begged Him not to let me have any sons. God must also have a sense of humor since I am now a Daddy to three daughters. I now have a lot of gray hair, too. I'll never have as many "parent experience" years as my sister, but with a 5-, 8-, and 12-year-old, I've already accumulated a quarter century of "Daddy years". As the hormones start to be activated in our oldest daughter, however, I'm worried that teenage girls can be more unsettling and wearing than any wolf pack of toddler boys.

Even though the girls only total twenty-five years in age, we've already celebrated 75 birthday parties. This seems to be a precursor to the trouble and expense we'll go through when the girls plan their weddings. My wife, Suzie, doesn't merely plan elaborate parties. She carefully choreographs them as Oscar quality shows. Birthday parties must be socially correct and yet show imagination and individuality. The events are scheduled for the Saturday nearest the girl's birthday, unless it interferes with soccer, gymnastics, art lessons, Brownies, community service, or a conflicting party scheduled by another Mommy.

Suzie has even scheduled a party for a March 28 birthday on July 20! I, however, insist on a separate party for each girl on her exact birthday. This is my family's tradition. The party doesn't have to be anything exotic, but a date is a date, and I grew up having your birthday as a special day. My wife's family usually ignored actual birthdays and had family "birthmonth" parties. They merely lumped whoever was born in the general season into the birthday celebration. It used to annoy me that they served birthday cakes with poorly scrawled icing writing: "Happy Birthday - Insert Name Here".

A traditionalist, I insist on an individual birthday cake, card, and visit from Grandma on each child's birthday. This worked out when Alexis, our firstborn, was little, but things changed when she started nursery school. We also now had to have a party at the school with her 20 other classmates. Suzie wanted to bring in simple decorated cupcakes and milk but was advised by the nursery school dietician that the toddlers were suffering from "cupcakeitis" from overdoses of birthday cupcakes every week. Our three-year-old celebrated her class birthday with dietary correct cranberry juice and celery stalks with "Happy Birthday" written in cream cheese.

We had also accumulated neighborhood toddler friends. Naturally we had a separate birthday party for the "locals" and their mommys. At first, these informal parties were primarily an excuse for the moms to meet for coffee and bagels, but the parties became more elaborate and extensive as more children were born.

Birthday parties now had themes; An English Tea Party, a Nature Party, a My Little Pony Party, a "Doubledare Party"-- where each child was a contestant in a series of contests, an Olympic Birthday Party, and so on. Suzie would scour magazines and the grapevine to come up with clever and creative new ideas, foods, and games. One year our house nearly lifted off its foundation when Suzie strung 400 helium filled balloons along the ceiling.

Mommy always managed to keep things festive, creative, but controlled. My assignment was merely to make sure there was enough milk, and to take pictures. The rest is a blur. Someday, an archeologist will view our home videos and think 20th century civilization consisted of nothing but little girls in fancy dresses ripping open wrapped boxes, saying "wow!", and then blowing out candles. The other future mystery will be trying to explain why each guest is blindfolded, spun around until dizzy, and then sent crashing into a wall with a sharp pin extending from their hand.

The sleep over party theme invariably raises its ugly specter around a child's twelfth birthday. I guess all Mommies and Daddies go through this rite of passage, but Daddies should be particularly warned in the "Guidebook for Perfect Daddyhood" to book a private hospital room for a couple of days recovery, particularly if the birthday child is a girl. I plead temporary insanity and ignorance. I'll never forget the consequences of having 12 preteen girls in various stages of hormonal change at our house for a weekend. I'll never forget the uncontrolled giggles, the tears, the screams, fights, and stupid tricks. Why? That was me! The girls were just being girls.

Sleep over parties for twelve-year-old boys are a lot simpler. As a former Boy Scout leader, I remember how easy it was to entertain boys. We could pass an entire weekend of sleepless bliss with just three items: an endless supply of pizza, video games, and horror movies. Gifts were simple too, -- pizza coupons, video games, and horror movie tapes. Boys traveled light. Maybe three of the dozen boys would remember a tooth-brush and change of socks and at least two others wouldn't even bring a sleeping bag.

Girls are much more complicated. Alexis and Suzie wanted a Hawaiian theme sleepover party for Friday night. I wanted to go to the beach on Saturday and suggested a beach party instead. We talked about the alternates for a bit, and then I innocently suggested, "Why not a Friday night sleepover and then we all go to the beach Saturday morning? After all, what's the big deal?" Suzie tried to elbow me, but Alexis thought it was a super idea. Finally, Suzie agreed. Then, I found out Alexis had invited, not the usual 4 or 5 close girlfriends, but a whole dozen. Oops! Suzie omi-nously suggested we hold off telling the girls about the beach plans until we got through Friday night.

The Friday came all too quickly. The first guest, Katie, arrived with a steam trunk full of clothes, queen sized mattress, makeup barrel, boombox radio, and 66 cassette tapes. Uh, oh. Thirty minutes and eleven more guests later, I had more merchandise in my den and living room than Sears. When the Ryder rent-a-truck pulled up to our house with Ariel, I was tempted to pack my own sleeping bag and hitch a ride out of town.

In retrospect, I should have just let the truck run me over. The next few hours, with 12 giggly girls in the house, in addition to Mommy, 8-year-old Erin, and littlest sister K.C., are a blurred nightmare. The girls seemed to divide into two groups - those who were already boy crazy, and those who were certain boys were just crazy. The first group couldn't stop giggling and talking about how cute Pauly or Billy was, and the second group just wanted to play Barbie. While the first group tried to act "cool" and "grown up", they all snuck upstairs and got a few minutes "Doll fix", combing a Barbie or American Girl doll while their confused hormones boiled and bubbled.

All of the girls loved Alexis's "goody bags". These specially made goody bags contained erasers, a makeup mirror, and the ultimate 12-year-old girl treasure, nail polish. They screamed with delight. I couldn't scream. I was nearly overcome as 144 bottles of nail polish were simultaneously opened. For the next 45 minutes, the group painted each others fingers and toes, as well as an elbow, two belly buttons, and our dining room rug. The temperature dropped 9 degrees when they all began waving their hands to dry their fingers.

I volunteered to get a breath of fresh air and go get the pizzas and milk. I arrived home with several pies and a half pint of milk. Everyone sat around the dining room wearing Hawaiian leis, eating pizza, and admiring each others glistening nails and toes. The girls spent the next hour watching each other pretend to be video rock stars, dancing to music tapes, trying to mimic Madonna. I was getting both bored and embarrassed when I realized a few of the preteen "mini-Madonnas" were borrowing my socks to make themselves look bigger. I needed an escape, so I volunteered to get more milk from Seven-Eleven.

It's a five-minute drive, and I made the trip several times, buying a half pint of milk each time. Raza, the prototypical Seven-Eleven manager, finally asked me why I was coming in so much that night. I explained we had a dozen twelve-year-old girls over for a sleep over birthday party. They drink a lot of milk. He suggested I buy more than a half pint of milk at a time. I almost hit him, but he was right. I was just desperate. I wondered if I would be able to wear socks again without laughing. I bit the bullet and bought a whole pint of milk this time and returned home.

The endless party night continued. Around 11PM, everyone gathered in the living room to watch a video, Forest Gump. While I admit this is a very good movie, I didn't realize it was nearly three hours long. Two of the girls fell asleep on the floor before the movie was over. During the last half hour, it became harder and harder to hear the soundtrack over the growing snores. The movie had several very emotional scenes, a "four Kleenex" tearjerker. Twelve-year-old girls seem to have leaky eyes. Six trees were sacrificed to make enough tissues to dry everyone's eyes. By the closing credits, the entire living room was literally flooded with water. "Wow," I thought, "that's a heck of a lot of tears." Then, my wife noticed that the bathroom toilet had overflowed. My own tears joined the group.

Finally, at 2:30AM, sleep time was formally announced. And formally ignored by two twelve-year-old zombies. Two of the girls insisted they were going to stay up all night and tell scary stories.... and they proceeded to keep everyone else awake the rest of the night with noise, laughter, boy tales, and sarcasm. My wife and I gave up coming back downstairs to tell the group to be quiet. It didn't seem to make any difference, even when I threatened to sacrifice Chris to the Hawaiian volcano god if she didn't go to sleep. Around 5AM, even our daughter Alexis gave up being a gracious host and stumbled upstairs to the quiet sanctuary of her own room.

We slept for 2 hours. When my alarm clock went off at 7AM, my wife stumbled out of bed and proceeded to paint a "happy face" on her weary head. She cheerfully ran downstairs and shook each girl awake.... very, very firmly! "Rise and Shine!!!", she shouted, "It's time to GET UP!!" Actually, it was time to get up. The party wasn't over yet. Suzie had scheduled a filling breakfast, and then my final treat - a morning at the beach! All of the 15 girls thought this was a great idea. By now, I thought my beach idea was insane, but kept my mouth shut in fear of the group stomping me to death.

Each of the girls called their homes to get permission and a bathing suit and towel. All but one girl could make it. Within a short while, moms were stopping by our house with towels and bathing suits for their kids. None of the moms said anything particular about the beach party plan, but they all looked a bit strangely at me. One mom came to pick up her daughter. She was already scheduled to be at a Saturday morning lesson. She apologized that her daughter couldn't go to the beach. She then leaned over and softly told my wife she felt sorry for her but realized this must be our first sleepover party experience. "Yes, "my wife confirmed, "How did you know?"

The mom looked at me with a dubious look in her eye and replied, "I figured you two might not have much experience yet with teenagers. Only a real idiot would schedule a morning beach party following a teenage sleep over party!"

My constantly supportive, sympathetic, and reassuring, wonderful wife was quiet for about five full seconds, then calmly replied, "Yes, but I married him anyway."

CHAPTER 15

DADDY AND THE SANTAHOODS

Christmas is an exceptionally long holiday season at our home. Our family Christmas season usually starts the day after Halloween and continues through the January "white sales". Christmas reluctantly ends when I get my last post-Christmas "greeting card" --- from Visa, Master Card, and American Express reminding me once again that I am not only Santa's helper but am financially responsible for an entire sleigh full of gifts. I am tempted to forward the bills to the North Pole, but nevertheless, this Daddy is truly glad to be a Santa's helper. And yes, there really is a Santa Claus.

I don't quite understand why there is so much controversy about whether Santa Claus is "real". Most adults can happily remember when, as young children, we first met Santa. I can still remember hearing his sleigh bells late one Christmas Eve and rushing downstairs to find my Mom, Dad, Uncle Bill, and Aunt Dorothy standing in the living room by the fireplace. "Hi, Big-Boy," my Dad said, "you just missed him. Santa's already gone back up the chimney. Look, he ate the cookies you left him, and I think there might be some gifts for you and your sister." I glanced at Uncle Bill as he wiped cookie crumbs off his chin, then leaped towards a pile of brightly wrapped packages. Maybe Uncle Bill had been Santa

81

that year, but I wasn't going to say anything. I didn't want to risk forfeiting Santa's new gift for me, a Super-Duper Deluxe Little Professor Chemistry set.

My children have their own "Santa Is Real" confirmation story which I use to remind myself not only that Santa lives, but that there is a God, and He has a sense of humor. That special Christmas occurred when Erin, our middle daughter was three years old. Our family traditionally spends Christmas Eve at my mother's house, which is located only a few blocks from our own home. It is one of the few times in any given year when my sister's family and mine are together. Suzie and I were getting ready to drive over to Grandmas and had just about gotten the coats on to each of our three daughters when Suzie noticed that Erin didn't look so good. Suzie asked Erin if she felt OK. As a reply, Erin merely bent over and threw up. This was not what I expected Erin to give us for a Christmas present.

Dr. Mom took Erin's temperature and diagnosed Erin as a feverish virus victim. I then made the typical Daddy ruling, "That's too bad. You stay home with her, and I'll take the other two girls to Grandmas. Bye!" and quickly fled the house before being volunteered to help clean up Erin.

The rest of evening passed quickly. Seven-year-old Alexis enjoyed playing with her older cousins (four boys - which is the primary reason I seldom visit my sister) and everyone enjoyed watching our cute little 9-month-old daughter, K.C., propped up in the corner. Grandma has a player piano. As part of our Christmas tradition, we get out the rolls of Christmas carols and sing honky-tonk versions of "Here Comes Santa Claus", "Silent Night", and "Yellow Bird". Yes, I know "Yellow Bird" isn't exactly a popular Christmas Song, but the music roll accidentally got put into the box with the Christmas songs in 1967 and neither my sister nor I had the nerve to tell our Dad he made a mistake. Instead, for over twenty years, we've bravely sung, "Yellow bird, up high in banana tree..." wondering how the banana tree would look if it had ornaments on it.

We then exchange and open family gifts, being very careful not to tear the wrapping paper. Instead, we have to smooth out and fold each piece so it can be reused. After all, Grandma grew up during the Depression. I think some of the wrapping paper actually dates from the 1930's, but has so many folds and tape repairs, it's a bit hard to make out the Shirley Temple pattern anymore. Finally, we spend the next hour politely smiling and quietly wondering why some of the crummy gifts "we" got seem to be clones of what we gave "them" the year before. After swearing we won't buy any more Christmas gifts for our relatives at Cheap Johns, we all stand in a group while Grandma takes a photo of us with her 1952 vintage Kodak Brownie Camera.

The annual Christmas photo is another bizarre Christmas tradition. Grandma is not famous for photography or cameras that actually work. She only takes one or two photos a year, and the roll of film presently in the camera dates back to April 1983. If the film doesn't altogether decompose, we can plan on seeing the photos when she finishes the roll in 2004. This story is true. Grandma was given the camera, and a 36-exposure roll of black and white film in 1952 when I was born. I finally saw my baby picture when I came home from the hospital with my own child in 1983. It had taken Grandma over 30 years to finish the roll. At least I was smart enough to buy Grandma only a 24-exposure roll. And I gave her color film this time!

I had just unwrapped by fourth frog-shaped wicker basket from my fourth nephew, when I noticed that K.C. was missing. She couldn't have crawled away by herself, but the corner where I had propped her was now filled with a pile of carefully folded used Christmas wrap, and a ball of recycled ribbon. Oops, my mistake. The ribbon "ball" was K.C.'s head. K.C. had fallen asleep, and my youngest nephew Danny had wrapped her up as a gift for his mom figuring it was a not just a cheap gift, but a neat way of getting a baby sister.

I carefully picked K.C. up, unwound her, and told everyone it was time for me to take the girls home. "After all, they will want to be asleep so Santa Claus can come," I added. Seven-year-old Alexis, however, was in no mood to go to bed. She was busy making origami frogs out of bits of Christmas wrapping paper. Actually, she and Grandma has fought over whether making Japanese origami paper animals was an appropriate or wasteful use for Grandma's treasure trove of hoarded used Christmas paper. My nephew (and future lawyer) J.J. resolved the conflict by pointing out to Grandma that Alexis wasn't wasting paper, but artistically and cheaply making reusable animal shaped Christmas bows!

This explanation fit in with Grandma's financial savings lifestyle. After all, the wrapping paper did cost money (probably 69 cents for 2,000 square feet in the 1960's) and could still be used. Grandma is not one to waste money - even at the age of 80 she was still putting $200 per month into a savings account for when she "got old". Anyway, Grandma and Alexis continued to eye each other suspiciously, but I agreed to let Alexis stay while I briefly left to take K.C. home, check on Erin and Suzie, and return for more of the festivities.

As I left with K.C. tucked on my shoulder, ever-frugal Grandma handed me 58 cents. I looked at the five Mercury head dimes and eight "Wheatie" pennies and asked, "Wow, Mom, you must have finally opened the family vault! What's this, a tip or your Christmas gift for Erin?"

"Don't be an idiot, Robert, there's a special sale on pickled herring at Grand Union. It's a tradition to eat a bite of herring for good health in the new year. Pick up a small jar on your way back."

I pocketed the change, grumbling that Grand Union was four miles out of my way, but personally pleased thinking I'd actually pulled a fast one on "exact change" Mom. The old Mercury dimes were worth at least a quarter each and "Wheatie" pennies were becoming scarce. It was only when I found out the herring actually cost $1.39 that I realized Mom had already prorated the value of the collectible coins and had given me exact change after all. Damn, she's good!

I still had the partially wrapped but sleeping K.C. with me as I was finally driving home, when I noticed a station wagon stopped in the middle of the street on my block. It wasn't hard to notice the car. There was a five-foot tall red and white lighted reindeer mounted on its roof, and loud vaguely familiar strange music blaring from a hood mounted speaker. I pulled up behind the wagon and stopped. The passenger door of the wagon opened slowly, and out stepped..... the Jolly Green Giant?!? A heavy-set guy (?) at least seven- feet tall, wearing a white fur trimmed, short green felt dress walked towards me. I was too shocked to throw my car into reverse and flee, so I rolled down my window, leaned out and said, "Ho, Ho, Ho, Green Giant! Looking for the vegetable patch?"

If looks could kill, I'd have been a compost candidate, but "Mr. Green" apparently was just tired of hearing the same joke repeated over and over. He apologized for blocking the road and explained that he and his partner were having trouble locating a particular address on the block, 10 Hawthorne Road. "You mean there's two of you out here?" I asked wondering where the Candid Camera was hidden. Then, I noticed another oddly dressed behemoth running across the front lawns. Wait a minute... it was Santa Claus!!!! Santa spotted the Green Giant and me and ran over. "Sorry, Mister. Do you happen to know where 10 Hawthorne Road is?"

"Actually, 'Santa', there is no 10 Hawthorne Road. Would you mind filling me in a bit as to what you and the Jolly Green Giant are doing?"

"Yo, I'm not the Green Giant, I'm an elf. I'm one of Santa's helpers! Do you understand me?", Mr. Green roared.

An elf on steroids, I thought, but replied only, "OK, OK. How can I help you?" That question stumped us all for a minute, but eventually I made a deal with Santa and the Elf King. They could follow me home and use my telephone to call for directions if they would also spend a minute visiting my sick daughter, Erin. It turned out that Santa and his Elf body-guard were college students who had a list of families to visit on Christmas Eve. The Elf said he was on a football scholarship and Santa was studying business management. They used this assignment to help earn room and board at the school.

Santa and his helper followed me home and walked with me to the front door. I fumbled with the keys, then handed K.C. to "Mr. Green" as I needed two hands to work the lock. Mr. Green took K.C. then said, "Wow it's a baby! I thought it was a liquor bottle. And you thought we were strange. Why do you have your kid wrapped up like that?"

Fortunately, the door opened before I could answer. Santa, me, K.C. and our smart alecky elf walked in. As luck would have it, Suzie was sitting in the living room with Erin resting on her lap. "Hi Erin," I softly called. "Santa heard you were sick and made a special trip just to visit you."

Erin sat up, and both she and Suzie's jaws dropped wide open. For the first time in her life, my wife was speechless. The seven-foot elf handed K.C. to Suzie and said, "Merry Christmas! No Backs! Can I use your phone, please?"

Meanwhile, Santa was having a nice little talk with Erin. He told her he was sorry to hear she was sick and said he was trying to get all the toys she had requested in her letter but was troubled about the request for a Super-Duper Deluxe Little Professor Chemistry set. Erin explained the chemistry set wasn't actually for her, but for her Daddy. (It seems her Daddy's father had thrown out the set when Daddy was a boy, after Daddy accidentally melted the family cat trying to make a hairless version so no one would be bothered by allergies.) Santa glanced at me as if he somehow remembered hearing about my aborted science career. Santa straightened up, then handed a candy cane to Erin. "Keep the faith, Erin, and try not to brag so much to Alexis that she missed seeing Santa. We both already know how ticked off she's going to be."

Santa and his elf bouncer huddled for a minute, then asked me where 10 Hathaway Drive was, the correct location instead of the non-existent 10 Hawthorne Road. Fortunately, it was only a block away, and I walked outside with them to return to Grandmas and my soon to be upset oldest daughter. Santa's rooftop plastic reindeer shown brightly, and the loud strange music boomed from the car speaker. "Santa," I asked, "That doesn't sound like any Christmas carol I know. What song is that?"

Santa and the elf-lord laughed as they drove away. "You are an idiot, after all. That song's the old Christmas special classic, Yellow Bird! MERRY CHRISTMAS!!!"

My only thought was Santa Lives! – and. I'm sorry about the chemistry set.

CHAPTER 16

THE CAREER GAME AND DADDYHOOD

When I was young, life was simple. Most boys my age wanted to be either a policeman, fireman, astronaut, or a cowboy. Most girls wanted to be teachers, nurses, or mommies. There were no job descriptions called information technology managers, or periodontal hygienists. We also drank whole milk without the foggiest notion what cholesterol was. I never saw my Dad's copy of the "Rulebook for Perfect Daddyhood", but I'm sure it was a lot thinner than the revised version I supposedly was handed when I became a Daddy. But, like Father - like Son, I bet he misplaced his copy too. There were many times I wish I hadn't misplaced my own copy. The overdue fines are probably enormous. Needless to add, I'm still winging it and am too much a macho man to simply ask for directions.

Today, life is increasingly more complicated. I imagine that my Dad's copy of his Daddyhood guidebook had a brief section on how to help your children plan for a career as an adult. His version was probably simple: 1) go to school, 2) get a job, 3) work 40 years, 4) retire and move to Florida. Easy advice, but a bit cryptic and it didn't explain the ulcers that many dads suffered from in the 1950's. I used to think men had ulcers issued to them as part of their employee benefits package. I didn't realize that the family father's stomach problems were caused primarily by trying to cope raising with children like me. It was only after I had my own children that I realized the true message my dad was really trying to tell me when he said, "you'll get yours".

One clue to the cause of my Dad's ulcer came when I was about eight. Dad was an engineer and was trying to explain to me what he actually did in the office every day. I asked him if he liked his work. His answer surprised me because he only answered, "Don't ever become an engineer". "That's it?", I wondered, "Then how come you've worked as an engineer your whole life??" Dad cringed and then asked me what I wanted to be when I grew up. I looked up at him and proudly answered, "An undertaker. Why not? Everyone dies, so I'd never be out of work. Besides, I could probably collect a lot of change from their pockets before I buried them." My Dad didn't respond to my stated career goals. He just turned a strange shade of green, held his stomach, and backed away.

Ten years later, I no longer wanted to be an undertaker. I just didn't quite know what I did want to be, so in the meanwhile I went to an engineering school and ultimately ended up working at the very same engineering company my Dad had worked at.... except he had now retired and of course, moved to Florida. Out of respect for my Dad's advice, my degrees were in science rather than engineering. Another ten years passed, and I was still working at that same company in New York City, but Dad was now gone, and I still didn't know what I wanted to be when I grew up. I could not see working for that company for another thirty years. After careful consideration, I quit and tried something else. I tried a 2 -year gig in Saudi Arabia as a geotechnical engineer for the U.S. Army Corps of Engineers.

Fifteen years and five jobs later, I'm getting good personal experience with such terms as "downsizing", "corporate restructuring", and "company relocations" as American business continues to give ulcers to the workforce while destroying the notion of career plans. Times have also changed for the better too, with more opportunities for women and minorities. The glass ceiling is finally being shattered as females take on more corporate "power" roles - but I'll bet that more women are also getting ulcers as a result. Computers and telecommunications enable flexible workdays and working at home possible. "Career" choices are expanding as new specialties come into demand. It just seems that everyone is a consultant rather than actually doing the work.

Unfortunately, career counseling is a bit confusing for this Daddy of three young daughters. I find it hard to give advice as to which direction to guide the girls. Each of them has their own talents, but it's a bit difficult to predict what the world will be like tomorrow let alone in twenty years. My wife, an artist, has been able to build her own career steadily while balancing her time as Supermommy and domestic goddess. Her influence and genes hopefully have rubbed off on each of the girls.

Our oldest daughter, 13-year-old (going on 29) Alexis, was born with a crayon in her mouth. From the time she could sit up, she spent countless hours in Mommy's art studio drawing while her mother did her own artwork. Alexis has never hesitated to say she was going to be an artist and has already sold paintings and won awards for her work. Nicknamed "Ali" from my year in the Saudi Arabian desert, she also has a good aptitude for science and math and does well in all areas. Ali has the talent, training, and perseverance to succeed, and I don't worry about her. Art comes first, but to give a bit of credit to influence from Daddy's environmental career, Alexis has mentioned she'd be interested in concentrating on wildlife art. She's even designed her own business card, and I keep suggesting to my wife that she start subcontracting her work to Alexis. I think Suzie's afraid of the potential competition. She entered one of Alexis's drawings at an art show a few years ago, not realizing 10-year-old artists were not permitted to be in the show. Alexis's painting sold....

and Suzie's didn't. It was probably the first time one of the artists spent her award prize money on Barbie clothes.

Erin, our 9-year-old middle child, has constantly amazed me with her uniqueness. As a toddler, she made her presence well known. She would have given my Dad a Magnitude 7 on the Richter ulcer-earthquake scale. We were tempted to nickname her Beetlejuice. There are times I've said that if we had Erin first, we wouldn't have any children now. Actually, she is a wonderful girl, and has many talents -- including a very active imagination. Her unique career plans will be a guidance counselor's nightmare, however, since Erin seems to want to do everything. She too, wants to be an artist, but also a teacher, professional swimmer, chef, environmental scientist, and musician, before settling down to get married when she's 20. Actually, she would make an excellent teacher and is sure to be in demand as a babysitter. (Providing of course, you don't mind if she gives your children tattoos while you're out for the evening.)

My own feeling is that Erin would be a fantastic defense attorney. She is a natural showman of pure absolute self-proclaimed innocence --even if caught red-handed. She is a true defender of the democratic system. Her most common expression is "It's not fair!" -- particularly if she sees her sisters getting something she wants. She has a special defense lawyer's talent for shifting blame. "I didn't do it! Someone else must have done it! You can't prove I did it! Anyway, you weren't home when I did it!" Well, maybe she needs some more practice... Erin has a Master of Science degree in Excusology but may have skipped more than her share of classes in Common Sense 101. Actually, she is a smart young lady and, if God allows, she will make an outstanding teacher if that's what she decides. She also will probably be able to see through every excuse her students give her.

Our youngest daughter, six-year-old Kathleen, already has her career goals etched in stone. K.C. is going to be a gymnast-ballerina-cowgirl-artist.

(I guess uniqueness runs in the family.) This pint-sized dynamo is probably going to end up a professional clown and has actually performed with me as my dummy in our ventriloquist act. She has a maniacal laugh and amuses herself with the dumbest jokes, but sings, dances and tells stories like a pro. One thing she will never be, though, is a maid or interior decorator. She used to just laugh whenever we asked her to pick up her room. I'd ask her again, and she'd just giggle and say, "I can't do that!" I figured she was just waiting for her sisters or me to pick up her room for her, but I became impatient. "K.C.," I finally yelled, "how come you can't pick up your room???"

She giggled some more and answered, "How can I? Daddy, it's attached to the house!"

K.C. inevitably has piles of toys and clothes scattered everywhere and is always emptying out another closet in search of more props for her favorite game, "Dress -up". Maybe she has potential as a fashion model or display artist, but her taste in dress-up clothes usually borders on the outrageous. She mixes gold lame vests with pink chiffon slips, high heels and five scarves. I thought my own fashion style was more conservative, but a few years ago I had an interesting lesson that my fashion tastes weren't always apropos. There was a designated clothes bin at her nursery school for "dress-up". One day, when I went to pick K.C. up from her class, I noticed several of the children playing dress-up. One boy was wearing a lime green, wide lapelled size 40 tuxedo. Another boy was wearing a peach fuzzy, tan, and purple colored size 40 sports jacket and pants as well as a 5-inch-wide tie with smiley faces on it. My favorite suits! My best tie! I tried to ask for my clothes back, but the teacher said that she thought a circus had donated them. I could almost hear the beginnings of an ulcer forming in my belly as I sadly got back into the car empty-handed.

There are times when I have interviewed for a new position or new challenge. One question that the invariably is brought up deals with handling stress. I've worked under ultra-high-pressure situations where critical decisions have to be made accurately and quickly. I've met impossible deadlines and gotten teams to work effectively under grueling conditions. I don't bother talking about the hazardous sites or safety issues. I just look the interviewer in the eye and tell him I'm a Daddy to three daughters so if I'm still alive, I guess I handle stress pretty well. To me, the most difficult and yet thoroughly enjoyable career is being a Daddy. (Besides simply taking the dog out for a walk.)

CHAPTER 17

DADDY GETS VOLUNTEERED

Five years ago, I was dozing through a local property owners association meeting when my wife, Suzie, raised my arm. Our Village had just established an environmental advisory board and Suzie felt it would be good for me to get involved. At the time, I was employed on a natural gas vehicle fuel program for Brooklyn Union Gas - a natural gas utility. My education and background experience, however, was in geology and environmental science. Even though I was qualified to be on the environmental advisory board, I was reluctant to have been "volunteered". I preferred to spend my free time being Daddy to our three girls instead of going to meetings. Suzie reminded me that sitting with them on the sofa watching 'The Simpsons' and 'Muppet Babies' cartoons for three hours each night was not a meaningful contribution to responsible Daddyhood. "Besides," Suzie said," the Village estimates it only will take up about six hours of your time each month."

The first year on the "Board" went by quickly, and as it turned out, I wasn't so "bored" with the Board after all. The other volunteer members were nice people, especially Bob, who turned out to have the same crazy sense of humor as me. There was even another geologist, Brandon, who volunteered to study water resource concerns - my own specialty, leaving me to try to address land use instead. Brandon and I enjoyed "rock talk" and worked on a report recommending a new well reserve system for the Village. No pay, but it gave me a chance to polish my technical writing skills.

When the Village needed an inventory of all of the open space properties, the task was assigned to the Land Use Committee - me. The original estimated six hours volunteer work per month began to escalate to six hours per week. I had to stop watching the TV with the girls, but they also got "volunteered". Between the four of us, we used up a dozen colored pencils, hand coloring a four-foot by nine-foot map of the town, showing all the types of open and green space remaining. My "expert committee" consisted of a 9-year-old, a 5-year-old, and a 2-year-old. And a 40-year-old - me. The girls taught me to color well.

During the next year, I was volunteered to give public presentations on the inventory my "committee" conducted. I was petrified of public speaking, so used my daughters as a practice audience. They were merciless. "Daddy, stop stuttering. Daddy, you're not up to date on your facts. Keep to the text, Daddy, and stop using your Kermit the Frog voice". Slowly, I became increasingly more comfortable talking with people. I found out people don't usually bite the speaker, and that my zipper was almost always up.

During one of my presentations, a resident innocently suggested I consider whether one area of open space in town could be designated a nature preserve or bird sanctuary. I was again volunteered to investigate this possibility. It was a heck of a bigger task than anyone ever expected. I had to give up my lunch hours, weekends, and half my sleep. Meetings with boy and girl scout troops, church groups, school clubs, wildlife organizations, colleges, Village, County, and State agencies, etc. Letters, papers, telephone calls, faxes, photos. Although I always had a terrible aptitude for remembering names, I soon realized I could recognize over 400 of the different kids who had been "volunteered" to help on the project.

My wife and daughters were constantly drafted to help me out at the designated site. Picking up litter, taking photos, planting flowers. Every weekend we came home smelling of compost and dirt. At nights after work, the girls, Suzie, and I made art posters and signs for the nature area. Neighbors were "volunteered" to help build bird houses. My simple volunteer work had developed into nearly a full time second career. As much as the bird sanctuary site began to develop, my own yard and garden became more neglected. My surviving perennial plants even pulled up their roots by themselves and hitched a ride over to the sanctuary. The plants left me a note saying they don't see me at home much anymore.

In the meanwhile, Bob, my fellow board member, somehow got me volunteered to my church's mission board with the false promise "Rob, it's only about 4 hours a month of your time." Bob's a natural salesman. The following year, he even managed to volunteer me into donating some of my blood at a hospital. "It's for a good cause" he said, "and besides, you get free orange juice and cookies."

"OK, OK, OK!" I replied. "I've been too busy to eat lately anyway. I just hope the patient doesn't fly off the bed when she gets my blood in her veins. Over half of my body fluid is pure caffeine."

The bird sanctuary project was a success thanks to the efforts of hundreds of local residents, kids, my own family, and major support from the local Audubon Society group and Hofstra University. I gave a few lectures and talks to nursery and elementary school groups about the environment, nature, and the bird sanctuary. One group of fourth graders was very attentive when I showed them several different types of live turtles during a talk about ecosystems. When I mentioned there were turtles at the new bird sanctuary, one boy seemed very surprised, and a bit upset. I then told him there were also squirrels, mice, lizards, and many kinds of animals at the sanctuary. He was unusually quiet for a moment and then softly asked me, "And they're all dead?" I then realized I needed to carefully explain the difference between a sanctuary - and a cemetery!

One drawback to this volunteer effort was that I became known as the "Village bird brain". So much for respect. Each Spring, there are invariably several instances when neighbors drop off a baby squirrel or injured bird at my house with the irrational logic that I would know what to do with the animals. I don't! Actually, I'm not much of a bird watcher either. My daughters are learning to spot different bird species. My own favorite birds are usually chicken or turkey but sometimes duck, and an occasional rock Cornish game hen. I'm learning, though, how to tell the difference between a cardinal and a crow.

I recently asked my wife whether she was ever sorry she volunteered me for the environmental board. She agreed that it took up much of my free time but said that when she found my unread copy of the "Rulebook For Perfect Daddyhood", she realized she would have to do something drastic to make sure I followed its guide plan. She had my misplaced rule-book! "One of the basic rules," she commented, "is to teach your children how to do something you enjoy doing. You're helping them learn skills as well as values. It's worth the effort." Suzie the PhD. Mommygoddess was right, of course, but this bird brain still can't figure out how she tricked me into taking these Daddyhood classes without me even knowing it.

CHAPTER 18

SOCCER DAD

When I last counted, my wife Suzie and I had three daughters. I'm too tired to be absolutely sure, and I don't always see them or my wife. I just see the backs of their heads as they drive by. We communicate mainly by waving to each other as we constantly drive the girls and their friends back and forth to assorted lessons, practices, games, and programs. Raising three children is a wearing task for any household. Somehow, sending the kids out of the house "to play" is simply not allowed in our time-pressed suburban culture. As children, our baby boom generation leisurely roamed the streets and town parks, having what we thought of as fun - playing tag, ring-o-leaveo, hide and go seek, red light\green light, and war. (Well, maybe playing "war" was not such a hot idea but no one ever got permanently killed in our games.) Our simple games were usually carefree and unstructured. One of my wife's favorite games was "boomer cars." The rules were simple. Each child would tuck their arms under their jackets, so the sleeves were empty. Once everyone was armless, all the kids would spin around until they were dizzy and started clunking and bumping into each other. The last kid still standing was declared the winner. Anyone who threw up was disqualified.

While we were out "playing," our Dads were either at work or puttering in the garage tool room and our Moms were home making dinner or cleaning the house. We were totally unsupervised. We were free to play. No matter how exciting a time we had, or how active we were, or even if we actually met an alien from Mars, it was just between us kids. Sometimes if we got too rowdy, one of the elderly residents in the neighborhood would scold us or call us "undisciplined rapscallions." When we finally got home, each of our parents would ask us, "Where did you go?" and we would say "Out." They'd ask, "What did you do?" and we'd simply reply, "Nuttin." Mom would then simply say, "O.K., wash up for dinner." God bless typical 1950's style family communications.

Times sure have changed. Although most of us kids have survived to become adults in spite of our lack of supervised play, we now also realize that many of us had no concept of safety or the risks we took. I guess many of us formerly "unsupervised rapscallions" are now concerned parents who don't want our own children to get into as much trouble as we did. Besides, with the pressures of two working parents (or single parents) trying to earn enough to raise a family, we need to spend what little time we have with our kids as "quality time." So why did organized sports ever take control of our lives??? In particular - girls soccer. I never saw any instructions written in the "Rulebook for Perfect Daddyhood" stating I had to enter my daughter in a girl's soccer league.

Not so long ago, there were few organized activities for kids. Boy and Girl Scouts, 4-H clubs, church youth groups, and little league baseball. Today, everything under the sun is offered and each activity is meticulously scheduled, planned, and orchestrated to build "self esteem and valuable skills." Church and scouting organizations have fierce competition from organized leagues of baseball, softball, lacrosse, football, volleyball, karate, tennis, gymnastics, swimming, ice hockey, field hockey, street hockey, and the biggest, most intense, time consuming and bane of every church pastor - "GIRLS SOCCER!!"

Girls' soccer leagues have completely taken over our community. Our suburban town has a total population of about 20,000. Our public school system has an outstanding reputation for its sports programs and has had several County and State Champion soccer teams. The school system provides intramural as well as varsity opportunities for the students, and many students win soccer scholarships to a variety of colleges. Our Village Recreation Department, however, is determined not to be a second-class competitor in the sports world. Over the last decade, at least six different soccer leagues have been started for girls in the town. Each spring and fall, girl's soccer season turns our entire village into a competitive free-for-all, and the body count continues to climb.

There are several levels of girls' soccer leagues in our village ranging from the beginning Novice League, to the Tournament League, to the Traveling League, to even the Superstar League. One father was so upset his daughter wasn't selected for the Superstar League that he even created another league - the Superduperstars of the Future Traveling League. I guess he was rewriting his "Rulebook for Perfect Daddyhood" with an extra section on creative ways to gain soccer scholarships. Even though the facts prove that there are less than 600 girls between 5 and 15 in the village, there are at least 120 teams of 12 girls in the leagues. Serious scholarship questing Moms and Dads sometimes have their daughters play in 2 or 3 leagues at once so the kids have a better chance at being a "champion" on at least one of the teams.

When my daughter Erin was in second grade, she realized her body wasn't built to be a gymnast like her older sister, Alexis. Erin was taller and bigger boned than most seven-year-olds and didn't have the petite stature or flexibility needed to turn her body into a pretzel on a balance beam. She was strong and a fast runner, though, and when she heard some of her friends were joining a soccer team, she asked Mommy and me if she could too. "Sure," I naively replied, and I brought her down to the Recreation Department to sign her up.

What an experience! There were 600 second grade girls, their moms, and their dads - all of them screaming, jostling, pushing, and fighting to sign up for the Fall Trophy Fest Girls Soccer season. As I filled out the application, I noticed an option of fees - "basic registration fee, insurance fee, field use fee, uniform fee, referee's fee, ball fee, and a "participation" fee. The participation fee, $35, was a sneaky way of getting Dads to sign up to be coaches or assistant coaches. The fee would be waived if you "volunteered" to coach.

Since I didn't know anything about soccer except that this was the sport where the ball has spots, I paid the additional fee along with the myriad other fees and looked forward to having someone else teach Erin the rules of the sport. One other fee had me puzzled - the "trophy fee." I asked what this fee was for and found out each and every girl gets a trophy at the end of the season. Even second string players on last place teams get a trophy. Of course -- it helps build the girls' self-esteem. It also builds a healthy bank account for the local Village Recreation Department Official Soccer League Outlet Store that happens to sell trophies.

I then asked the League Director if Erin would be on the same team as her girlfriends. Instead of a simple yes or no response, I got a half hour lecture about how all of the new candidates are pooled according to their ability and a lottery system is used to select teams of equal caliber talent carefully and fairly. "Wait a minute," I replied, "Erin's only 7, she hasn't played soccer before. We registered so she can begin to learn how to play."

The Director sneered at me. "You mean she's never played on a soccer league before? Some of these girls have already been competing for five years." Five years experience by the age of 7? This was the first of many lessons I learned that season. There is an incredible amount of behind the scenes politicking and competition to get the "Big Tournament

Trophy" at the end of the season. The purpose of a few of the coaches wasn't really to teach the girls the skills of the game, or to teach them how to work as a "team player." These coaches had only one goal - to ensure that their own daughter was the star of the first place team and to see that their daughter got a full scholarship to an Ivy League school by playing soccer.

As luck would have it, Erin did get assigned to the same team, the "Village Donut Stallions," as her friend. We showed up at the first practice and met her teammates. Coach Bruno introduced himself and his daughter -Brunhilda, to the team. "Hi girls," he said, "are you ready to win? The team rules are simple: stop anyone from the other team who comes toward you with the ball, kick the ball to Brunhilda, and keep out of her way. Also, each team member has to eat 3 dozen donuts every week. Any questions?" I could tell it was going to be an interesting season.

The girls practiced for two hours, and by the end of the session, I could tell which girls knew what they were doing, and which girls didn't have a clue. Two girls had problems understanding why they weren't allowed to stop the ball with their hands. One girl kept forgetting to run up the field when she got the ball. One clueless girl couldn't even figure out which direction she was supposed to kick the ball. Brunhilda's only problem was that she kept screaming "Give me the ball! Give me the ball!!" and elbowing her teammates whenever they got near her. Erin did OK for her first practice, and enthusiastically ran up and down the field. Whether she had the ball or not didn't seem to matter to her.

Erin was assigned as Center Halfback, Brunhilda was Center Forward, the two girls who kept using their hands were made goalies, and "Clueless" was designated Left Forward Reserve which meant she wouldn't be allowed on the field unless the Stallions were ahead 10 to 1. The rest of the girls grumbled about their assigned positions. It seemed every girl wanted to be a forward so they could score the winning goal. It also turned out that the girls were embarrassed to tell their dads they were "only" good enough to be a fullback.

Coach Bruno was firm and told the girls that every one of them should practice during the week because the first game was the next Sunday at 11AM. First game??? Some of these girls couldn't even figure out which limb to put their shin guards on yet, and they already had a game coming up. I cringed a little when I realized the game was scheduled in conflict with our church service. I figured I'd better say an extra prayer on Saturday evening.

The week sped by, with Erin and me out in the backyard every evening trying to learn how to kick, stop, and pass a soccer ball. I was still wondering why a full game had been scheduled so early in the season, when so many of the girls still didn't even understand the game. I was also wondering why I was spending 20 hours of my limited time teaching Erin soccer when I didn't even know how to play the game. Where was Mommy during these practices? She was driving Alexis to gymnastics, and our youngest daughter, K. C., to dance lessons. Then we also had church choir, art lessons, and swimming lessons. Our car never left town, but we still traveled over 50,000 miles each year. We spent more time dropping off and picking up the kids than we did sleeping. We even had to start packing our own box lunches so we could eat in the car as we drove back and forth. Suzie and I began to write little napkin notes to each other and stick then on each other's lunch box. One of Suzie's notes said "Hello there, I am designated driver #1. Please remember to get gas for the day shift driver. XOX" God bless typical modern family communications.

On Sunday morning, I felt guilty about not going to church, but proceeded to drive Erin to her first soccer game. I purposely avoided driving by the church since I didn't want anyone to notice we'd were ducking out on God's time. The Village had seven different soccer fields set up to hold the games. It took Erin and me twenty minutes to find which field her team was going to play on. I was shocked to see that there were over 12,000 people in the stands. Wow, I thought, I guess there's plenty of seats at church this morning. Our trusty Village Recreation Department also was making a fortune selling coffee, donuts, and souvenir pennants to the spectators.

Erin's game was a riot. Literally. Within five minutes of the kickoff, not one girl remembered to stay in their assigned position. A tremendous knot of 20 seven-year-old bodies rolled back and forth across the field with the ball, oblivious to boundaries, end lines, or the goals. Every once in awhile, the ball would pop free of the body mass and then Brunhilda would scream, "Give me the ball! Give me the ball!" There was fighting, kicking, and screaming from the stands too as each and every parent saw their dreams of a full college soccer scholarship fading away.

The thirteen-year-old Official Village Recreation Department Soccer League Referees blew whistles, threw flags, stamped their feet, and finally just stood in bewilderment as the game went on. The game reminded me of the 'boomer cars' game my wife used to play. I was getting dizzy just watching. I heard the man next to me saying the Lord's prayer, and turned to ask him if he thought a 'Hail Mary' might be appropriate. Wait a minute! It was the pastor of my church! "Reverend Jim!", I exclaimed, "What are you doing here??? Who's giving the sermon today??"

He looked at me a bit sheepishly and replied, "Actually, no-one. It seems everyone in the congregation has at least one daughter on one of the soccer teams, so no one ever shows up at church during soccer season. I got tired of preaching to an empty church and decided to join the rest of you." I noticed Reverend Jim didn't mention that his own daughter, a second grader, was also in the Girl's Soccer League....

CHAPTER 19

SWAMP STOMPING WITH DADDY

I guess by now you realize that one of the secrets of successful "Daddyhood" is for Dads to do things with their children. This does not mean do their homework for them, buy them the pony or video game they beg for, or give them money so they can go shopping with their friends. It took me awhile to learn it was more important to spend time with my children than to just buy them things to keep them occupied. When my middle daughter, Erin, was seven, she thought getting "things" would be a great way for Daddy to gain her enduring love. She continually begged me for some cash so she could go shopping for more toys. It didn't matter that her closet already held more toys than Toys R Us. I finally decided to give her a lesson. I gave her my credit card and told her she could use it as much as she was able to pay with from her allowance.

Erin returned home empty handed two hours later. "Daddy," she said, "I can't believe how much things cost when I've got to pay for them myself. It's a whole lot more fun when your there to help me decide." Wise child, I thought, and I was very pleased with my "Daddying" skills. Two weeks later, however, the delivery truck from Toys R Us tried to drop off her $600 order of Barbie clothes and Breyer horses. Then Erin confessed and asked for her next three year's allowance. Wise child, dumb Dad. Unhappy truck driver.

The key is not to do things for children, but to do things with them. Most importantly, try to share experiences where you also have the opportunity to have some instructive fun. My wife and I have three daughters. I don't think they will ever realize how much it has pained me to play 6 gazillion hours of Barbie dolls with them. Dressing and undressing 50 assorted 12-inch dolls with proportions that are totally inhuman (before liposuction or Pamela Anderson). Zipping and buttoning 6-inch long pink dresses, 10-inch long golden gowns, or those tiny, stupidly tight stretch pants which just will not go over Barbie's rubbery legs. My nickname is not "Thumby" for no reason.

Dressing dolls and setting up Barbie's dream mansion for the ten thousandth time was not my idea of a sharing experience with my young daughters. Still, they loved it. The genetic makeup of females must include tiny, cute, pink, and frilly chromosomes. As I tried for the seventh time to tie a two-inch gold, satin halter top onto Bodacious Barbie, I began to think maybe I'd have more fun if I could convince Frederick's of Hollywood to market a special doll-sized line of lingerie. Daddies everywhere would beg to play with Skipper. It gives new possibilities to the game of "dress up". Then again, I don't think Mommy would exactly approve.

It is a bit difficult for Daddies to come up with creative ways of having quality time with children. Part of the problem is the typical Daddy's lack of experience. We're usually at work during the day, sleeping at night, and trying to keep the house from falling down on weekends. It used to be the Mommy's job to raise the kids. Now, unfortunately, it seems to be more and more the Nanny's job since Mommies are now working to prepare for the time Daddy gets laid off - again. I certainly did more than once.

Besides my collection of frogs and beer cans, there is little evidence of a male in our house. Of course, all four of the females blame me whenever mysterious piles of dirt appear in the kitchen or muddy footprints are found on the carpet. I admit I'm a dirt magnet - it must be a male genetic trait, but I don't enjoy being followed around by a four year old wielding a dust-buster. I like having daughters instead of sons. With daughters it's easy for me to figure out which lunch box is mine - it's the one that's not pink. The girls are being raised under the influence of the all-powerful and omnipotent Goddess of Mommyhood. This leaves me few opportunities to teach my daughters anything. Actually, Suzie says I have value by demonstrating the perfect example of what can go wrong when left to Daddy to do it when he doesn't even read the "Rulebook for Perfect Daddyhood". OK, I guess I'm good for something!

I finally realized that the only way I could enjoy an opportunity to "bond" with my daughters was to separate the three of them. Divide and conquer. Uh, I mean spend a special time with each of them alone. I mean really alone - no sisters, no Mommy, no friends, no telephones, no interruptions, and no constant distractions from time with Daddy. Old boy scout that I am, I instantly decided to take each girl camping. Just me and my daughter, enjoying nature in the woods. I told my wonderfully supportive wife, Suzie, about my wonderfully innovative plan. She reminded me about my woefully bad back, ticks, poison ivy, snake bites, rainstorms, food poisoning, the Jersey Devil, and monster rocks.

I should have anticipated her initial reaction. Many years ago, B.C. (Before Children), I had coerced her into a camping trip canoeing down the Delaware River rapids with a group of my co-workers. Suzie's idea of the wilderness is when I don't mow the lawn for 5 days. The canoe trip was a nightmare. The group was not Boy and Girl Scouts, but city slickers and 30-year-old teenagers who got drunk and were too hung-over to paddle. Most of them lay moaning in the bottom of the canoes or rowed in circles. Suzie hadn't been able to sleep the entire night after seeing a raccoon- which she was positive was a mountain lion. She also hated the woods, loathed the bugs and mosquitoes, and learned the hard way what poison ivy really is.

I tried to make it easier for her. I told her to just sit in the front of the canoe while I did all the paddling. All she had to do was warn me where the rocks were as we went down the rapids. For the next three hours all she did was scream, yelling "ROCKS! ROCKS! ROCKS!" every 20 seconds. The only times I found out where the damn ROCKS! ROCKS! ROCKS! were lurking was when our canoe crashed into them. In the meanwhile, I had to tow the other three canoes behind me since all the rest of my fellow campers had fallen asleep.

I had my first Daddy-Daughter camping trip when my oldest daughter, Alexis, was seven. It was a bit primitive since I had little camping gear -- just a hand-me-down pup tent and a Cabbage Patch children's sleeping bag. Ali had also packed two of her "My Little Ponies" and her favorite stuffed animal, "Froggy". We camped for a weekend at a New York State Department of Conservation camp, "Mongaup Pond", nestled in the western Catskill Mountains. Alexis was a perfect companion. We hiked, swam, went swamp stomping in search of frogs and newts, cooked hamburgers, and had a campfire, sang camp songs while eating toasted marshmallows, and shared quiet times. When I came back to the camp site after gathering more wood, Ali had even scratched a big heart in the mud with an "I love U Daddy" printed in the middle. A truly perfect weekend and a testament that some of Daddy's ideas do work. All of the girls have gone since camping with me. We've gone through a number of tents, sleeping bags, and other equipment, but the memories last.

Then we packed the car, carefully putting all our dirty clothes in a giant plastic garbage bag and drove home. As we pulled into the driveway, Suzie was standing at the front door. I thought she was waving to us, but she was actually trying to flag us down. Mommy blocked us at the door, refusing to let us inside the house until we had been hosed down. She said we reeked like dead skunks in a smoky swamp. All of us, Froggy and the My Little Ponies too, scrubbed down in the back yard, and our clothes were sent to the compost heap. I admit we were a bit dirty, but I didn't think it was that bad until an EPA official called to inquire about a toxic waste spill reported at our address.

Over the years, my supply of camping equipment and Daddy-Daughter camping memories has grown significantly. I've also learned that each child is absolutely unique. Whereas Alexis thoroughly enjoyed being alone with me, Erin - our middle child, preferred to immediately search the campground for other girls her own age. She spent most of the time with her new-found friends leaving me to wash, cook, and clean-up. I still enjoyed the camping, but the anticipated bonding experience with my daughter was replaced by free cans of beer from the other parents. (Not a bad trade, actually). Erin's favorite time included extensive swamp stomping (with me and her 6 new buddies) and hitting me in the head with her pillow to stop my snoring. We were again hosed down and fumigated when we returned home to Mommy's clean, domestic oasis.

As the years have gone by our simple pup tent has been replaced by a Sears Craftsman 6-Man Mount Everest Super Arctic Survivor model, and three foam and air mattresses. Added to this is a deluxe portable gas grill, 400 flashlights, and an increasing collection of sleeping bags. Traditions include stopping to visit at the New York State Trout Hatchery and eating Sunday breakfast at the Robin Hood Diner. As the girls have gotten older, we've added bicycling and tubing to our weekend excursions as well as stopping at the occasional roadside garage sale or vegetable stand.

Although Alexis and I still camp out alone, I usually bring my youngest daughter, K.C., along as a buddy for Erin. Erin enjoys being "big sister"' and also enjoys telling K.C. how to do the chores. Last year, Erin even caught her first fish, a small perch, which we put in a bucket and proudly brought home to show Mommy. Perch, however, don't travel too well in the trunk of a car, and instead of a live perch for a potential pet, we had a dead perch and another example of why Mommy sends all of our clothes and camping gear to an industrial cleaner each time we return from camping trips. At least our pet turtle, 'Big Red', enjoyed the perch. He ate it for dinner. As long as he doesn't develop a taste for my Doritos, he can stay with us.

No matter how much we try to stay clean, whenever we get home my wife immediately complains about how dirty or bug-eaten we are, and how filthy our clothes have become. Even clothes we haven't worn immediately get thrown into the washtub and everyone gets thrown into the shower. Even the car has to take a bath. It was a bit frustrating hearing over and over from "Mrs. Clean" that I had once again earned the "swamp monster" award for filth. This summer, I was determined to prove to Suzie that Daddy and daughters could stay clean for an entire weekend in the woods. Erin, K.C. and I packed the car, and kissed Mommy goodbye. Instead of driving to Mongaup Pond, however, we drove to Grandma's house.

We dropped off our freshly packed suitcases of clean clothes and picked up the garbage bag of worn out clothes which I had stashed there during the year. Then we went camping. We swamp stomped, fished, ate by the smoky campfire, swam in the pond, and rolled in the mud, made a sand and mud sculpture of an alligator on the beach, and had a great weekend. K.C. even caught her first fish - a small pickerel. She was a bit disappointed when I told her to throw the little fish back into the pond. I didn't realize the consequences of not personally see her do it.

When Sunday afternoon came, we showered twice, threw out all our dirty and worn out clothes, dumped our sneakers and even threw out the old towels. Before we went home, I stopped to vacuum the car and then we drove to Grandma's, took another shower, aired out our sleeping bags in the dryer and changed into fresh clean clothes. Erin and I sniffed each other carefully and could detect nothing that indicated "eau de swamp".

Satisfied that there was no trace of camp odors on us, we then went home. I thought we had successfully been able to prevent Mommy from dousing us with the hose, but as soon as we tried to cross the threshold of the front door, Suzie screamed and threw a bucket of lava soap at us.

"Don't come in!!!" she yelled. "You smell like dead fish!!!!"

I started to protest, but the soap suds were already in my throat and making me gag. Then Erin turned to me and said, "Daddy, I think Mommy's right. Something does smell yucky." I tried to figure where my careful plan went wrong. Then it dawned on me that K.C. did indeed have a peculiar strong odor coming from her. The putrid smell turned out to be the remains of a dead fish. My littlest daughter had been so proud to catch her first fish, she had brought it home- in her pocket. She had even showered with it and again pocketed it in her clean new shorts that had been carefully stored at Grandma's. It didn't seem to matter to her that the pickerel had been caught on Friday evening and it was now Sunday afternoon. Or that Saturday had been sunny and hot. We took K.C. into the back yard, removed the decayed fish from her pocket, and hosed her down. Next year, when we go camping again, I'm adding one more item to our "get ready for camping checklist" - sew K.C.'s pockets closed before we leave home.

CHAPTER 20

DADDY GETS COOKED

I try to be a "good" daddy to my three daughters. My wife thinks I'm merely winging it, but I'm just following the instructions in my "Rulebook for Perfect Daddyhood". My tattered "Rulebook", however, must be missing a few pages. There is no mention of whether "the Mommy" or "the Daddy" is ultimately responsible for putting food on the family table. My natural inclination is to let the Mommy do the cooking. In our family, though, this has not always been a successful or wise venture. To put it politely, my wife, Suzie, has never showed a natural affinity for food preparation. Like oil and water, Suzie and cooking don't mix well.

When we were first married, we received the usual wedding gifts of kitchen utensils. As we unwrapped each box, Suzie kept asking, "What's this???" and I'd reply, "This is a blender. This is a crock pot. This is a tea kettle. This is a can opener." I suspected trouble when she then innocently asked me, "O.K.... What are they for???" We ate out a lot.

Suzie's first attempt to use our new kitchen utensils was memorable. She is a creative artist, so she decided to make a new recipe as a surprise for me. She served me something she called "Chicken De'alto". It looked a bit odd sitting on my plate oozing sticky green fluid. When I took a small first bite, it bit me back! Well, actually it was just pieces of chicken neck

112

bone sticking into my tongue, but it did cause me to rename her recipe to Chicken Di'sastero. Apparently, she didn't remove the plastic bag of neck and giblets from the bird's cavity before she put the entire bird into the blender.

Our first Thanksgiving was another clue. We invited 'Big Bill' for turkey dinner. Bill was a seven foot tall Notre Dame graduate with an athletic appetite. We bought an 18-pound turkey. Suzie and I both worked and were worried that we wouldn't have 5 hours free time to cook the turkey on Thanksgiving Day. We got the bright idea to cook it the day before. Suzie stuffed it, wrapped it tightly in aluminum foil, and carefully put it in the oven, setting the temperature at a "perfect" 370 degrees, and set the timer for 4 hours, then left for work. I came home at lunch, noticed the oven was off, so discreetly reset the timer for 4 hours and returned to work. Suzie came home about 4:30, also noticed the oven was off, and reset the timer for another 2 hours. Neither of us actually could see the wrapped up bird, but Suzie figured if we simply followed directions, it would be fine. Since the turkey was too big for our refrigerator, we also left it in the oven overnight.

The next morning, Suzie again turned on the oven to warm up the turkey, but turned the control knob the wrong way. Big Bill came over about 3 in the afternoon. When Suzie finally opened the oven to get the turkey, all that remained was a lump of melted aluminum foil surrounding a pile of blackened bones. Suzie had turned the oven control to 'self clean' and accidentally incinerated the bird. I scraped off as much of the melted aluminum foil as I could and pried some of the meat out of the crevices, rescuing about 6 ounces of what might still be chewable. As I set the platter down on the table, I mumbled, "I hope you like dark meat." We also served carrots, bread, and cranberry sauce. Big Bill ate cranberry sauce and carrot sandwiches. He declined future invitations to eat with us unless we promised to order takeout from the local Chinese restaurant.

Many of our home cooked meals had the same unique quality. As a precaution, I began eating a quick dinner on the train ride home. My wife began to hate cooking. No matter how carefully she followed recipes, no matter how high the quality of the ingredients, the results were frequently dismal. Her Jello would never gel, her brownies were always burnt or soupy, and the chicken was always chuck-able. I had little experience at cooking, but this was a matter of survival. To me, the four basic food groups had always been coffee, beer, chocolate covered donuts, and Doritos. Fortunately, inside of every Man's typical primitive gene pool is the chromosome of barbeque!!! All little boys like to play with fire and burning raw flesh on a grill just adds to the fun. It's one of the few things that males dominate. Besides, I could gracefully give my wife a reason not to cook.

Things settled down until our first child was born. Suzie breast fed our daughter Alexis as long as she possibly could. She said it was a healthier alternative than my suggestion of barbequed formula. This extra couch sitting period gave the new Mommy goddess time to read 6,000 magazines and books on health, lifestyles, parenting, psychology, and religion. The new Mommy became an advocate of health. My daily barbequed meat days were increasingly replaced by boiled pasta and vegetables. My whole lifestyle changed. I stopped going to hockey games because instead of sharing beer and hot dogs with my buddies, I now had to bring pocketfuls of broccoli and juice packs. Carrot stick anyone???

Shortly after our first child was born, we moved to a larger home in a different community. Being new residents, we joined a neighborhood group, Welcome Wagon, as a way to meet and get to know our new neighbors. One component of this group was a gourmet club where four couples met on a monthly basis at each other's homes for a deluxe home cooked meal. We joined reluctantly. The 3 dinners at the other member's homes were fantastic, but Suzie became more and more nervous as the time approached for our turn. On the night we were scheduled to entertain the gourmet club, I came home to find a perfectly set table. Suzie proudly served a wonderful lobster bisque, duck a la orange, saffron flavored wild rice, and black forest cake for dessert.

I was amazed. The food was outstanding and drew raves and bravos from our guests. As fate would have it though, when one of the wives was helping to clear the table, she noticed a suspect pile of catering cartons in the kitchen... and no dirty pots. No wonder the food was so good. We had catered the dinner and were banished from the gourmet club. In retrospect, we did the right thing. Of course, I could have just pulled a handful of sliced veggies from my pocket and accomplished the same thing. "Carrot stick anyone?"

As we added more daughters to the family, our Mommy and Daddy roles continued to evolve. I began to pitch in more and more with the cooking. I admit our family is a bit out of the norm. We rarely eat out anymore and seldom order fast food delivery. Our family eats most meals together. We don't have a microwave. We like salads and fruits. We eat to live rather than live to eat. Suzie approaches cooking reluctantly and has yet to successfully bake a brownie. I discovered spices and marinating and enjoyed mixing and creating recipes. I burned out 2 home-made ice-cream machines from overuse, discovered the joy of making jelly, and used to make a dynamite chili until our tummies surrendered. I enjoy turning my home-grown tomatoes or blueberries into a variety of foods, although blueberry sherbet invariably stains our Tupperware.

I have two weak points. I can't get the knack of baking cakes or breads, and can't stomach looking at or smelling lunch foods, especially meat, before 8AM. As a result, someone other than "the Daddy" has to bake the birthday cakes and pack the school lunches. I thought this might be the Mommy's job, but she is carefully grooming the girls to fend for themselves. The main rule is no one is permitted to just pack 6 Twinkies and 12 Snickers bars for lunch. Juice packs have to contain real juice, not "ecto-cooler". Our middle girl, Erin, has a gene I suspect was not inherited from her mother. She likes to cook and is good at it too. At age 9 she made a terrific home-made shrimp scampi that would make Julia Child proud, and frequently volunteers to make us lunch on Sundays. Her only payment is that this time counts towards her home chores, and she doesn't have to do the dishes.

Making nourishing lunches is not difficult. Getting everyone to eat them is another story. K.C., our youngest child, is a particularly finicky eater. We constantly have to prod her to try a variety of foods and are constantly amazed that a forkful of anything new merely has to start moving towards her mouth when she can immediately conclude she doesn't like it. For six months, she would only eat food that was white. She then switched to only one particular variety of egg bagel. Recently, the only food she seems to eat is plain spaghetti. In spite of her reputation as a female "Mikey" who doesn't like to try anything, the one constant food that has remained in her diet is chocolate ice cream with chocolate syrup. I have to purchase it by the 55-gallon drum.

If parents have children in schools or are members of any organization, the time eventually comes when someone wants to put together a cookbook of favorite family recipes. These requests for recipes are usually directed towards the family mommy. My wife used to submit the only recipe she inherited from her mom, lovingly called "heart delights". These delightful morsels consisted of real butter, chopped nuts, chocolate, coconut, six tons of sugar, and held together as a thick paste by a dozen raw eggs. YUM! Actually, they were delicious - just diet deadly. My own research has revealed that the recipe was invented by a group of high school students called "Future Cardiac Surgeons of America". When Suzie's treasured family recipe was summarily rejected by a health-conscious nursery school cookbook editor, Suzie was crushed--- and her dad had another heart attack.

The following year, Mrs. Maria L., our girls' wonderful teacher, sent K.C. home with a printed request for recipes for the first-grade student cookbook. This time, however, K.C. gave the request to me rather than Mommy. K.C. whispered gently, "Daddy, please don't let Mommy know about this. I don't think she can stand the pressure." I thought about submitting Mommy's infamous 'Turkey Flambe' I but decided to create a new family heritage recipe instead. Something wonderful, to match my talents and unique creative gifts. I rummaged through the pantry, inspected my spice drawer, and thought. I wrote out a recipe for a new soup and practiced making it with my daughter. She helped me cut and prepare the ingredients, fry and stir, and we had a neat time together as it cooked. When it was done, I ate a spoonful and was surprisingly pleased. I began to put the rest away when she stopped me. "What about me?? I haven't had any yet."

I replied. "K.C., you won't like it. I wouldn't want you to try this. It's too special." She begged me to let her try it, so I gave her a small teaspoonful. The spoon rose towards her mouth, which this time actually opened and swallowed the soup. "Hmm," she said, "Actually it's not bad, Daddy. Thanks for letting me try some. Just don't tell Mommy I did. I don't want to ruin my reputation." And thus, was born: "Daddy's Frog Pond Stew".

DADDY'S FROG POND STEW

Ingredients:

1 chicken breast (or 2 frogs' legs), 1 can cream of asparagus soup, 1 cup nonpoisonous swamp greens (or spinach leaves), 1 egg, ½ cup mushrooms, 1 stick fresh asparagus stalk, ½ pint light cream, 1 teaspoon Frog's Leap wine, 2 Tablespoons butter, salt, pepper

Directions:

Cook egg to hard boiled and set aside. While it is cooking, either catch a large bullfrog (or use a chicken breast, it tastes like frog). Cut the meat into small chunks and fry in butter. Open can of soup and place in large saucepan. Add light cream. Add meat. Clean spinach (or swamp greens --throw out any poisonous ones) and break into small pieces. Clean and slice mushrooms. Add spinach leaves (or swamp greens if you're really daring) and mushrooms to pot. Add 1 teaspoon Frog's Leap wine. Add spices to taste. (If I'm invited, add extra salt.) Cut asparagus stalk into 3" sections and gently cook in separate pot. When stew has simmered for about 25 minutes ladle it into bowls. Add hard boiled egg slices so they float like lily pads. Add asparagus sections as semi-submerged logs. Keep lights low when you serve.

CHAPTER 21

CONVERSING ON DADDYHOOD

I am constantly amazed how quickly my daughters are growing and maturing, changing, and learning. As I watch them play or listen to them talk, it reminds me of my own childhood, it's just a lot noisier. Especially the talking. My ears might sometimes hurt, but I do enjoy listening to their unique perspectives on the world. One activity which my nursery school aged daughters did reminds me how quickly we forget our own childhood. It is the typical greeting for 4- year old's, "Pick - Up". I watched a group of several nursery school aged boys and girls stand in a row and pick each other up. Up and down, up and down again, giggling and talking. The shortest child was then passed around like a sack of flour. I asked my daughter why she was doing that. Her answer was, "Because I can!" It is a ritual greeting most adults have forgotten, although the recent fad of teenage 'moshing' at rock concerts is similar. I can vividly imagine starting a public meeting with, "O.K. everybody, let's introduce ourselves. Start by picking up the person standing on your right."

Kids do talk a lot, and it pays to be a good listener. Every day is an opportunity for Daddies to learn something about their children. Whether it's a milestone event or an everyday routine, it's also a chance for Daddies to learn a little more about ourselves. Most young boys, when asked what they want to be when they grow up, do not instinctively reply, "a Daddy". Somehow, it's not as glamorous as being an astronaut, fireman, baseball player or movie star. Even so, more men wind up becoming Daddies than become policemen. Actually, Daddyhood is a combination of many professions and deserves more credit than it gets. Being Daddy to three girls gives me many chances to be a detective (Which one of you girls left her 'My Little Pony' toys all over the den floor?), a doctor (Your tummy will be OK, Princess, but next time don't eat the entire bagful of Halloween candy by yourself!) or a coach (Kick the ball again, sweetheart, but this time towards the net, not into the street!).

I find it sad that many men miss the special opportunity of being "Daddy". They may be Fathers, but being a Father isn't equal to being a Daddy. Being a Daddy is a special period of a man's life. It begins several months before the birth of your firstborn. (For some reason, the news "You're going to be a Daddy" is usually delivered by the soon to be Mommy.) Panic sets in as most men realize they have no experience with babies and aren't prepared for Daddyhood. My advice is simply, don't worry about it. The new baby doesn't have much experience with you either so you're both on a learning curve together. Daddyhood can be a fun trip and can be more rewarding than frequent flyer miles. Daddies who spend time being with their young children build a solid relationship that can last a lifetime. This is more important than just spending money on your children. Those relationships last until the kids get their own credit card.

If communicating is the key to successful relationships, however, my own ship sometimes founders. It's not all my fault. I didn't suspect the troubled waters ahead when my wife and I taught our three girls how to talk. The first word six-month-old Alexis said was "Da-da" and I was convinced Ali was a pure genius. How else could she have been able to learn so quickly? I had spent many years trying to teach my dog, Penny, to speak. All I could get Penny to do was to answer a few basic questions. When I asked her, "Penny, what's on top of a house?", she'd answer "Roof". If I asked Penny what texture sandpaper had, she'd answer "Ruff". (It was hard to work those questions into everyday conversations.) Mostly I just sat with her scratching her ears as I watched TV football, thinking 'smart doggy".

The new baby changed my life. I was delighted to hear Ali's tiny voice echo through the house. "Da-da, Daddy, Daddy." I frequently scratched her ears as a reward, thinking "smart baby." Soon other words came- "ma-ma", "milk", "bottle", "Froggie", and "Why are you watching football on TV when you have me and Mommy to talk with and entertain you?" Uh-oh.... this is a no-win question.

The precedent had been set. My wife, Suzie, is frequently referred to as the protective saint of conversation, the supreme goddess of the spoken word. There is a clear genetic reason for this. A recent study by the Women's Institute for Conversation revealed that the average female speaks 2,657 words per day. Every day. All year long, including holidays. The average male, on the other hand, utters only 625 words a day. Excluding football season. With a wife and three daughters, I'm statistically outtalked by over 10,000 words a day. In reality, my wife skews the bell curve and can easily manage to verbalize an average female's monthly allotment in a two-hour conversation. And, of course, each and every word is a precious gem that I must listen to, or I'll discover I accidentally agreed to take all the girls to another 4 hour long ballet performance scheduled for Superbowl Sunday.

Now that the girls are all in school, my wife has returned to teaching on a part time basis. In spite of hectic schedules, we still eat dinner as a family. This used to be the period when we could all have a turn telling each other what we did during the day or something interesting we learned.

Now, I only get to ask one question - "What did you do in school today?" and I not only get a lengthy synopsis of my own daughters' academic and social activities, but also a detailed rundown on the trials and tribulations of each my wife's 139 students. Dinnertime sometimes extends for 3 hours. It's hard for me to get a word in edgewise. The girls all jockey for position, tongues revved up at the starting gate waiting for an opportunity to zoom into the conversation speed lane. If I have any questions, I have to raise my hand. Our youngest daughter, K.C., usually insists on starting off the "What I did in School today" marathon sessions. At age seven, she doesn't have quite the stamina to sit through the lengthy discourses by her older siblings and Mommy. If she doesn't go first, by the time it's her turn, I sometimes find her face down in her mashed potatoes, snoring.

Thank God I'm a good listener. I do enjoy hearing each of their stories and the challenge of trying to remember who did what. I'm also relearning all of the school subjects I had forgotten since I was in elementary school. K.C. was amazed at how smart her Daddy was and how much I know about Theodore Roosevelt. She thought I was the smartest Daddy in the whole world as I rattled off fact after interesting fact about TR's presidency, war record, and the National Park System. I amazed myself too, until I realized I was merely repeating what I had heard from K.C.'s older sisters a few years earlier during their respective term paper assignments. They had spent weeks during dinner table discussions discussing what they'd learned.

From these dinnertime university sessions, so far, I've completed fourth grade history, introductory Italian, nearly flunked seventh grade math, and am well into Biology. The only time I turn off completely is when I'm about to put a forkful of tasty, well salted, medium rare sirloin steak into my mouth and my oldest daughter Alexis begins to talk about her Biology class. I do not want to hear her graphic description of the new film on advanced techniques for heart operations while I'm trying to swallow.

Since Suzie and the girls dare not miss any potentially vital telephone calls when they're out of the house, we have a telephone answering machine. I have a real philosophical gripe with these machines. I suspect they are an evil plot hatched by the phone companies to force us to make even more phone calls. I have endured endless games of telephone tag, trying to reach a real, live voice rather than a taped "beep", and all the time our phone bill racks up another call charge. I detest "call waiting" for the same reason. Not only does the caller get charged to find out we're already talking to someone else on the telephone, but now we're stuck with the responsibility and cost of calling them back.

We do find the answering machine useful for one purpose. If the girls are home while my wife is out, she calls them every hour - just to make sure everything is OK. The younger girls, however, are not permitted to answer the phone by themselves. This is a leftover order from the time 3-year-old Erin misinterpreted my instructions to answer the phone for me while I took a shower. I told her if the phone rang, I'd dry off quickly so I wouldn't get the floor wet and get Mommy mad, and to simply tell the caller I'd be with them in a minute. Sure enough, the phone rang, and she announced "Hello, this is Erin. My Daddy said that if anyone called tell them that he couldn't come to the phone because Mommy got excited when he ran around the house without any clothes on." Apparently, Reverend Jim's wife was only slightly upset.

The girls have been instructed not to answer the phone until the message unit plays through and Suzie identifies herself that it's safe for them to pick up the phone and talk. When I get home in the evening, it's been my assigned job to play back the phone messages. Because my wife has activated the machine to screen calls, her entire phone conversations with our daughters are now recorded. Playing the tape back at fast speed

123

makes the voices sound like Alvin and the Chipmunks on estrogen. I now have the added "privilege" of hearing another 1,500 words of high-speed conversation that typically go:

Mommy: "HloErn,thszMme."

Erin: "HIMMEHWRU?"

Mommy: "Mfn.Hwzskl2dy?"

Erin: "GD!MyTECHRWZSKNDWHDATSTNBIO!"

Mommy: "DdUdoOK?"

Erin: "FCRSE!IGT100!!CNIHVACKE?"

Mommy: "No,hvaglsfmlk."

Erin: "OKMME!"

Mommy: "IlvU,Ern"

Erin: "ILVU2MME!"

Surprisingly, I'm starting to be able to understand what my wife and the girls are saying to each other. I always had a flair for understanding foreign languages-- like modern chipmunk. Speed listening is a gift I never thought I'd need. I was more surprised to learn the typical topic of the conversations. Many times, they tell each other what they have been doing at school!!!?!?? It's the same stories I'm going to hear again at the dinner table that night. I finally asked my wife why she has the girls describe their day during dinnertime when she already knows what they've done. She replied it was so their Daddy could share the experience with them. "After all," she sweetly added, "You're a good listener."

Daddyhood ends the day your child calls you "Dad" for the first time instead of "Daddy". It's a 'listen-up' warning. The first time that a Daddy is referred to as "Dad" or "Pop" by his child is a traumatic experience for many fathers. Without warning, you've been downsized. Your 'baby' is letting you know the relation has changed. Not only do they now want their own phone, but, like young bucks, soon they'll be challenging you for control of the herd. Worse yet, they might also announce they're thinking of joining a different herd. One where nose rings are more accepted. I suspect it's their revenge for the time Daddy explained to them the facts about Santa Claus. Well, it wasn't my fault I finally had a chance to talk, but at least they listened.

CHAPTER 22

DADDY'S SHOCKING SHOPPING SAGA

The years of Daddyhood continue to whirl quickly by. With three active daughters, I've been gaining a unique perspective on time. First off, I'm realizing I'll never have any time just for myself. I thought I'd get at least 2 hours a day back to myself once the girls were housebroken, I mean toilet- trained, and I no longer had to change diapers. If I want privacy, I now have to wait 2 hours to make an appointment just to go to the bathroom. My wife thought I was merely having typical middle aged prostate troubles when she noticed me getting out of bed every night around 2AM to go to the bathroom. She didn't realize it was the only available time slot left.

Perhaps I'm still winging it without my long lost "Rulebook for Perfect Daddyhood", but frankly, sharing a bathroom with four females isn't fun. I'm pretty tired of seeing 350 varieties of shampoos, conditioners, shine enhancers, and split end treatments crowded around my poor lonely bottle of Head & Shoulders in the shower. How can girls use so much of this stuff? (I wash my hair once a month, whether I need to or not.) Since each of the girls insists on having Rapunzel- length hair, I've gotten group rates from Smitty, our local plumber. Smitty has to come over at least once every 3 months to snake out our drains from 12 pounds

126

of hair washed down the shower by the girls. Smitty has put his daughter, Jen, through Ivy league college thanks to his plumbing business. Jen was a popular neighborhood babysitter and got a whopping referral fee for letting him know which houses had a new baby girl. Smitty knew that within five years, he'd have a new client too.

Due to my male genetic heritage for household chore incompetence, I've been fired from laundry, dishwashing, vacuuming, and most duties around the home. I cook out of necessity, after convincing my wife that the four basic food groups are coffee, Doritos, hot dogs, and little chocolate donuts. I guess it's a man thing, but I really don't trust men who like folding laundry. Actually, I don't think laundry was meant to be folded. Its natural state seems to be in a large pile dumped on the bed. Once, I was with my middle daughter, Erin, trying to sort through a clothes mountain that had formed on my bed. Erin was really upset that Mommy had assigned her the task of sorting laundry as her household chore. I explained to her Daddy's way of folding laundry. "First, Erin, close your eyes, grab any three socks, then roll them into a ball. Next, take all the panties and stuff them into your little sister's shoe rack. Finally, hang Mommy's blouse on a hanger, but only after you turn it inside out."

Erin looked at me dumbfounded. "Daddy, that's all wrong!"

"Precisely, Erin, "I replied confidently, "And that is exactly why my own Dad showed me how to do it this particular way. It's a secret men have shared from father to son for generations. If you continually screw up household chores, Mommies will eventually stop asking you."

"Thanks Daddy. You're the greatest! And to think, Mommy refers to you as thoughtless and clueless."

My remaining primary responsibilities for household chores are taking out the garbage, bundling the papers for recycling, and food shopping. This is fine by me. I get to be out of the girls' hair and into the fresh air.

Food shopping was my personal safe haven, but I was recently blasted by an unanticipated female land mine - "girl friend things". It is a gruesome tale, and I warn all men not to read any further.

My daytime job is with the United States Environmental Protection Agency in their Superfund Division. Part of my responsibility is removing toxic and hazardous wastes and chemicals from dump sites. I love the danger and dirt. I am used to seeing all sorts of 'environmental nasties' in the field and have gone through extensive emergency training to prepare for unusual situations. No amount of training, however, could help me prepare for the upcoming family emergency situation. I had just gotten home from work when my wife, Suzie met me at the front door. "Robert," she beckoned, "we've got an emergency. Go to the store and get a box of "girl friend things".

"What 'things'?", I naively asked.

"You know, the monthly visit, the period, the girl friend...we need more."

"Didn't you buy a box last month?"

Suzie hit me in the ribs and confided, "They're not for me. Now go!"

"Oh, good grief," I thought, "I'd rather drink a drum of toxic stew than be caught buying a box of tampons. This is not what real men stand in line at 7-11 to buy." Instead of trying to get the nerve to ask for tampons at the 7-11 counter, I drove to Pathmark, hoping to hide inconspicuously in the crowd. I grabbed a cart, then wandered up and down the aisles looking for the feminine hygiene section. My heat pounded in my chest and my throat became dry. I had no experience doing this, I guess you could say I was lost in virgin territory.

Finally, I turned down aisle 8 and there they were. All of them. Billions and billions of varieties, shapes, and sizes. I was totally flab-bergasted. This wasn't simply a "pick up a quart of milk' quick mindless decision, this was a feminine hygiene version of Home Depot. There were pads, liners, shields, fresh weave, overnight, long odor absorbing, super plus, satin or smooth, flexible, flushable, portable, cardboard (!?!!), scented, mountain fresh, ultra thin, gentle glide, silk glide, slim fit, comfort design, curved maxi, secure hold, biodegradable, with baking soda, wrap around, light days, naturals, and maxi with wings. I was hopelessly lost. What the heck are 'wings' for? No, I didn't really want to know. I just wanted to get out of there quick.

What was I supposed to get? I sometimes have trouble remembering if we're a Brillo or SOS family. I couldn't remember what brand or even the color of the box of the things in our bathroom closet. I stood there trying to decide if 'cottony dry cover' or 'comfort weave' were attributes I'd want if I were a woman, when I suddenly heard a voice call, "Hi Rob, what are you doing?"

"Oh God," I thought, "Please let the big asteroid hit Earth right now. A sudden plague, maybe?" I quickly turned away from the feminine hygiene hell and faced the caller. My miserable luck, it was Patricia, our neighbor! Beautifully sweet, super smart, ever elegant, Patricia-- dressed appropriately for food shopping in full makeup, high heels, and a full-length mink coat. I thought of Bogart in a '90s movie version of Casablanca, "Of all the Pathmark's in all the towns in all the world... and she has to walk into mine.... Hide me, Rick! Hide me!!" I couldn't ignore the fact that I was standing in front of 300,000 boxes of tampons. Patricia is always a treat to look at. On the other hand, it was not the most comfortable spot to make small talk.

"Good evening, Patricia, so good to see you. How's the family? You're looking wonderful as usual **PleasehelpmeI'matyourmercyIneedtobuy someofthesethingsnow!** Now, I'll turn my back and you just throw them in my cart. So good to see you, must run, ta, ta!"

Bless her elegant heart, Patricia rescued me without even a blink. As soon as I heard the sound of a box land in my cart, I blew Patricia a kiss goodbye, and proceeded towards checkout line, quickly dumping 30 boxes of tissues and 48 bags of Doritos into my cart to hide the feminine 'things'. I rolled into express checkout, casually dumped the tissues and 'things' onto the belt, and pretended to read a National Enquirer magazine article, "Giant Alien Cotton Swab Drains Lake Erie" until the checkout girl had completely rung up and bagged my purchase. Relieved from feminine hygiene purgatory, I handed her a fifty, said "keep the change", and ran to my car with the bags. I sped home and handed the bags to my wife. "Please don't ever make me do that again," I begged.

"OK," she sweetly replied, "but I think you're just being silly. By the way, your mother called and asked you to pick up a box of bladder control pads the next time you go food shopping for her. Have fun!"

CHAPTER 23

DADDY GETS PLAYED OUT

I've given up trying to bond with my three daughters through organized sports activities. Nearly a quarter century of marriage to my artistically talented wife has finally purged any interest I had in baseball, football, ice hockey or golf. She has never shown an interest in sports and could not understand my enduring infatuation with entering physical competitions where, for the sake of a small brass plated trophy mounted on a teak or marble base, I would allow my body to be tackled, cross checked, or broken and bruised.

Actually, I never considered myself to be a sports "jock". I am not a big person, and do not have a natural athletic build. I earned a couple of athletic "letters" in High School (on the tennis and track teams) and played ice hockey (intramural only) in college, and was a member of a softball team while stationed in Saudi Arabia in the early 1980's. The team, however, was composed primarily of female nurses - the only coed team of 26 in the league, which was my primary reason for joining. Mostly, my interest in sports has been limited to rooting for the Mets, Islanders, or Jets, while sitting on the sofa eating Doritos and beer.

Hey, it works for me. It doesn't, however, work for my wife Suzie - the Mommygoddess of our three daughters. Suzie's main interest is the arts, especially the art of conversation. She doesn't appreciate any activity where the noise of a crowd drowns out her talking. She feels it is her personal responsibility to immediately fill any silence or void in a conversation. We were once banished from a Superbowl TV Party after Suzie kept trying to engage everyone in a group conversation. She was getting more and more frustrated that the other couples were merely watching Phil Simms throw another touchdown pass rather than respond to her Oprah Winfrey impersonation.

Finally, she blurted out, "I can't believe 8 grown people are just going to sit here watching the stupid TV for 3 solid hours and not talk." Apparently, 7 of those people had those exact plans, and 6 of them stayed to watch the rest of the game. On subsequent Superbowl Sundays, if I wanted to watch the game, I had to tape it under the excuse I wanted to tape the Budweiser Frog commercials for my frog collection.

My attempts to pass on an interest in sports to my growing daughters have included twelve years of gymnastics lessons for my oldest daughter, yearly swimming lessons for each child, and a notorious turn as assistant soccer coach for my middle daughter's team. Despite some success - and a few broken bones, gradually their interests have evolved to jazz dance lessons, ballet, music lessons, art lessons, and even cartooning. I agree that there is some physical endurance needed to be a good dancer, but somehow, these activities weren't what I intended with my efforts to "bond" as a daddy- besides, I don't think I'd look too good in a tutu.

At the age of 8, my youngest daughter, K.C. has determined that she is someday going to be a Broadway dancer. When auditions for a new original musical were announced by our local Village Community Theatre, Mommy discreetly checked if there were parts available for children. Brad and Ruby, the Directors, Producers, Writers, and Chief Cheerleaders for the amateur group, urged Suzie to have K.C. audition. "Don't worry about it, all children who try out are guaranteed a part. After all, how do you explain to an eight-year-old they're not 'good enough'? By the way, parents are welcomed as well."

The auditions were held at our local church on a Wednesday evening, which conflicted with my wife's art lessons. Needless to say, Daddy got volunteered to bring K.C. to the audition. Actually, I got hoodwinked by my lovely, and devious-when-she-needs-to-be, wife. She told me to bring K.C. to church to watch a TV show. This sounded like a great way to share a moment with my little ballerina, so I showed up promptly with a six pack, bag of Doritos, daughter, and chocolate milk pack. We followed a raucous group of kids and adults into a large room where we were given cards to fill out. "OK, I thought, they merely want to know a little about us so we can rate the TV shows we watch."

The first question was: 'Please state your acting experience." While K.C. was busy drawing pictures of dancing bears and singing birds on her card, I carefully wrote on mine: Rob has over 40 years acting experience. He started out acting as an innocent infant, then bewildered child and befuddled teenager, before accepting the role of clueless husband and dim-witted Daddy. To the second question: 'How would others rate your acting experience?', I wrote: Rob has his mother fooled, but his wife is hoping he eventually starts acting in a responsible manner. Question 3- 'Singing experience?' Answer 3 - Rob sings the blues whenever he gets another credit card bill.

I handed in our cards and asked Brad when we would be able to start watching the TV show. He looked at the cards, then at me, looked back at the cards, and finally said, "It's a little early. First we want to hear K.C. sing."

"Oh, good grief", I thought, "the beer's starting to get warm.", but dragged K.C. over towards the piano and said, "O.K. sweetie, sing!" No response. Nothing. Not a peep. "K.C., K.C., K.C., my favorite youngest daughter. Sing for Daddy." Again, nothing. Absolute silence for a full minute until she finally peeped, "But Daddy, what song should I sing?" I was getting desperate. I knew that 'Baywatch' was going to start in five minutes and I'd miss it if we didn't get our act together.

I quickly said, "How about '*Me and My Shadow*', the song you danced to during Talent Night at Family Camp?" K.C. smiled, nodded her head yes, and softly began a slow tap version of 'Me and My Shadow'. Unfortunately, no one could hear her. She sounded as almost loud as a mime, so I got behind her as her "shadow" and began 'strolling down the avenue' with her, encouraging her by calling, "Louder, Princess, sing your heart out. Do it for Daddy!" When she was finally done, Brad and Ruby clapped politely and said, "Thank you. We'll call you next week to start rehearsals."

"Rehearsals?" I asked, "What rehearsals? I already know how to watch a TV show! It's a basic male instinct! What do we need rehears- als for?"

Brad came up to us and explained, "Rob, we're not here to watch TV. We're putting on a new musical play by the name of "The TV Show". You and K.C. just auditioned to be in it." He looked at K.C. and then said, "You were great K.C., but is your Daddy always this slow?"

K.C. handed Brad my precious six-pack and replied, "Its O.K. I think I can work with him."

I couldn't plead my way out of this predicament, or even get my six-pack back. K.C. and I each received copies of the script and were told to learn our lines by the following Saturday. K.C. was thrilled. She got the coveted role of 'Kayote Kal's Kid's Klubhouse Pardner #3', while I was assigned the part of 'Henry Bigsby - Chairman of the United Communication's Company TV Network'. K.C. had one line, actually one word, "Hamburger", which she was supposed to say in reply to a question from Kayote Kal. K.C. learned her word in the car on the way home and was very pleased with herself. I was in a bit of a personal fuddle and was not pleased with myself. I had a slightly larger part. Actually, I think there were more lines for Henry Bigsby than there were words in the entire unabridged edition of Moby Dick. On the other hand, it was an opportunity for me to share a bit of time alone with my littlest daughter, who was also growing up very quickly. Reluctantly, I decided to give it a fair try.

Over the next few weeks, K.C. and I met a different breed of people - actors, dancers, singers, and even technicians and stage volunteers who stayed behind the curtain but were critical to get the curtain open and closed when needed, the right costumes sewed, and the lights and sound working like a fine-tuned clock. Like clockwork, during every scene I messed up my lines. My brain had no clue on when to respond to a cue, and I was told I invented a new musical scale whenever they had me sing.

The "bonding" experience was not what I expected. I didn't exactly spend much time together with my star daughter. Each week K.C. and I went to rehearsal together and then split up for the next 3 hours. She's go on stage for the first 6 minutes, say "Hamburger" right on cue, then sing 'Whistle a Happy Tune" with 'pardners' 1, 2, 4, 5, and 6, and finally run off to the waiting room to play video games while the adults struggled through their own scenes. While she seemed to disappear, I felt as if I were under a police interrogation lamp rather than a spotlight. I continued to blow my lines and discovered my natural voice range was limited to one note, and it was a flat one.

The choreographer, 'Aku', then would spend another 40 minutes with me trying to show me how to move and dance on stage without resembling a three-legged zombie. I felt it was useless and kept either banging into the wall or hitting the curtain. I asked him why a talented choreographer like him would waste his time trying to work with me. He explained, "Actually, choreography is only my hobby. I just got my degree in Biology from Hofstra University. My graduate thesis topic is going to

135

be comparing maze learning techniques between you and laboratory rats. So far, the rats are ahead. Way ahead. Shall we try again, or would you like some cheese first?"

After a few weeks of rehearsal purgatory, the night of our big performance came. I don't actually remember the details much, but the other actors were great, and I didn't fall off the stage more than twice. I told Brad and Ruby that it was a refreshing experience for me to have been in their show with my daughter K.C.. Brad replied, "Well, we're glad you joined us. K.C. was terrific, but Rob-- don't give up your day job."

On the way home, K.C. told Mommy how much fun it was being in the show with Daddy during the last few weeks and that she enjoyed being with me so much. She said she was proud to watch me trying to learn how to sing and dance, and even won thirty-two dollars on the pool. "K.C., what pool are you talking about? We hardly spent any time together at all, you kept disappearing somewhere right after your scene. What were you doing?"

"Daddy, I was watching you the whole time! It was great!! I was with all the other the kids watching you on the closed-circuit TV. We had bets on how many times you'd mess up. I won the big pool!"

"Sweetie, you were all betting I'd blow my lines? How many times did you bet I'd mess up?"

K.C. sweetly smiled and replied, "Well, Daddy, let's put it this way... Don't give up your day job."

CHAPTER 24

DADDY GETS TREED

Of all the different types of jobs I've held during the last quarter century, my work as a hydrogeologist with the US Environmental Protection Agency (EPA) has been the most interesting. I get issued free work clothes and am constantly learning new things. I like the opportunity of being out of doors and meeting new people. Sometimes I encounter people I really didn't plan on meeting or under situations I didn't intend. Well, such encounters sometimes help the day from being boring. What does an environmental scientist and a county prisoner have in common? A penchant for Day-Glo orange clothing, apparently.

A few weeks ago, I joined two other scientists from the EPA to take water samples from the Hackensack River in New Jersey. We stopped our small boat behind a heavily fenced building complex in Hackensack and began to unpack our equipment to take samples. To the dismay of fashion editors worldwide, we were wearing EPA Day-Glo orange windbreakers and matching pants -- the same "notice me" hue worn by inmates from fashion wastelands such as Sing Sing, Attica -- and the County jail. For about an hour, we worked quietly. Then someone walked by and, in the words of one police officer, "freaked out." How was I to know our boat had been docked behind County jail property?

We continued our work, oblivious to our surroundings. Moments later, law enforcement officers countywide lurched into full-alert mode. A bulletin was broadcast: *Three inmates have escaped from the County jail and are headed south toward Newark Bay in a wooden dinghy. They are wearing orange prison jumpsuits.* "It's 'Papillion' all over again!!," the County police captain said at the height of the fracas, referring to the movie in which Dustin Hoffman plays a sensitive, bespectacled prisoner who escapes from prison.

County police dispatched all available units and several scent-tracking dogs to spots along the riverbank. Patrol cars with sirens yowling sped to the nearby bridge, the designated lookout post. Officers blanketed both sides of the highway interchange and at least two other cars were dispatched to comb the area. Meanwhile, jail security guards did a head count and realized nobody was missing. The mystery was solved forty minutes later, just as jail officials were beginning to wonder what sort of inmate wannabes had been hanging around their facility.

Later, a helicopter spotted us in Secaucus, quietly motoring down the river -- but looking an awful lot like escapees. As we saw the helicopter fly overhead, my partners waved, and I asked them if we could dock to find out what all the excitement was about. Sheriff's officers rushed to the scene just in time to see three befuddled EPA inspectors docking to investigate the fuss. "Hi," I called, Want some Coke????" In retrospect, I guess it was an unfortunately poor choice of beverage words. A shotgun and 2 pistols suddenly pointed at us as I wondered if they were hard core confirmed Pepsi drinkers. We slowly raised our hands. "Need directions?", I politely asked. "They didn't understand what they did wrong," the police spokesman said. "They were very confused, to say the least."

'Confused' is a major line item in my job description. After showing our identification cards, we were finally sent on our way -- still wearing our orange jackets and pants. "I suggest the EPA gets you a new uniform," the policeman said. "It's not such a good idea to dress like an inmate if you're hanging around a jail." I told the officer that next month I would wear my green Kermit the Frog outfit instead, but I hope I don't get mugged by the Audubon Society.

That minor brush with fate led me to wonder about my family 'roots'. Did my ancestors have similar encounters? I'm sure my family tree had its typical crop of fruits and nuts, but as I began to assemble the data and records, I soon realized there wasn't much more than a Charlie Brown Christmas tree rather than a deep rooted Elm. My tattered copy of "The Rulebook for Perfect Daddyhood" stressed the importance of sharing activities with your children so I drafted my 3 daughters to help me.

This legendary guidebook for raising children was written anonymously by one of my ancestors, referred to as "Daddy I", and the treasured guidebook has been passed down from father to son for generations. It is rumored to contain all the secrets of having a great and lasting relation with your children without resorting to taxidermy when the child starts becoming a teenager. Unfortunately, I misplaced the copy my own dad gave me, and I suspect he didn't read it either. Probably none of the men in my family actually have read the book (it's a male thing, akin to asking directions.)

Alexis, my oldest at 16 going on 29, immediately structured a detailed four semester science research project involving 34 genealogical societies and engaged the National Archives to provide complete census records searches of our family name back to 1790, while in her spare time she would alphabetize and cross reference all directories from Germany, Holland, and Ireland. She also wanted a sample of my blood for DNA analysis. Erin -- my 12-year-old and soon to be teenager, grabbed our family Christmas card list and telephone book and began to call all of our relatives for information, then spent the next week in Internet Chat rooms trying to sell family secrets.

K.C., at age 9, took a more direct approach. She picked up her crayon box and paper and disappeared for 2 hours. When she returned, she proudly showed us the family tree she had already completed! It was a little lopsided, but very carefully written. Alexis, Erin, and KC with their birth dates across the bottom, then 'Daddy' and 'Mommy' above them, connected by purple lines. Not our given names, but literally Mommy and Daddy. "Daddy's" birth date was correctly written, but I noticed 'Mommy' was missing a decade. This didn't bother me, and Suzie immediately raised K.C.'s allowance, but the next level of entries did. Above my name was clearly written "Grandma" and "Pop-Pop", and above that were two "Great-Grandmas" a "Great-Grandpa" and a "Great-Pop-Pop". Again, K.C. didn't bother with names, but my side of the tree went back at least six generations of "Great-Greats" until she ran out of paper.

My wife, Suzie's historic side, was a bit simpler. Above "Mommy", K.C. had merely written the word "God". I asked K.C. why she wrote just "God" above Mommy. She simply replied, "Because you always tell us she's the Goddess of Mommyhood. She must be God's child."

"Good conclusion K.C., I always wondered where Suzie gets all of her advice from. But what about her brothers and sisters or Grandpa Mason and Ma Carol?" I asked.

"They must be children of a *lesser* god."

"Please don't repeat that at family reunions, K.C., but I guess it explains why so many of Mommy's relatives are named 'Cain'."

Actually, K.C. said it was only a draft version and later added several cousins, Barbie, Ken, and Skipper as well as a few Beanie Babies to her unique version of the family tree. She even brought a copy to school and got her entire third grade involved on a similar family tree search. Their teacher gave them an impromptu homework assignment to bring in family tree data from home. One redheaded Irish girl, Meghan, came in the next day with a neatly penciled tree that connected her with generations of Juans, Antonios, Carlottas, Marias, and similar Spanish sounding names. There was also a dotted line connecting her to a small box merely labeled "other household occupants". When questioned, Meghan explained that Juan and Carlotta were the household help, and she loved the way they took care of her and always had time for her. The 'other household occupants" were merely her blood relatives. Anyway, she liked tacos and the more exotic life.

For the rest of us, it was a continuing, long-term effort to track down ancestors and cousins we never knew existed. There were a lot of dead ends, and frustrating blanks. It seemed as if my family had scattered into the abyss of history. I found out my grandfather had 2 sisters in addition to several brothers, but somehow no one knew what happened to them. Still, it is a worthwhile experience. I located the town my father's mother came from in Ireland as a sixteen-year-old at the turn of the century.

I found out my mother's grandfather owned a German beer tavern in Brooklyn and her father worked as a brewer's mechanic for several Brooklyn breweries. This led me on a self-appointed quest to sample as many of the beers and 'micro brews' currently available in search of Grandpa's favorite beer recipe. The Mommygoddess, however, made me abandon this research effort when I came home with a half- ton of beer-making equipment to try to set up "Grandpa's Golden Ale" basement brewery.

While my wife's family roots extend considerably back in time, my own family name turned out not even to be our own. It's an English name given to my grandfather by the customs agent who couldn't understand German pronunciation. One of his sons even spelled the name differently so many direct relations have different versions of the name. On top of that, it turns out we're not quite German, but Pomeranian, a closely associated, nearby country that no longer exists. When I told this to the girls,

K.C. was convinced we were a breed of dog and drew us a family crest which looked like a cross between a poodle and Barney the Dinosaur.

Still, my daughters were happy to see the diversity of family names connecting across time and some of the varied occupations and cousins they have across the land. We've identified nearly five hundred "relatives" on both sides. One newly located cousin was even nice enough to send me a copy of a photo of my great-grandmother. Most important to them is that several of the surviving stories highlight the accomplishments of the women in the family- nurses, war veterans, teachers, wage earners who had to raise children alone after their husbands died or abandoned the family. These same sources also pointed out some of the frailties and foibles of a few of the men- prisoners, gamblers, run-aways, car accident victims, drifters, rumrunners, etc.

I gathered the girls around the extensive family tree and pointed out many of the names and stories I'd been able to document. I asked them if they had a better appreciation of their part in the continuity of life. "Yes, Daddy," they all replied, "and we're especially glad you only had daughters".

"Why is that?" I asked.

"Because," Alexis answered, "based on the information we've been uncovering, I suspect there's a genetic defect in most of the family males that makes you all act weird. Besides, none of us like beer. It must be a male thing. We did find out something interesting though. Daddy, you remember that book you always tell us about on raising children?"

"Oh yeah, 'The Rulebook for Perfect Daddyhood'. A true classic. All of the men in my family have passed it down for generations. Did you find out who the author, 'Daddy-1', really was? He was the one male in our family who really contributed the most."

"Yes Daddy. The author was Great *Aunt* Eva."

"Doh!!!!! It figures....."

CHAPTER 25

BIG SISTER
AND DADDYHOOD

There is a special breed of human known as Big Sister. I grew up with one and can testify that they have a lasting impact. No matter what life's twists and turns throw at me, what I have become is somewhat the result of having a Big Sister. I may be graying and in the midst of long-term Daddyhood myself, but somehow, I still feel like a small child that is constantly getting advice. Even without my lost "Rulebook for Perfect Daddyhood" to guide me, I usually can successfully wing it in trying to raise my daughters. At least I thought so until I realized I was getting plenty of advice from the great number of females who have taken on the role of Big Sister.

My Big Sister, Maureen, had already staked out her place in my parent's household by the time I was born. She had enjoyed unlimited access to Mom and Dad, a dog, her own bedroom, tons of toys and dolls, a nice wardrobe, an even an allowance more than appropriate for a five-year-old. I have heard that, originally, my sister was looking forward to having a new little baby in the house. She even built a small box for me next to her doll house. She had literally hundreds of dolls and spent countless hours changing doll clothes. Maureen looked forward to changing a real baby. She was disappointed that I turned out to be a boy - none of her doll

143

clothes fit me, although she did dress me up and bring me out trick-or-treating as a three-year-old Raggedy Ann on Halloween. When one of the neighbors looked at me and said he wouldn't give me candy since I didn't have a costume on, I pulled off my wig in frustration and yelled, "I'm a BOY, dammit! Tell him, Maureen!!!" Her only reply was, "Now, you know better than to curse...... 'Roberta'!"

Still, she did bring me in to her kindergarten class for show and tell. I have been told I only cried a little during my sister's attempt to put a dog leash on me. It was a warning of what our relationship would be like for the next 12 years. We fought like cats and dogs, except at Christmas, other holidays, and birthdays. I especially looked forward to her birthday as this was the one day of the year I could hit her once for each year, give her an extra hard pinch "to grow an inch", and a swift kick "not to get sick".

One of the first things Little Brothers and Little Sisters learn is that Big Sisters are older, wiser, more experienced, and have already done everything before so there is no way to impress Mom or Dad. My first baby steps? She's done that and can even hop backwards. My first words? She's done that and can count to 10. Actually, it was only years later that I finally realized us "Little uns" have to give a lot of credit to those Big Sisters who paved the way for us. They were the barrier breakers who wore Mom and Dad down so we could get our independence a bit earlier. It is only now that I know the true feeling of an impending parental heart attack when the first child goes on a first date or drives my car for the first time. GULP. I know it will get easier with the next child, and I'm sure I'll be too exhausted to notice when my littlest one changes from driving me crazy to driving my car. She'll have her Big Sisters to thank.

Big Sisters have more internal strength than us "Little 'uns". It comes from facing life's everyday challenges without the protective guidance of an older sibling. My Big Sister wasn't a dainty female, but rather the 'Tom Boy' that taught me to throw and catch a ball, climb a tree, and discretely hide my lima beans in my napkin until I could throw them in the toilet. We shared a love of hating lima beans. Years later, I noticed she was serving lima beans to her own four boys. I asked her why and she replied, "It's a tradition. I'm letting them learn a lesson in creative ways of making lima beans disappear." She was right. At my house, my three girls and I all throw our lima beans onto Mommy's plate when she's not looking.

On the other hand, who else but Big Sister would save her little brother's Lionel Train set for over fifteen years until he had children of his own to play with it? Or, who else but a Big Sister would disappear into her basement for a few minutes and drop a pile of vintage 1960's Mad Magazines onto her Little Brother's lap when he confesses that he still gets a kick out of reading it? What else is in that basement? My lost 'Rulebook for Perfect Daddyhood' maybe? Before my wife and I began our own family, my Big Sister dropped off 26 boxes of baby clothes her four boys had outgrown. As I lugged the boxes down to my basement, I shuddered to think of the day we might really need them. Wouldn't you know, we had 3 girls.

Big Sister is also the one who is more adept at repairing plumbing or wiring a lamp and is the one that teaches the 'Little uns' the value of volunteering. She's the one with a strong faith and demonstrates that it means more than just sitting in a church pew on Sundays. Big Sister is also the one who volunteers her time on numerous charity and church activities. She also volunteers my time, your time, and all the kid's time, but does it in a way that you don't really mind. You learn that sacrificing sleep or missing a TV program is insignificant in comparison to helping the community, friends, or those in need. You also learn that life happens while your busy making plans.

No matter what rules and guidelines parents set up in an attempt to raise children the "right" way, it was usually up to Big Sister to either enforce them or break them. My Big Sister had a knack for enforcing them on me. She learned how to tell time quickly so that she could promptly call to our Mom and Dad to put me to bed at 7:30 on the dot. If I was playing outside, she was the one who cautioned me to get home before the streetlights went on or I would "get it" from Dad. (What was "it", anyway???? I never recall actually ever getting "IT" from my dad.) If one of my vegetables somehow rolled off my dinner plate, I could guarantee it would be Big Sister who would scoop it up and hold it under my nose saying, "Look what we found, baby brother! My, oh my, someone sure is sloppy tonight. Here, let me feed you!"

Probably due to our similar genes, both my Big Sister and I have some musical talent. Maureen took piano lessons and was surprisingly good at them. However, our early rivalry came back to haunt me. We both sang in the church and school choirs. However, since my Big Sister was also playing the piano, I wouldn't. I was a real macho mini-man. I refused to play an instrument that a girl, especially my stupid Big Sister, played. Instead, I stupidly opted to take accordion lessons knowing full well I'd never be invited to many polka parties. Maureen played well enough to be invited to play at our annual Christmas family parties, where she astounded me by playing a lovely rendition of "Silver Bells". So many notes and both hands working independently! Meanwhile, no one asked me to play "Texas Hayride" and I can only pound out a Christmas carol on the piano using my right hand, and only if I tip the piano on its side first.

The male versus female rivalry is as basic as life itself. I'm sure I'm left-handed only because my Big Sister is right-handed. (This made sense to me when I was six). I guess I was also jealous that Big Sister was Daddy's girl. I always wished I was bigger than my Big Sister so I could hold her down and tickle her to death like she frequently did to me. One summer, she spent a month away at a Church camp and came back 20 pounds heavier. Her diet had consisted of nothing but bread, butter, and

146

sugar sandwiches! Before I could even begin to mock her, she gave me a steely look and whispered, "Tickle fight, dog breath?"

A few years later, when my Big Sister stood at the door in her high school prom dress, I was stunned into silence thinking how pretty she actually looked and wanting to kill her date if he dared touch her. As we grew up, our rivalry ebbed and flowed with the tide. Her favorite nickname for me was "Pest" as I trailed along or intruded on her space. We did team up on one occasion when we bought a baby rabbit and hid it in a hat box to surprise our Mom with a gift for Easter. Our Mom was sure surprised when she went into the room to clean up and a small, furry creature flipped out of a box she picked up. Her scream, "ARGHH! A RAT!!!!" was heard three blocks away. My respect for my Big Sister increased when she accepted a large share of the blame, while I merely stood there and suggested we name the rabbit "Rat".

Somewhere along the way, my childhood goal of getting revenge and beating up my Big Sister faded away. It ended when she married and moved out to begin her own family, leaving me to deal with Mom and Dad on my own as a young teenager. Holy Cow! What a revelation! It finally dawned on me how much a Big Sister could be worth, and it was a treat to visit her, have a cup of coffee, and hear her chat about her boys. I could still tease her about her quickly graying hair, but she laughed and reminded me I'm only five years behind her and "You'll get yours". It is Big Sister who also keeps accidentally calling her first-born son by my name whether she's mad at him or not.

When I was away in college, it was Big Sister who wrote me a touching and heartfelt letter breaking the news that our lifelong family dog, Penny - the best damn dog in the world, had passed away. It was also Big Sister who drove my future wife 180 miles upstate to visit me at college for the weekend. Later, it was Big Sister and I who stopped in at our old high school to visit our former teachers and show off her little sons.

(This was traumatic for me when one of the teachers mistakenly thought I was her Older Brother!)

I guess it was inevitable that I would marry a girl that was also a Big Sister. My wife is the oldest of five children, and functions as surrogate Mom as well Big Sister. She can also juggle six tasks at once and is famous for giving advice. I know I need to have more than an hour of time available if I ask her a simple yes or no question. My wife is also a terrific Mommy to our girls, as is my Big Sister to her sons. As our families have grown, it's been interesting to see the types of girls my nephews are attracted to - Big Sisters. It has also been marvelous to observe the Big Sister role my own daughters fill with their younger siblings. Alexis leads by example. K.C., our youngest, is luckiest since she has two Big Sisters to run interference for her. Then again, perhaps Erin, my middle girl is luckiest since she is both a Big Sister as well as a Little 'un and knows both sides...

The 'Big Sister' role never ends, no matter how many birthdays the Little 'uns have under their belts. I am also sure that when the day comes that Big Sisters are welcomed into heaven, they quickly become Guardian Angels, and the world is a better place because of them. One special one, however, will be asked to stay awhile and rest a bit, and play Silver Bells for the other angels.

CHAPTER 26

SANTADAD.COM

Recently, I was going through a box of papers I had inherited from my sister when I came across a letter which I had written at the tender age of nine to Santa Claus. I was surprised to see the letter - a reminder that older family members sometimes volunteer to share the duties of the "real" Santa. Santa is real but could use some help. After all, Santa lives in the North Pole and can't possibly visit all the good children in just one night. It was surprising that my big sister had intercepted my letter to Santa and helped make my Christmas merry.

It was just as surprising to see that I had written a real letter! Even if it was 'Charlie Brown' style writing with smudges and cross outs, I had used a real pen, paper, a genuine 3- cent stamp, and even a real envelope. (The envelope was one my Dad had taken home from his job, but the address under the corporate logo had been crossed out and rewritten with our home address in Garden City, Long Island.) I thought, "When was the last time you received a real letter?" Nowadays, our fast-paced lives have no time for simple letter writing. We try to communicate via fax, phone, and e-mail. And 'post-its' in school lunch boxes. Somehow, we are all so busy communicating that we never get the message across.

I blame computers. I have one in my office but had historically been resistant to getting one at home. The price was always well beyond what my meager salary could afford. If my family really needed some computer help, I could use my office computer. Besides, I didn't want my daughters on chat rooms or wasting their time playing computer games. If they needed some information, they could go to the library or ask Mommy -- the human reference encyclopedia and all-knowing Goddess of Mommyhood. The girls refer to her as "Mommy Britannica" -- the unabridged version. The only time she was stumped was when my daughter Erin once commented, "Just how stupid is Daddy, anyway?" Suzie replied she couldn't find the appropriate reference point.

I wasn't proud we didn't have a home computer, but life had its financial limits. Several years ago, I mentioned this fact to my pastor's wife, Chris. It turned out Chris was a real computer buff and decided I needed an education in 20th Century technology. She showed up at our house with a small computer for us to 'borrow'. Chris asked me if I knew 'DOS'? When I answered, "Dos? It is German? *Was ist Dos?* Mochten Sie eine tasse Koffe trinken?" she said we'd be better off with 'Windows'.

I was dumbfounded, but before I could politely decline and tell her I already had windows as well as storm doors, my daughters all pleaded "A computer!!! Can we keep it? Wow! Please, please, please??" It was as if a stray puppy had suddenly appeared on our doorstep. How could I resist their pleas? And so, little by little, life changed.

The little '286' model had very basic word processing (Word Perfect 0.5) and rudimentary spreadsheet software (Lotus 0.9+) as well as several simple games - Pack Man, Defender, Space Invaders, and Digger. We named it "Big Blue". I thought the girls would spend considerable time learning how to type or prepare a spreadsheet, but it turned out they had already mastered keyboarding -- in elementary school. In a short time, Alexis had already prepared a fully integrated and cross-referenced spreadsheet of her entire My Little Pony collection and Erin had already calculated how much my old coin collection would be worth when she inherited it. K.C., still pre-school but already starting to read, was up to Level 7 on Digger and climbing!

Digger, a simple computer game where a character chomps through tunnels to find diamonds and sacks of coins, was our passion. The background music was "The Chicken Dance" and we filled all the top 200 score historic record list within a few months. KC, Erin, and I became adept at the mysteries of "Digger". It was especially gratifying for KC that she could consistently beat her oldest sister in a game of Digger (and Erin didn't mind).

A few years later, it dawned on me that our little "Big Blue" 286 computer was on its last legs. We couldn't even buy the old-style floppy discs anymore, and most of the ones we had were too warped to use. Fortunately, my father-in-law had just inherited a bigger machine from a defunct company he had represented. It was a whopping "386" and could use the new smaller discs. Unfortunately, when we transferred all of the data from "Big Blue", Digger became corrupted and wouldn't work. The screen would come up and then freeze. The Chicken Dance soundtrack sounded like a funeral dirge. Digger was dead, and the 386 killed it. We were devastated and it took the magic out of our relationship with the 386. We wouldn't even name it.

Later, we found out the 386 computer was not only a Digger killer, but it was also frustratingly slow. It took 12 minutes to boot up and you could only type about 8 words a minute before the screen froze. I began calling it lots of names, but it merely sneered at me, burped, and took its sweet time. At least I still had my "real" computer at work. It had every software capability (but didn't have Digger.) As time went on, I more and more frequently had to bring my daughters homework reports to work, reformat them and print them out. Eventually, both Erin and Alexis

151

stopped talking to me. They were upset if I edited any of their work - which would cause them to get lower grades than before I got involved.

For the next Christmas, I decided to try and replace the Digger game. I went to several stores, but no Digger. It turned out it was no longer even manufactured. It had been replaced by newer, more modern, and complex, exciting (blast and kill) strategy games nearly ten years earlier! One store owner could sense my disappointment and suggested I try to obtain a copy through a "freeware" or "shareware" service on the Internet. I did many Internet searches, but it seems Digger didn't have the worldwide popularity our household thought it would.

I occasionally found references to 'Digger' on computer chat rooms where the writers were moaning that they couldn't find a working copy, and how much fun it used to be to play the simple game. Occasionally, someone reported a rumor that they heard someone was trying to rewrite an updated version, but no one ever really knew who or where. Then, fate led me to a new world - E-BAY!! This site is actually the world's largest auction flea market. Anything you can possibly spell will be found for sale at any time. In anxious anticipation, I tried an E-BAY search for "Digger". The response was short, "No Listing, Please Try Again". Rats, no listing for the elusive, long lost Digger.

I thought that maybe it was the E-BAY system that wasn't working properly. As a test, I tried a search for "Johnson Brothers Heritage", our dinnerware pattern that had been discontinued several years ago. To my surprise, seven items were currently for sale! Most had photographs of the dish, and all of them looked better than the chipped and cracked, discolored set we had been using for the past 20 years. Suzie and I never had the money to replace the set. I bid on a few different ones, and a few days later, I was notified my "bids" had been accepted and I was now the "proud" owner of 3 butter dishes, a cup, and salad bowl. I had them mailed to my office, then carried them home and slipped them into our stack of dishes. My wife, Suzie, never noticed or commented, so a plan was hatched.

Over the next few months, I occasionally checked the E-BAY web site and inexpensively purchased several more pieces of the dinnerware. Suzie never noticed that our plates were mysteriously breeding in the cabinet, and our chipped and cracked dishes were gradually healing themselves. Our old set was looking better and better. It was fun playing secret "Santadad" and giving her these unnoticed gifts. I let the girls in on the secret and told them to see how long it took for Mommy to notice.

Suzie hates to cook and is known for serving lunch and dinner on paper plates. By the time it actually dawned on Suzie that we didn't always have 4 large serving bowls, our dinnerware service had grown to 22 full place settings, with 32 assorted serving pieces and 2 butter dishes. I remember the day she noticed very well. It was the same day she dropped off several boxes of all of the Johnson Brothers Heritage dinnerware to the Salvation Army. She told the clerk she was tired of looking at it all those years, but at least it seemed indestructible. We now eat off paper plates. She wonders why I don't talk much anymore. I've been in therapy.

I switched from Johnson Brothers to searching for turn-of-the-century Heckers' Flour advertising cards, My Little Ponies, and Kermit the Frog neckties. They are always good for anytime, anyplace, holiday gifts for either Suzie (Heckers'), the girls (My Little Ponies), or me (Kermit). "Santadad" has a special closet where these gifts are carefully hidden. "Santadad" is always ready with the perfect gift – especially for ME! Whenever one of my children comes up to me and asks what I'd like for Christmas or Father's Day, I simply reach in the closet and pull out a Kermit the Frog necktie or frog watch and say, "You want to make your Daddy happy? Give this to me, it's exactly what I'd like." So far, I haven't had any complaints. It is a better system than my neighbor, Tom, used. His young son came up to him and asked what he'd like for Christmas.

Tom asked how much his son was planning on spending, and his son said, "Oh, about $10.00"

"Fine", Tom said. "I'd simply like a nice, crisp $10 bill."

"OK", his son replied, "Can I borrow $10.00?"

I'll stick with my own system. It saves last minute shopping trips, and I can spread out purchases throughout the year. The year flew by, and I again had my computer at work upgraded by the company. It now could talk with me and connected me via e-mail automatically to everyone in the universe. I tried ignoring most of these messages. When the computer began giving me urgent and loud reminders that I wasn't answering my 3,000 e-mail messages per day, I turned its volume control to mute, wishing I could also do this at home.

As the next Christmas approached, I tried once more to find Digger through a computer search. One reply message read that a Ukrainian computer buff had reworked the classic Digger program so it could operate on the new high-speed computers. Digger lives? I, at long last, decided it was time to get a new home computer after all. I went to Chris and asked her if she had any suggestions. Chris advised me to pray. It works for her husband. She then asked how much I was willing to spend on a new computer and I casually offered "about" $500. Chris said that for $500, I could certainly buy a good 'Barbie' or 'Pokemon' computer, either of which would still be faster and more powerful than our troublesome '386' dinosaur.

Eventually, we budgeted an amount only twice as high as what I paid for my first car twenty years earlier. Actually, I already had a head start saving. Each year, our family saves all the money we find in a special Found Money Bank. On January 1, we open the bank and count all the coins. Usually, the girls and I split the findings (averaging over $30 per year!). Last year, the girls decided to keep all the Found Money together for our new computer. I had already saved $38.52. It turns out this year was going to be an even better haul for the Found Money Bank, primarily due to K.C.

K.C. was on a quest to pick up every lost penny on Long Island. After school, she and her friend Kristen often go with Mommy to 7-11 to buy milk. (This used to be my job, but Suzie fired me after observing I was going to 7-11 8 times a day for milk and always only coming home with just a pint at a time. It was simply my way of getting out of the house whenever she started to ask me to do something.) K.C. and Kristen would then dive under the counters to collect lost change, usually coming up with at least 8 pennies and a dime (as well as assorted bits of beef jerky and used gum.) My wife is a stickler for 'fairness', and if one of the girls found more than the other, she would make up the difference from her own change purse to keep things equal. So much for altruism. When K.C. and Kristen figured this out, they secretly teamed up where one child would sneak all her coins to the other so that Mommy would have to give them the maximum amount possible. The girls were easily collecting an extra dollar a week with this subterfuge.

On top of this, the girls jointly agreed that this year, none of them wanted any individual gifts for Christmas. Daddy was told to apply all the gift funds to a good family computer. Erin was most insistent. It seemed that her cousin Kate no longer called her on the phone. Worse, Kate was now spending time "Chat rooming" with one of Erin's friends via computer. Since we had no "real computer", Erin was fast losing friends. "Santadad" came through with a Christmas promise to get a "real" computer by the close of the Millennium.

After much shopping, we finally had bought and set up a decent home computer system and printer. It was one Chris promised me wouldn't be obsolete for at least 7 minutes after we bought it. For Christmas, my wife was finally able to view the digital camera photos of my nephew's wedding from the previous year. (The same one's I'd already e-mailed several months earlier to all our relatives from my office computer.) The Christmas stockings were rather empty (except for mine which was stuffed with 6 different Kermit the Frog neckties), but the girls were all happy. There was, however, a small bump in K.C.'s stocking. She unwrapped a plain computer disc and gave me a puzzled look.

"Put it into the computer, Princess, then press 'Enter.'" K.C. did, and suddenly the screen lit up with a series of tunnels and the music of The Chicken Dance. Digger was back!

"Thanks, Daddy. This is the best Christmas ever. Want to play?"

CHAPTER 27

DRESSING UP DADDYHOOD

If Seven - Eleven sold clothing, I would never have to shop anywhere else. If it seems as if I have spent a good portion of my 'daddyhood' years at the local 7-11, you're right. Raising three daughters over the last 17 years has meant a near infinite number of daily trips to buy a quart of milk. Yes, I know it would be more efficient to buy milk in gallon containers, but then I wouldn't have as many excuses to flee my female filled noisy home 4 or 5 times a day. I know I have only three daughters, but some of their friends have been over so many times, they've been informally adopted, especially daughter #4, Maggie. Whenever the domestic noise level gets too high or my wife, the goddess of Mommyhood, remembers to tell me "Just one more thing". I suddenly stop and say thoughtfully "Oops, I think we're out of milk again. I better go to 7-11 and get some right now." I leave quickly, before they can react by giving me a never-ending list of other food items we need. I'd rather make 8 separate trips to 7-11 and pick up each item one at a time.

Actually, it's a typical Daddy's way of doing things. Seven - Eleven has all the basic food groups a Man really needs, caffeine, nicotine, alcohol, cholesterol, and sugar. When they started carrying Dunkin Donuts, I was tempted to bring my sleeping bag and just move in. I do see a lot of other Daddies in the store, the occasional frazzled Soccer Mom hurrying in to buy 8 large Slurpees every weekend for her team, and the glazed eyed 10-year-olds begging for more Pokemon or Baseball cards. The local 7-11 can also be an adventure, especially when my own children discovered the floor is a "lost change factory". There are usually several pennies, nickels, and the occasional quarter laying in the corners or under the counters, undoubtedly dropped by commuters rushing to catch the approaching Long Island Railroad train at the station across the street.

With their natural fixation on "Found Money", each of my daughters has gone on treasure hunts with me to 7-11. While I get the milk or read the local weekly paper - the *Garden City News*, from its rack, they dive under the counter or inspect each corner of the shelves. Usually, they find at least enough change for me to pay for the local paper. However, I prefer to simply read it for free and put it back on the rack for the next Dad and let the girls keep their findings (split with me 50-50 since I sometimes have to act as a diversion if a customer is standing on a quarter without realizing it. It's my job to bump him into the Big Bite bin while KC scoops up the coin.)

The years of Daddyhood have flown by. No longer do I have to make an emergency run to 7-11 to buy Huggies baby diapers for my children. Instead, I now have to make emergency runs to buy Depends adult diapers for my mom. I used to think how rich I'd be once my daughters were all toilet trained. Little did I know that I'd soon be facing the same situation on the other side of my lifeline. Between those and the four gross of Tampons we seem to go through every month, it's no wonder I detest shopping. Still, I'd rather buy these necessities than ever, ever, go clothes shopping with or for my daughters ever again.

It must be a result of countless childhood hours of dressing Barbie or My Little Ponies, but it seems females have a united plot to drive males crazy shopping for clothes. As young boy, I distinctly remember wearing the same tee shirt and jeans every day for three solid months, then turning the tee shirt inside out and wearing it for the next three months. My wardrobe has expanded since then, but I can shop for a year's clothing supply in 37 minutes at Sears and still have time to look at lawnmowers.

My basic wardrobe consists of 26 frog-print ties, 12 frog-printed tee shirts, 3 nightshirts - 1 Tweetybird, 1 Grumpy the Dwarf, and 1 Mickey Mouse (who says I can't have fun in bed?), 5 pairs of Levis jeans, a 10-year-old bathing suit with matching tee shirt, a couple of old sports coats, a 1980's vintage short sleeved shirt, and a suit so I can look great when buried when the time comes. It's a great looking Ralph Lauren suit I made the mistake of buying in 1983 immediately on my return from a year in the Saudi Arabia Desert. I forgot I was dehydrated at the time. Within a month, my body had ballooned back to its normal fubsy condition, and the suit never fit again. I'm going to let the undertaker figure a way of getting me into it.

My wife worked in the fashion display field for several years, and still tends to pin "For Sale 50% off" signs on me whenever I get dressed. Then she dusts off my shoulders and mutters something about plaid and stripes don't match. The reason the 'Regis' look, black on black with gray, is so popular is because it's simple and basic- (and hides a lot of coffee stains.) Who wants to look like a Millionaire, anyway?

With girls, it's different. Each piece of clothing must be carefully screened for the perfect balance between fashionable and stylish. Would Barbie approve? Does the dress nip and tuck all the right attributes flatteringly? With most guys, as long as the zipper works, the pants are fine. With girls, God forbid there's a missed stitch or crooked button. With guys, we simply read waist and leg size and know the pants fits. I pull a pair of pants labeled 34x32 and I know they'll fit (just a little more tightly than they would have 20 years ago). Female sizes are a mystery. They must have been made up by a sadistic fashion designer. Female clothes sizes seem to just be numbers with no basis in reality. Just as I'm getting used to seeing my girls grow from size 2 to size 3 to size 6 to size 10, they suddenly started the numbering system all over again. My littlest daughter K.C., (a Size 8) now wears a bigger size than her oldest sister Alexis, (a Size 1). I don't believe 17-year-old Alexis shrunk in the wash.

To make it more complicated, not all of these sizes are 'standard'. Many of the size labels are merely the whim of the manufacturer. Those that want to sell a bunch of clothing should cut the clothes in all sorts of sizes and simply label everything Size 5. They'd make a fortune. The "magic" numbers are the odd numbers reserved for princesses and junior teens, while the 'even' numbers are set aside for their matronly misses and moms. (Susan Lucci, however, has a firm lock on a perpetual Size 3 Petite which is probably why she finally was awarded an Emmy.)

When Alexis celebrated her sixteenth birthday, we were sucked into the Long Island tradition, the Sweet Sixteen party. The tradition was started by the catering industry. She invited seventy of her closest friends allowing us to invite thirty of our closest relatives. Alexis, Mommy, and the girls spent weeks scouring the halls of Roosevelt Field and every other shopping mall in Nassau County to find the right dresses. My gasoline bills for the month were nearly the same as our mortgage payment. They did finally find the outfits they wanted. The day of the party, I got out my 'good clothes'-- frog green colored shirt, blue frog patterned tie, and brown corduroy jacket. Thinking I looked good, I told them I was ready to go. Wrong. Mommy, Alexis and even K.C. told me to go change. It turned out my trusty 15-year-old corduroy jacket had finally died. The liner was trailing behind me, and change kept falling through the hole in its pocket.

While K.C. scooped up the change and added it to our Found Money Bank, I drove downtown, bypassing 7-11 reluctantly as well as Sears, and parked in front of Lord and Taylor instead. I entered the store, and low and behold -- right in front of me was a rack of sports coats. My arm brushed against one and I jumped. It was the softest, smoothest Ultrasuede I'd ever felt. I picked up a tan one marked 'Medium - Regular' and put it over my frog green shirt. It fit and felt great, but I noticed my shirt was frayed badly along the collar. Oh rats. I floated down the aisle in ultrasuede heaven, and picked up a new shirt, (size 'Medium'), then splurged and scooped up a matching pair of pants as well as a new tie (size "Regular" and with a subtle frog pattern no less!) I watched as the cashier range up the charges (and burned through my credit limit) and was home within 25 minutes. I didn't even ask if Lord and Taylor had a lawn mower department.

The party was great, but frankly I don't remember what any of my girls wore. All I know is that my ultrasuede jacket was a hit. The guests kept brushing against me, then stroking my arm up and down. Some of them even purred. It was cool! Erin, my wise middle child figured out why I was suddenly so popular. "Daddy, you feel just like a Beanie Baby." No wonder Ty has sold so many of the stuffed animals! Well, I'm not one to fight success. The next week I went back to the store and bought four more of the jackets (all size 'Medium') in different colors. I figure I'm set until the year 2060 and anyway by then the only thing I'll be wearing is Depends (size Medium).

A few months later, my oldest daughter Alexis began shopping for a dress for her junior prom. This was an ordeal beyond belief. It became the "Quest for the Perfect Dress." She and Mommy went to every store in creation, trying on every style and size imaginable: 1,2,5,7, petite, short, junior, misses, trendy, trashy, floor length, short, midi, maxi, ensemble, empire, drop waist, and on and on. Nothing was acceptable. It had to be the perfect color for her eyes, the right material for her skin, and the exact cut to flatter her figure.

Week after week, Mommy and Alexis made pilgrimages to shopping centers with high expectations but came home empty handed and frustrated. At long last, they came home one Monday evening happily announcing they'd found the Perfect Dress! I was pleased to be reunited with my family again and asked to see it. "Sorry Daddy, it needed a minor repair, so we had it put on reserve for pick up later, but it's STUNNING!" and Alexis handed me a receipt. My luck, I got volunteered to pick up the dress.

The store was nearly an hour's drive away. The following Friday, I took off from work and drove out on Long Island to the store with the Perfect Dress. The building was a huge factory style warehouse covering nearly 100,000 square feet and was filled floor to ceiling with 30 gazillion dresses. It was definitely prom season. There were at least 5,000 teenaged girls and their moms scurrying around the store, each bleary eyed, searching desperately for their own Perfect Dress. Models wearing this minute's seasonal fashion statement were walking around spraying customers with samples of perfume. When I got doused for the third time with "eau de toad", I fell on the floor clutching my throat screaming "I'm melting, I'm melting!', but the teenage girls were oblivious as their personal Prom Dress Crusade continued.

I waded to the front of the counter and handed the cashier my receipt for Alexis's dress. She turned towards a rack of 3,000 dresses and began leafing through them. After a few minutes, she looked at the receipt again, then turned back to me and said, "I'm sorry. The dress wasn't picked up within the 48 hours it was on reserve. We put it back on the sales floor."

"You put it back?" I screamed. "How could you put it back? I have the receipt!"

It turned out I didn't have the receipt. I had a ticket for repairs, but the dress hadn't actually been paid for. The cashier asked me to describe the dress so she could have one of the clerks check the floor to see if was still there. "I have no idea what the dress looks like. All I know is that it is the "Perfect Prom Dress". The cashier laughed and said that described the dress perfectly, as well as any of the other 30 gazillion dresses in the store. I was stumped.

I called my wife and then had her call the cashier. Women have certain communications skills that men lack when it comes to clothing, because within 10 minutes the cashier knew exactly which Perfect Prom Dress to look for. Unfortunately, within 10 minutes more, she returned with the sad news that the dress must have been sold. "So, give me another one just like it," I naively said.

The cashier looked at me as if I was a typical male. "It's not that easy", she replied. "It was a special dress, size 1.025, petite but developing." I was developing a headache but asked her what she meant. She just turned away and returned a few minutes later with a rather pretty gown. "This is the best I can do," she explained. "It's the same dress in gold rather than blue. I took it off one of the mannequins." Blue, gold, what's the difference, I thought. It will match her hair rather than her eyes. I bought the Perfect Prom Dress Number 2 and made the hour's drive home.

I no sooner got into the house with the Perfect Prom Dress Number 2 than Alexis came home from school, took one look at it, and dragged Mommy and the dress back to the store. It seems the gold color didn't quite match her blond hair, and a gold dress wouldn't go at all with silver shoes or silver pocketbook. Little did I know…. I went to 7-11 to try and cool off by the Slurpee machine. Later that night, they returned with the Perfect Prom Dress Number 3 (size 3 junior short) in their hands. Success at last! It was a different style, a 2-piece outfit, than either Perfect Prom Dress Number 1 or Number 2 but looked fine to me. Alexis tried it on and screamed. "OH DAMN! They forgot to remove the security tag!!!" Sure enough, on the top piece of the gown was a large gray plastic disc. It could not be removed without a certain tool.

The next morning, I was again volunteered to spend 2 hours driving back and forth to the dress store to get the tag removed. I arrived at the store just as it opened. I parked and brought the top piece to the store and asked the security guard if he could get the manager to remove tag. The

163

guard took the piece, then returned a few minutes later with the manager. The manager looked at me suspiciously and asked how I got the dress out of the store without the security alarm setting off.

We then got into a fifteen-minute argument about whether I stole the dress, their stupid alarm system, where was my receipt, their stupid alarm system, checking credit card purchases, and why would I steal just the top half of a dress then bring it back to have them remove the security tag did I really look that stupid? At last, we agreed on something, and the manager removed the security tag while the security guard unhandcuffed me. On the way home, I celebrated my Perfect Prom Dress Number 3 legal victory with a Supersize Big Bite and Cherry Slurpee from the only retail store that really understands me.

Mommy and Alexis were happy with her Perfect Prom Dress Number 3, (although I was slightly leery that Ali's date was more interested in getting Ali out of her Perfect Prom Dress than seeing her in it.) Anyway, we survived Prom Number 1 and the Perfect Prom Dress Number 3 has now joined the Sweet Sixteen, Confirmation, and Spring Fling dresses in the hall closet, (never to be worn again), right next to Mommy's Prom Dress, Graduation Gown, and Wedding Gown (also worn only once each.)

CHAPTER 28

POKEYDAD 2000

With the new Millennium, it was time for my annual Government provided HMO physical. This was a real treat ---which I looked forward to almost as much as filing my taxes every year. At least the physical exam was "free", but you get what you pay for. I thought that the reason my body was becoming less user - friendly was due to advancing age or occasional exposure to toxic or hazardous substances from my work with USEPA Superfund sites. I didn't realize the cumulative damage was primarily due to exposure to Daddyhood and Pokemon.

After getting probed, prodded, plucked, pricked, hammered, thumped, photographed, sprayed, tattooed, and sampled, I was called back by the assigned Government HMO Doctor to review the results. "Mr. Abbey, I have some rather bad news," Doctor 'X' explained, "Your tests have revealed a dramatic change for the worse over the last year."

"Thanks, Doc," I replied, "especially since my name's not Abbey. Are you sure those are my results? Computer mix-ups have been known to happen, even in the Government."

"Mr. Avery," Doc "X" continued, "the test results show you're partially deaf, you have the beginnings of osteoporosis, and your blood has elevated levels of lead, caffeine, and nicotine. Your lungs are normal

--- for a 135-year-old, and your Cholesterol levels have suddenly jumped to 4,800."

"I'm glad I'm not Avery either, but it sounds like me anyway. Is that good or bad?" I asked.

"Well, put it this way Mr. Levy, your arteries bear an uncanny resemblance to processed American Cheese."

"Cheese?" I thought... "That explains it. I've had a serious case of Pokemonitis, but hopefully it's over now. My children are now Pottermaniacs."

Doctor "X" looked at me suspiciously, but my 3.5 minutes of free Government HMO annual health advice were up so he merely told me to get more exercise and check with my primary health care provider's HMO web site, www.hmoquakers.com\deaduck.html, if I wanted any further information. "See you next year, Mr. Alvarez."

It's been that kind of year. Being the Daddy to three quickly maturing daughters is slowly killing me. The previous year, my youngest daughter K.C. became hooked on 'Pokemon', the collectible craze of 1999. Pokemon is a game in which you collect, train, and fight little creatures known as Pokemon. It is available as both a simple card game and a computer game. The games were released a while ago in Japan, and since then their popularity has soared. Not even the Beanie Babies were as popular! There were Pokemon toys, games, snacks, clothing, plush characters, lunch boxes, and, I imagine, many, many more. Who could resist them? There's something about the Pokemon that made them impossible to avoid. What was it? A huge and excessive marketing budget!

This Japanese cartoon creation invaded the US with a greater impact than Pearl Harbor. The cartoon consisted of 150 different 'pocket monsters'--- varieties of fantasy animals that evolved with different strengths and special talents. Pokemon is a game that puts you in a magical land. The land is overrun by the little monsters. Pikachu, Charizard, Charmander, and Squirtle were among the more popular Pokemon. Kids collect and keep these monsters in a magical red and white 'pokeball' that can comfortably hold a Pokemon no matter what size it is. I wish my closets were like that. They then use their Pokemon to fight with others using special powers. All across the fantasy land are several gyms that are led by gym leaders. The gym leaders help train Pokemon trainers to beat the tar out of each other. (Confused? So was I, but I'm sure this makes sense to the average 10- year- old.) I think the goal is to become a Pokemon MasterCard before your parents' Visa and America Express cards melt down.

The game was primarily a series of 'collectible' cards that had the primary purpose of separating families with as much money as possible in the shortest time permissible. K.C. became a Poke-addict and joined 100 million other young children in a quest to amass a complete set of the 150 Pokemon trading cards.

The darn cards, however, were priced slightly more than my first car. This wasn't the same as throwing down a $5.00 bill for one of 600 different My Little Ponies for my oldest daughter Alexis or tossing another $5.00 for one of 26,486 Beanie Babies for my middle daughter, Erin. This was like burning $7.99 for a pack of 10 pieces of colored cardboard, and then another $3.00 for clear plastic collectible card insert holders so your nine-year-old wouldn't actually touch the cards and "ruin" them. Actually, I wish I had kept my Mickey Mantle Rookie baseball card in a plastic holder rather than using it as a noisemaker on my bicycle. I could have retired by now.

Pokemon made one marketing error they quickly corrected. Originally, there were only 150 different cards, too small a number to sufficiently drain Daddy's wallet. To make up for this limited (?) number of characters, there are now many different versions of the game, including Green, Gold, Red and Blue. I expect there are more, so that there are now 2,955,000 separate versions of the 150 different Pokemon characters. Now, in each version, the game is the same, but it doesn't have the same mix of monsters. Therefore, to collect all the Pokemon, you will have to find someone who has a different version of the game. (Or buy the other version, and another Game Boy if you can convince Daddy to fork over his wallet or not pay the mortgage.)

I resisted the Pokemon blitz as long as possible. K.C., however, had other ideas due to the intense Pokemon national marketing campaign. Pokemon cartoons were broadcast five times a day, and I wound up taping countless hours of episodes at her insistence. There were rumors that Japanese kids had gotten hypnotized by the special effects watching Pokemon cartoons. I don't know if this is true, but one time I sat down to watch one of the shows and woke up four days later wondering what the story was about. The darn cartoons were made as an episodic series that never seemed to either make sense or end. When 'Pokemon-The Movie' was released into theaters, I reluctantly joined 10 million other Daddies and their children to sit through 75 minutes of what seemed to be an oriental water torture to adults, and about as exciting. (The kids, however loved it.)

K.C. is no dummy and found a way to use her own marketing talents to build her own Pokemon collection. She made colored drawings of many of the Pokemon characters and traded them with other kids for their cards. She was developing quite a following for her artwork and was taking special orders during breaks in her summer music program. While this was going on, I attended my 30th High School Reunion and happened to talk about K.C.'s artwork to a classmate, Kathy, whom I had not seen for many years. As luck would have it, Kathy's career was making voice-overs for television and radio, and she was the actual voice of Pikachu for the Pokemon cartoons. (No, that was not her normal voice!) We spent the rest of the reunion in an animated conversation, me using my Kermit the Frog and Muppet voices while Kathy responded in a hundred various Pokemon or Looney Tunes voices. It was a great reunion, although our table cleared out when we began doing a Rocky & Bullwinkle routine and sang the alma-mata song from Whatsamatta U in squirrel voices.

I got Kathy to autograph a napkin for K.C. and when I gave it to my daughter, she was ecstatic. "Pikachu's voice? OHMYGOD!!!" K.C. said. She was super impressed that I went to school with someone who actually made it big time. (I decided not to bring up Susan Lucci, John Tesh, or Nobel Prize Physicist Steven Chu as possibly better examples of my 'big time' high school alumni. After all, none of them had even made guest appearances on the Pokemon show.) When I last checked, there were 2,390,000 Pokemon web sites on the Internet, outnumbering the combined pages of Ms. Lucci, Mr. Tesh, and Dr. Chu fan clubs by a ratio of over 1000 to 1.

My diet and health took a turn for the worse when Burger King began a promotional campaign offering a free Pokemon toy with the purchase of a "Kid's Club Meal". There were 150 different Pokemon toys available. Each Kid's Club Meal consisted of a cheeseburger, small French fries, and soda, and a genuine Pokemon toy in its very own Red and White plastic Pokeball. Since I was doing fieldwork for a few weeks, I could not bring my lunch to work and stopped into a Burger King to buy a Kid's Club Meal for lunch. The place was Pokemonium, err, I mean pandemonium. There was a huge crowd fighting, pushing, and shoving their way towards the counter to order Kid's Club Meals – and Pokemon. What was surprising was the customers were all Daddies! Each one was trying to satisfy their kid's insatiable hunger for more Pokemon. When I finally got to the counter, I nonchalantly ordered 150 Kids Club cheeseburger meals – to go.

I sat in my car, ate about a dozen cheeseburgers and fries, and unwrapped my, err, K.C.'s new trove of Pokeballs. I ate a dozen more cheeseburgers, and it dawned on me that I didn't have one of each Pokemon, I had 10 individual ones, but also 6 Pikachus, 5 Charmanders, 2 Jigglypuffs, and 2 Sythers. Rats. For the next 2 months, I ate nothing but Kids Club Meal Cheeseburgers, and wound up with only 38 of the $^%^*$$! Pokemon characters. Each night I handed my new batch to K.C., who was becoming more and more agitated. "Articuno, Moltres, Zapdos and 4 more doubles. Well, I've got lots of trade bait" she muttered.

K.C. and her friends spent days trading Pokemon toys and figures with each other. Burger King even began a weekly Tuesday night Pokemon Party event, but most of the time it was just other Dads like me trying to complete our kids' collections through trades. We gave each other tips on better ways of stomaching 150 Kids Club Meal cheeseburgers (They go down better with beer. Never ask for extra mayonnaise.) As the summer slowly went by, my blood began to thicken and turn a cheesy yellow. Slowly, K.C.'s Pokemon collection became nearly completed. Finally, I came home with the last of the 150 different Burger King Kid's Meal Pokemon toys. Did I get a hero's welcome? Not on your life. "Thanks Daddy," K.C. said without looking up.

"What's up, Princess? I thought you'd be delighted I finally got Charizard! We made it! Your collections complete! Let's celebrate."

"Not now, Daddy, I want to read."

"A new Pokemon comic?" I asked.

"No, Daddy, it's a terrific book about a young wizard named Harry Potter! It's brand new. All the kids are crazy about it!!"

"But what about Pokemon?"

"Shush, Daddy I want to read!!"

I gave up. At least K.C. was reading a book, I thought as I walked away feeling my heart tighten again in my chest, what possible craze could start from something as innocent as that? Little did I know. Typical Daddydumb.

CHAPTER 29

DADDYHOOD AND PETS

I never needed the '*Rulebook For Perfect Daddyhood*' to remind me that all kids need a pet. I grew up with the best dog in the universe, Penny. When I was four, my family returned from a vacation visiting my grandparents to find a small black and white puppy huddled in the rain on our front porch. As soon as I saw it, I called, "Daddy, can we keep it?"

"No, No, a thousand times No!!!!", he automatically answered, but even at 4 years old, I knew he didn't really mean no. My surprisingly softhearted Dad brought the puppy inside, where I promptly named her "Penny" because I had also found a penny that day. I then fought with my sister about whose dog it would be. Even more surprisingly, I won this argument in spite of the fact that my sister was five years older than I was. It turned out that my sister thought the puppy looked more like a drowned rat than a canine and didn't really want it anyway. She only wanted to fight with me over ownership so she could keep me in my rightful place, low man on the family totem pole.

Anyway, Penny was mine and as a frisky wire haired terrier mutt, she was delightful company, obedient, a great listener, and liked to get her ears rubbed. She never asked for much, just a bowl of water, can of food, and a couple of walks a day. In return, she gave steadfast loyalty, lots of love, and a playmate whenever I needed one. Yes, my family had other occasional pets too-- a parakeet, a kitten, a bunny, a field mouse, and 300 fish (guppies), but Penny was a certified member of the family. She sat in the corner by our kitchen table during meals, watching my Dad eat every bite of his evening meal. She would give him the 'Puppy Dog Eye'; silently staring at him until she managed to get his attention. Dad would finally stop eating and a small piece of meat or roll would then be handed down to her with the usual comment, "OK, you win, now go lay down."

Penny was a major factor in my memories of a pleasant childhood. Many years later, when I left for college, I remember saying goodbye to Penny and thinking how old she suddenly looked. Not even 2 months later, I received a sad note from my sister that Penny had died. I was heartbroken. I remember thinking I had not only lost a dog and friend, but a big link with my childhood. I never got another dog, but figured if I ever had kids, I'd get them a dog. Hopefully, it would be as good as Penny.

I was wrong. The kids I got, the dog I didn't. Why? My wife and is allergic to fur. No dogs or cats are allowed in our home. Actually, with the fast-paced, stressful life of the '80's, '90's and new Millennium, I'm not sure our family really would have time to take care of a dog. Besides, while I am really glad there are "pooper-scooper" laws, it is another reason I'll pass on dog ownership. So, instead of dogs, our household has turtles and frogs--- Lots of them. When our oldest daughter, Alexis was in first grade, her teacher -- Maria Locopo, brought her entire class over to our house on a field trip. I gave the students a science demonstration on turtles and frogs and showed off our pets. The kids enjoyed it, I enjoyed it, and my wife even made a frog shaped backpack full of frog books, frog games, and frog puzzles for the class.

Alexis and her younger sisters, Erin and K.C., thought it was natural to have frogs and turtles around the house. Erin already has asked me if she can inherit the family turtles. They've also learned a bit about life and death – frogs don't live too long in captivity, but at least they've also seen tadpoles develop into frogs, and have released many into our pond. When the girls were very little, I had gotten a green tree frog, which was promptly named "Sticky" since it could climb the glass walls of its tank.

They loved watching "Sticky" hang around. (Actually, they really don't do much more besides that.) A few months later, however, I found "Sticky" dead in the tank. Not wanting to see the girls upset, I promptly went back to the pet store and bought a replacement. None of the girls realized "Sticky" was actually Sticky II, then Sticky III, and then Sticky IV. Three years later I was up to Sticky XVII, but the girls finally caught on when the store ran out of common green tree frogs, and I tried switching Sticky XVIII with a narrow mouthed toad. As a tribute to Sticky I through XVII, Erin named her stuffed frog "Sticky".

In addition to our own menagerie, I've been a volunteer leader at a local bird sanctuary not too far from my home in Garden City. My wife calls it 'Daddy's Big Backyard' because I seem to be spending a lot of time at the preserve 'playing' and coming home dirty. Actually, I work very hard on this project, but I also enjoy seeing the wildflowers, birds, lizards, rabbits, snakes, toads, and neighborhood cats that hang out at the nature preserve with me. Unfortunately, my volunteer work resulted in some people thinking that I am the 'Audubon Guy' and every year, people call me to help rescue a hurt bird or baby squirrel. Most of the time, I'm more like the Village Bird-Brain than I care to admit as I have "rescued" many baby squirrels, rabbits, and birds. These "rescues" are sometimes rescuing the baby bird from misinformed people who think the animal actually needs rescuing, when it's merely in need of a drink or dead tired trying to get away from all the people chasing it around and around while they try to 'rescue' it. (Actually, the first thing I do with "rescued" birds and animals is merely give them a bit of water, keep them warm, and call a licensed animal rehabilitation expert.)

I thought pet life was pretty much under control until this summer. Unfortunately, "Rescue Dad" happened again this Memorial Day weekend. My daughter K.C. and her cousin Emily found a baby bunny in the street. They brought it home and by the time I came home myself, the baby rabbit was already making itself at home in a cardboard box in our den. I no sooner got in the door than K.C. called, "Daddy, can we keep it?"

"No, No, a thousand times No!!!!" I automatically answered, but I didn't use enough No's.

"Daddy, Emily found a baby bunny in the street. It's in the den and we're keeping it, right Daddy? I love you!" K.C. responded, completely deaf to my thousand No's.

"Your cousin Emily found it?" I switched tactics, trying to reason with a 10-year-old. "Well, then let Emily bring it home! Her Daddy manages a pet store, and her Mommy works for the NY State Department of Environmental Conservation. The baby bunny just hit the Lucky Bunny Lotto! Both of Emily's parents know how to take care of it."

Unfortunately, Emily's Mommy nixed my evasive maneuver by packing up Emily quickly and driving off—without Bunny. Rats, just when I was going to beg her using my 'Penny's Puppy Dog Eye' look! I was stuck. We spent the next several hours with a pet baby bottle, canned pet milk, and a handful of alfalfa sprouts. The baby bunny sat comfortably in KC's hand, and they bonded faster than Crazy Glue. A few hours later, Baby Bunny was christened "Basil" and rested comfortably in a pile of soft cotton rags in Sticky XXVIII's former glass tank. Three days later, Basil had her very own genuine, certified $60 rabbit cage, with $40 worth of rabbit toys, $15 in alfalfa, a $5 deluxe water bottle, and a $9.50 rabbit blanket. All this in spite of my absolute ruling that wild bunnies are not pets and Basil was going to be released as soon as she was big enough to outrun a cat.

174

During the last day of school my middle daughter, Erin, called me at work and asked if she could bring home one of the gerbils from her science class for the summer. "Why not?" I said with good humor, "It's only for the summer and there's at least 8-cubic-inches of free space in the den. How much room could a gerbil take up?" Unfortunately, when I got home that night, I found out the truth. It wasn't merely 1 little gerbil visiting for the summer, it was 4 gerbils --- permanently. Erin couldn't separate "Big Momma" from her three new babies. By the next week, Big Momma and her babies; Roo, Bilbo, and Allegro were set up in their new $70 gerbil cage, with $50 in gerbil toys, $5 deluxe gerbil water bottle, $25 in gerbil food, and an $8 gerbil exercise wheel and I could no longer afford a summer vacation. My wife and I also found that we could no longer get any sleep. The gerbils spent entire nights running around on their metal exercise wheel ---their squeaky, metal exercise wheel. Their loud, annoying, squeaky, metal exercise wheel that was the only thing left of the $50 in gerbil toys that they hadn't completely chewed into dust.

Two months later, I found out that gerbils do a little more than eat, drink, chew plastic, and run on their squeaky exercise wheel. Big Momma quietly built a sawdust nest and quietly had four more babies. I didn't realize there was only a short window of opportunity where you had to separate the mommy from her children after weaning.... and I then changed Bilbo's name to Oedipus.... The next gerbil tank set me back another $72.50, but it had 2 locking lids – needed to hold back sex-crazed boy gerbils that could sense the presence of 5 lovely lady gerbils in the next tank over.

Meanwhile, baby Basil had now grown from hamster-size to guinea pig-size and was contentedly munching way on baby carrots, broccoli flowers, spinach leaves, and all of the good, healthy vegetable snacks my daughter, Erin, was supposed to be nibbling on. K.C. was even picking flowers from my garden so Basil could have some fresh greens. While baby bunny was being hand stuffed, I was outside defending my flower garden from 16 other neighborhood rabbits – one of whom I was sure was Basil's neglectful father. I was also carefully tending a flat of rare, wild blue lupine seedlings I was trying to grow for the nature preserve. These hard to find perennials have wonderful bright blue flowers each summer and attract hummingbirds with their sweet nectar. I had spent the entire previous autumn scouring rock outcrops along the New York State Thruway to collect some seeds.

By August, Basil was nearly full-grown, and as fat as a pig. She was getting harder for K.C. to hold and began to squirm if we even reached into her cage. It was time for her to be set free. K.C. resisted, but we were going on a family trip to visit colleges that my oldest daughter was interested in attending. We couldn't possibly take Basil with us. There was no more room in the car after packing the 8 gerbils. (I was all ready to hand out gerbils in little trick-or-treat bags at Halloween.) I brought Basil outside, opened the rabbit cage lid and waited. No movement. Nothing. Basil looked at me with Puppy Dog Eyes. "Basil, one of us has to go, and you've been volunteered." As gently as I could, I turned her cage upside down and Basil dropped onto to soft grass. "Remember, Basil, you're a wild rabbit. Live free and fly! Go forage." Basil made a weak, reluctant hop towards my forsythia bushes.

The trip was a usual Alvey household adventure. Just me, my wife, 3 daughters, and 8 gerbils in the car. For the Millennium New Years, we had vacationed at a friend's home in the Catskills. Ellen and Hank welcomed us graciously, but "Patty", our caged quail, was the hit of the century. Patty was another of Erin's science class animals that needed a place to hang out for the holidays. (She must have passed the word to the other lab specimens that the Alveys were easy prey.) Actually, the college trip had one benefit. While Alexis took a tour of SUNY Environmental College in Syracuse, the rest of us hung out in the Environmental Science

176

building. All of us. Including the 13 gerbils. (I guess 'Roo' can pick locks.) K.C. had used the entire remains of my retirement savings and bought a $3.75 pink plastic gerbil roll-a-ball.

While we waited for Alexis, K.C. put Big Momma into the roll-a-ball, sealed it shut, and let Big Momma roll around the Environmental Sciences Building main hallway. Big Momma loved her semi-freedom in the wide-open spaces, and rolled back and forth across the hallway, bumping into chairs, corners, and the Environmental Sciences Dean's leg. OOPS. The image of Alexis' application being shredded by the Dean flashed across my eyes.

Instead, Enviro Dean bent down, picked up the gerbil filled roll-a-ball and called out, "Whose gerbil?" K.C. raised her hand, introduced herself, and went to retrieve it just as Alexis returned from her tour. Enviro Dean turned to Alexis and said, "Well, you certainly must become one of our Environmental College students! Any girl that brings gerbils to school is the type of student we want!!"

Instead of politely asking if there were any gerbil scholarships available for poor children of government workers, Alexis merely turned beet red. Alexis, who had spent almost 12 years near the top of her class, studied 10 hours a day, did science research in addition to being a top notch gymnastics and ballet student, award winning artist, and who had spent 300 hours putting together the world's best transcript and resume, was being told she would be accepted to SUNY Environmental College merely because her little sister had 26 pet gerbils.

The trip home was a little less eventful. I was disappointed that Alexis had decided to not even apply to SUNY Environmental College, and that she made K.C. and I sit in the car with the 34 gerbils while she toured Cornell. Still, after 3 days we all made it home safe and sound. As I pulled into the driveway, I wondered if Basil had managed to adapt to her freedom, or whether I would find a limp bunny body on my lawn. K.C. got out of the car and carried the 47 gerbils into the house. I got out of the car and carefully walked into the back yard.

Suddenly, a rabbit hopped from the base of my apple tree. Basil! She looked up a second, then hopped quickly into my forsythia bush and disappeared. "Well, that's a relief," I thought. "Basil will be all right after all." Wait a minute… something was missing. I looked at the base of my apple tree again and realized Basil had just nibbled the entire flat of my prized wild blue lupine seedlings into stumpy nothings! My shoulders sagged. As I walked back into the house my only thought was that if I ever catch Basil, I'm going to change her name to– Hassenpfeffer! (cooked rabbit).

CHAPTER 30

ENCORE FOR DADDY

The 'Daddyhood' show must go on, whether I have a well-written script or not. The "Rulebook For Perfect Daddyhood" says to play with your children. This I am well qualified to do. For me, it's as natural as getting dirty. I seem to have a long-playing daddy and daughter act. My oldest daughters have their individual interests, but my youngest daughter has ensnared me with hers. After completing her debut role as 'Pardner #3' in the Garden City Community Theater musical, *"The T.V. Show"*, my eight year old daughter, K.C., caught a slight case of the acting bug. It was a small bug, but very suitable for my small daughter. She continued her dance lessons, started flute lessons, and returned to third grade as a confident veteran actress. She then "starred" in the annual Church Christmas Pageant, as "Sheep Number 7."

Of course, it helped that she only had one line to memorize-- "Baaaaaaaaaa". There is a Church policy of fitting in a part for everyone in Sunday School, and it's the only Christmas Pageant I know of that doesn't have the traditional 3 Wise Men. A few years ago, one of the Sunday School boys mistakenly thought the part was 3 Wise Guys after he watched too many gangster movies. During the Christmas Eve performance, he executed a "hit" on a Christmas Angel. Our Church Christmas Pageant now has the politically, if not historically correct 8 Wisepersons. And of course, 63 sheep and pigs, 24 shepherds, and the Holiday Innkeeper.

When the Church Christmas Pageant was over, Mommy complimented K.C. profusely, "K.C., you were terrific. Mommy is proud of you! What a great and sensational sheep, K.C.. You worked very hard and we're very proud of your effort." (The Goddess of Mommyhood is a strong advocate of building self-esteem whenever possible.)

I was still trying to figure out why the Church Christmas Pageant needed 2 Josephs --both of whom looked mysteriously like 9-year-old girls anyway. My only comment was, "K.C., you weren't all that baaaaaaad!" (Daddy is a strong advocate for inadvertently destroying the girls' self-esteem with poor jokes.)

K.C. merely laughed and sheepishly said, "Daddy, I've seen you act… Now that's really baaaaaaaaaad"

To be candid, both K.C. and I both had parts in 'The TV Show' musical. I figured my own "acting" career was already over. It had lasted the one play, although I had put on my acting resume the proud part as "Shadow" in the 'Me and My Shadow' duet and dance number K.C. and I performed at a Church Camp talent show. (She danced while I merely shadowed her.) For "The TV Show", I had played a failing businessman as well as uncle to 2 feisty nieces. I actually had a good time with the cast, in spite of not knowing which direction upstage or downstage was or following a cue with my line. The actors, actresses and kids were really a lot of fun to be with and it was a nice way of sharing a special experience with my youngest daughter. And so, the following year came, and we both decided to try out again. K.C. and I passed the auditions easily. Actually, the auditions were fixed. Any kid that attends the Church Sunday School on a regular basis is automatically given a part, however small based on the amount of kids in the Sunday School that year. Any male that has most of his limbs and can breathe at least part of the time is automatically given a major role.

My goal was to act with one of the other dads, Bill. Bill had been with the theater group since its inception, but he always got assigned a part as a dim-witted stooge. After four years Bill began to wonder if he was being typecast. "Not at all," the director, Brad, assured him. "This year I've got a perfect part for you, a real stretch. Your character's name is Curly, and you play a bodyguard with two other guys, Larry and Moe."

I was to be Moe, at least for the first week. Then, Brad called me and asked if I could play the Village Mayor instead. I was flattered to be given a larger part until I found out it was only because I kept sticking 'Curly' in the eye during the rehearsal and 'Larry' was jealous I kept missing him. The Director assured me being the Mayor was an easy part-- an incompetent, slightly dazed, oblivious town leader whose wife actually had all the brains. I wouldn't even have to act. Brad told me to just be myself.

So, I didn't even have to act. While 9-year-old K.C. learned her new line and role as Camper Number 5, I merely wandered around the rehearsals drinking coffee and chatting with the other members of the cast. I spent a lot of time doing Kermit the Frog impersonations with the many kids. If the kids had problems with remembering who was who, I was having a major identity crisis myself. I couldn't remember what part people were playing. There were several new faces, including the very talented John and Jen, but several others had returned from the previous year. Mary Kate no longer had the part as my niece. She was now a gangster's long time girlfriend. Abe was no longer a Cuban announcer; he was a Cuban gangster. Eileen no longer had four small character parts, she had four small character parts as well being a Sudsy Girl dancer. Eileen, one of the rare moms who looked good in a leotard and furry tail, was worried about being in a dance routine, especially next to 3 fourteen-year-old teenagers. I told her not to worry. After seeing the teenagers in their leotards, no one would even notice whether she was on stage at all. In spite of my attempt to make her feel confident, Eileen walked away muttering something about my success rate in building self-esteem.

George was no longer Kayotee Kal, but one of the crooked Village Trustees. His wife, Sue, was now my wife!?!? "Wait a minute," I complained, "this is a church play, and George is actually a licensed Minister. How can he just give his wife away? It sounds perverted." On top of this, my character was supposed to be seduced by "Lola" so he could be blackmailed into giving up control of the town to the gangsters.

Somehow, I couldn't get the knack of being seduced. Poor "Lola" had to try repeatedly, but no matter how close she pressed up against me, I was just too stiff, I mean rigid... No, that's not what I mean! Anyway, we practiced this one scene over and over, and just when I thought I could be convincing, I heard K.C.'s small voice call out, "Attaboy Daddy! Wait 'til I tell Mommy you finally got Lola'd!"

There was additional camaraderie among the cast and crew, but this had nothing to do with the actual play itself. Several of us shared serious life situations coping with our own older parents. Steve had recently lost his mother. George's mom had just entered an assisted living facility. Pamela's dad had taken a turn for the worse with broken ribs from a fall, and my own mom was continuing to decline from a failing heart and stroke. Each of us was able to share stories of our efforts dealing with the role reversal where we were now taking care of our parents. It was not surprising that we had reserved a line of spaces at the theater for our parents to watch the play from their wheelchairs. Later that spring, many of the cast even volunteered to sing at a benefit I was organizing, and we've become friends offstage.

Another reason to work in the Community Theater musicals is to see the other children growing up. Amanda, Meredith, Brooke, Farah -- each happy to get their one line and dance number. Nichole, playing a very mature Intern Julie to Mayor Swindel, and I kidded each other with Bill

Clinton jokes, until I realized she was 13 -- the same age as my middle daughter Erin. It's also fun to have many of the kids say "Hi" if they see me in the school or around the community. No matter where they see me, I'm usually asked to speak like Kermit the Frog.

As the six week rehearsal schedule flew by, I remember Brad's repeated question, "Rob, who are you tonight?" He kept cringing as I blew lines, then ad-libbed mercilessly. By the time of the actual performance, however, we had come to a mutually acceptable agreement. I would try to say at least one third of the lines he wrote. Lori, the choreographer, was just as frustrated with my lead-footedness, but compensated by having the other actors simply dance around me. The performances themselves were fun and I didn't have to write more than six apologies for inappropriate ad-libs.

After the play was over, K.C. and I went out into the audience to see our family. As I passed George, I overheard his mother say, "George, you were terrific Mommy is proud of you. What a great and sensational Trustee! George, you worked very hard and we're proud of your effort!" (George's Mom seemed to have read the same self-esteem script my wife used.) My family thought K.C.'s line and dance number merited an Emmy award, but my nephews J.J. and Danny wondered how come I wasn't in the play...

"What do you mean, not in the play?" I asked. "I was on stage nearly the whole time! I was one of the main characters!!!"

"Sorry, Uncle Robert, we didn't notice. We were too busy watching the Sudsy Girls...and Intern Julie."

After the show, the adults in the cast celebrated at the local watering hole, Leo's. It was a rather sobering experience for us all. Each of us had realized that no one in the audience actually cared a hoot what we said or did. Brad told us to relax, "The audience's main focus was on each of their own children. You were all just adult stage props. After all, you all love watching the annual Church Christmas Pageant, don't you?

"Yes, I do" I admitted sheepishly, "but someday my little girl will be the 'Star'…or at least one of the 8 Wise Persons."

Brad was right, and he didn't even notice I had done the entire second act in a Kermit the Frog voice. At least so I thought until Brad called the next year to tell me he had a part custom made for me in his new play-- as a dead body!

CHAPTER 31

THE ITALIAN TRIP AND DADDYHOOD

If my daughters ever have to write a back- to- school essay on how they spent their summer vacation during the summer of 2001, I'm pretty sure they'll select our family's trip to Italy as the topic. It was certainly a memorable experience; I just don't want to remember everything. Our Italy trip actually began over 18 years ago, when my wife and I planned a trip to Rome on our way back from my work in Saudi Arabia. It was going to be a wonderful vacation- perfect for a young, art loving couple, and a welcomed respite from being stuck in an empty desert for a year.

Unfortunately, my wife was too pregnant to travel extensively and we bypassed 2 weeks in Italy for an overnight in Amsterdam before heading back to the US and beginning life as Mommy and Daddy. Eighteen years and three daughters later, my wife and I decided to try Italy again. It would be the trip of a lifetime - except instead of a young, carefree couple, we would now travel as a family of five. It would be a reward for our oldest daughter's high school graduation, and a lasting memory with all the girls before she left for college. Our family would never be the same again. Considering the cost of this trip, my wife was more than correct.

My wife admits she is not a person who enjoys spontaneity. She likes to have things well planned. For six months, we carefully debated the merits of each of 24 Italian provinces, each of 630 cities, each hotel, each museum, each of 7,851 different churches, and each of the gazillion statues, ruins, and temples we would visit. Suzie brought home countless travelogues and travel guides from the library. She made so many lists of each possible attraction that I nicknamed her 'Fodor'. I admit I was slightly distracted by this planning. While I can appreciate an art museum, my primary target was to see Pompeii, the ancient Roman town buried by volcanic ash. Rather than debating about the merits of visiting Venice versus Florence, I debated which child to sell for medical research purposes so I could afford to pay for the Italy trip. My way of preparing for Italy was to watch the movie "Gladiator" three times and try to plan a budget that wouldn't break me.

If I learned anything during the Italy trip, it was that it did break me financially and that even the most careful plans go awry. As a bonding and Daddyhood experience, it was great, but it gave me new perspective on some things. Let me share a few observations. Never travel in a confined space with four females. The hormones go wild, and no male can survive a "group period" in close quarters. It is natural to be a bit cranky when suffering from jet lag, but I would rather be fed to the lions than have to deal with multiple cases of PMS again. It reminded me of the time our four pet girl gerbils hit maturity and decided to gang up on their mother. I couldn't put my wife and children into separate cages, but it seemed that, at times, I risked getting my toes chewed off.

Italian food is great, but you need time to enjoy it. My youngest daughter, K.C., ate nothing during the two weeks but plain spaghetti and chocolate gelato for every meal. Gelato became our passion. The hot Mediterranean climate, especially in July, dries you out quickly, and there are nearly as many gelato ice cream stands in Italy as there are Starbucks in the US. The Italians have a wonderful assortment of exotic flavors-kiwi, coconut, hazelnut, mango, melon, six types of chocolate, squid (not too popular with the tourists), pasta, and even volcanic ash. They serve these flavors in small cups with tiny plastic spoons, and the stores delight in piling 3 or 4 different flavors onto one cone or cup. The servers were constantly disappointed when K.C. ordered only plain chocolate, but she was kind enough to verbally rate the chocolates for them.

Erin, on the other hand, tried combinations like coconut- octopus-squash and then routinely passed them on to me while reordering hazelnut instead. I was in gelato heaven having discovered the delights of blueberry-spinach-palm tree gelato! Even Alexis enjoyed sampling different varieties 2 or 3 times per day. I scream, you scream, we all scream for ice cream- except the goddess of dietary correctness Mommyhood, who fought against our continual gelato cravings. "It's just junk food. You shouldn't eat so much of that stuff. Have a carrot stick instead." Really? I did not go to Italy simply to eat carrots.

There was one other cultural difference that my wife made an earnest effort to change. Italians serve food at a leisurely pace and at a late hour. Dinnertime in Rome usually starts at 8pm and consists of at least five different courses over a period of not less than 2 hours. While I've heard that "When in Rome, do as the Romans do", my American wife was determined to eat dinner promptly at 6pm and be done by 6:15 to no avail. Most restaurants didn't even open until 7pm, so at 5:59 I would throw her a can of Pringles to hold her over. She also spent two weeks trying to get the Italian waiters to at least serve all the courses together. I, on the other hand, simply began ordering large bottles of wine to the point where I didn't care if we ever had solid food and I could always nibble at my melted Master Card.

We made numerous excursions to see innumerable art museums. The art collections are truly fantastic but brought up another minor cultural problem. Labels. For some reason, the museums in Italy only have labels in Italian. Can you believe it? No English labels in the Italian museums! My wife wasn't exactly appreciative of this fact and spent two weeks trying to correct this deficiency. She bought English guidebooks at each museum, then spent the day reading each page out loud to us, describing in detail the pictures or statues we were supposed to be standing in front of. Actually, many times the painting or sculpture had been moved to another floor since the guidebook had been printed, but this didn't stop the art lecture. After awhile, the Bernini's, Borgheses, Balduccis, and Balbonis all looked the same and I'm not going to audit any art history courses anyway.

What the Italians lacked in English labeling, they more than made up for in plumbing. Everywhere, there were fantastic fountains, and we have a nice photo of us throwing money into Trevoli Fountain in Rome. I'm sure we wished for a chance to return to Rome, but none of us expected our wish would be granted when our passports were misplaced, and we missed the plane coming back from Florence. (Oh well, only another 2 or 3 million Lira onto the melted American Express card, but that's another story).

The Italians have a healthy regard for flowing water. Ancient Roman baths, street fountains, modern toilets and even bidets. While the eco-sensitive American Standard toilet uses a puny 1.2 gallons of water per flush, the Italian luxury hotels use a toilet that uses more water than Niagara Falls. We flushed our hotel room toilet on Sunday, and it continued to cycle and flow magnificently until Tuesday. My wife couldn't sleep with the sound of torrents of water flowing through the pipes overhead. Our younger girls marveled at the bidet and even made a bidet- fountain for their My Little Ponies to swim in.

Yes, My Little Pony, the American girl's popular pastime of the 1980's, joined us on our Italy trip. The toys were some of the 'must have' necessities that were packed by my young daughter in an attempt to get her suitcase over the weight limit. The necessities included six different cameras, books, a video camera, books, film, My Little Ponies, books, stuffed animals, books, and duct tape. Actually, I had fun with the My Little Ponies, and a highlight of the Italy trip was taking photos of My Little Ponies at Trevoli Fountain, the Vatican, on a rooftop restaurant, in the hotel swimming pool, in a gold jewelry shop, and in front of my melted Visa credit card. A memorable day ended when I took the family on a sub-way ride to Rome's only western style shopping center, and the girls found a store that sold *Italian* My Little Ponies. I paid for these with my quickly melting Discover Card.

There is never enough room in a suitcase to hold all your needed stuff. As our souvenirs accumulated, you could expand the suitcases by unzipping different compartments. The previous Christmas, we bought a new set of wheelable luggage in preparation for our Italy trip. Each person had a new, multi- zippered, expandable piece of black luggage for the trip. Wheeled luggage is a great innovation. As the five of us walked in a line dragging our new six pieces of luggage, it looked a bit like a wagon train, especially when I called out "Whoa - circle up" before trying to board a train or taxi.) Yes, six pieces of new luggage - one conveniently brought over to Italy empty so it could be filled with treasures procured via my melting Roslyn Bank Debit Card.

Pompeii and Ostia Antica were my favorite places to visit. Plenty of history, plenty of ruins, probably because both cities tried living well above their credit limits. As much as Suzie and the girls dragged me through art galleries, I dragged them through ruins. The absolute most meaningful experience was tagging along with a Midwestern American group at the Roman Forum that was giving an informal tour. The simplic-ity of the Maratine Prison, where both Saint Paul and Saint Peter were imprisoned before being executed by Roman Emperor Nero, the Coliseum where thousands were slaughtered or martyred for "sport", the temple of

Augustus, eating dinner at the ancient theater where Caesar watched a play before being assassinated-- all reminders that any difficulties we had during our vacation were actually insignificant in comparison (as long as our credit held out).

In order to save room for the return trip to the US, I used a technique recommended by my own Dad. I packed my suitcase with worn out socks and underwear, stained or torn shirts, and the bright red pants I'd bought in the 1970's that Suzie and the girls hated. Every night, instead of packing my smelly, dirty socks and clothes in a zip lock bag, I merely threw them out. Goodbye old shirt, goodbye frog boxer shorts, goodbye trusty old red pants. This method saved a tremendous amount of space in the suitcase for the much needed fifty-eight pounds of little bars of soap and shampoo my wife took from every hotel room in Italy to use as Mother's Day favors for nursing home patients on Long Island. I really miss my red pants, which I abandoned wistfully in Florence along with my razor and last spare pair of socks seven hours before finding out we were going to be delayed three days in Rome. (I looked and smelled like three-day old roadkill when we finally landed at JFK Airport.)

Our family also has a history of taking photographs. Each of us had a camera, and I prudently bought 18 rolls of film before leaving for the Italy trip. Alexis also brought a couple of rolls of black and white film so she could take "art photos" of various scenes. We never quite worked out a system for cost efficient picture taking. Instead, I noticed many times that all of us were standing next to each other taking pictures of the same thing at the same time. K.C. seemed to enjoy taking pictures of pigeons in the streets, while I took shot after shot of Roman ruins. Many of the museums prohibited cameras, so we wound up buying tons of postcards too.

Probably, the person who was happiest to see us return to America was Ron, our favorite photo developer, who could now afford an overseas vacation of his own on what we spent in photo processing. It was in this regard, however, that my wife's talents were a true asset. Within a week, she had filled and labeled 4 separate photo albums with pictures (and post cards) of our Italy trip. K.C. had also finished 12 scrapbook pages on Italy, and I had my own personal collection- receipts, bills, and melted credit cards. Even though the trip was memorable, I don't even want to bring the whole family to McDonalds for a while. I simply can't afford it if anyone wants extra fries.

Going through customs was also an experience. All they asked was whether we'd been on a farm and waved us through. I wasn't prepared for that. I was waiting to have my suitcases opened and inspected in detail, while we were grilled about possible smuggling. I had already listed everything we'd obtained overseas. The items included, 7 My Little Ponies, 3 Murano glass frogs, 68 Italian Museum guidebooks, Harry Potter and the Sorcerer's Stone (in Italian), 452 postcards, small glass mosaic necklaces, a bottle of Mediterranean Sea water, a tube of Italian sun tan lotion, volcanic ash from Pompeii, small plastic copies of the Pieta, Coliseum, and David, a shard of pottery from the Roman Forum, a frog magnet, 18 small plastic gelato spoons, a Broadway NY tee shirt (made in Italy!) and 468 small soaps and shampoos. Monetary value - $150. Memories of an overseas vacation with the family.   Estimated value - priceless.

CHAPTER 32

DADDY'S CHRISTMAS TRADITIONS

Christmas is my favorite time of year, and at our house it lasts from the day after Thanksgiving until Valentine's Day. Sometimes I even start as soon as Halloween trick-or-treating is over with. I wish it could last all year long, and frankly, it didn't bother me when my wife began putting up Christmas decorations in July at the department stores where she worked as a visual merchandiser or display artist. I have many good memories of Christmas from when I was a kid. I enjoyed having my Uncle Bill as Santa Claus, or getting more Lionel trains, or carefully wrapping a piece of coal as a special brotherly treat for my sister's Christmas stocking.

My mother took perverse pleasure in saving every piece of wrapping paper and reusing it for the next 20 years. I used to torture her by scotch taping the Christmas paper with double-sided tape to the box, then slowly and loudly ripping it as I sat on the floor across from her chair. "Oh, I'm sorry, Mother Dearest. Was that ripping sound my wrapping paper? Clumsy me.", and I'd watch her cringe at the loss of 18-cents worth of foil wrap while my dad tried to whack me for being a smart-aleck. It was a time for family, and whether or not Penny, (THE BEST DOG IN THE WORLD) actually climbed onto the dining room table and ate the

Christmas goose my mom had cooked for her own elderly dad, it was still a special time.

There was also a period when my dad's father lived with us after Grandma died. Pa was special too, and not just because he was a genuine veteran of the Spanish American War. He was an easy-going, quiet man who wouldn't complain - except if served sweet potatoes. It seems his Navy ship was quarantined for a month due to a smallpox outbreak, and the crew was reduced to eating nothing but sweet potatoes. What do you get a 90-year-old that he doesn't already have or need? For Christmas, we each gave him a bottle of apricot brandy - for medicinal purposes, and he joined us around the family player piano singing "Yellow Bird, High Up In Banana Tree" and other traditional Alvey Christmas songs. I remember he then started singing a salty Navy ditty, something about "Mary's chemise blowing in the breeze", when dad realized that Pa had taken a bit too much apricot flavored 'medication' and hustled him off for a nap. Other memories are more of a blur, but there was always a warm feeling of going to church for the Christmas Eve service and seeing if I could drip hot wax from the advent candles we held onto my sister's arm.

Time marches on. My grandparents have been gone for years and my dad died on Halloween 1985. After that, my mother, now referred to as Grandma, shuffled back and forth between my sister and my house for the holidays. Many things have changed as our family has grown. Some traditions, however, continue. My wife was the oldest of her family's children and as the oldest, she was able to claim "Christmas Day" at our house as a birthright. Sometimes my mother would join us, other times she joined my sister. Oh, the fights and arguments over the years over serving rights to Christmas dinner. We don't even talk to my wife's youngest brother anymore. He and his wife decided it was too far for them to travel to Long Island from New Jersey (but for some reason it wasn't too far for us to have to travel from Long Island to New Jersey). It was easier to simply stop visiting them at all rather than trying to figure out how much we'd age if we traveled "with" or "against" the time currents between New Jersey and Long Island.

My mother, a fiercely independent woman for over 80 years, had a minor stroke several years ago. As her heart and health slowly but continually declined, her care was more and more provided by my sister and me. I became a part of the "between" or "sandwich" generation - caring for my own kids on one side while caring for my parent on the other. It got to where I teasingly referred to Grandma as the Eveready Bunny with her pacemaker battery and asking her if I could use her to help jump-start my car. God bless my sister for the times she volunteered to help, and for making it an annual Christmas treat to "momnap" our mother every year for Christmas week since the health aides were off.

Live-in health aides were also a great help, and "St. Rose" was a spiritual blessing. Gloria and Norma became my buddies as we'd kid each other about my mother's latest stubborn streak, or how was I going to get "Grandma" to church to hear me sing in the "Messiah" concert? "Easy", I replied, "I'm going to prop her up on roller blades and boogie down the street with her". My mother's reply was, "So, when did you become such a comedian?", but she came with us in the borrowed wheelchair to hear me sing. She would not pay "good" money to buy or rent such a frivolous extravagance as a wheelchair. They cost more than $5.

Five dollars was the magic amount from Grandma. No matter what the occasion was, or how old the recipient, five dollars was all you could expect as a gift from Grandma. On top of this, you were required to write a thank-you note. In actual pen, not pencil or e-mail. Both my sister and I began to quietly supplement Grandma's five buck limit, especially when Grandma handed "St. Rose", her devoted live-in health aide, a five-dollar bill as a Christmas bonus. It got to be such a long running joke that we included as a verse in our family Christmas songfest: The Twelve Days of Family Christmas–

On the first day of Christmas, my family gave to me: A MY LITTLE PONY

On the second day of Christmas, my family gave to me: 2 CABBAGE PATCHES.....

On the third day of Christmas, my family gave to me: 3 CRAYOLA CRAYONS.....

On the fourth day of Christmas, my family gave to me: 4 TREE ORNAMENTS.....

On the fifth day of Christmas, my family gave to me: 5 BUCKS FROM GRANDMA!.....

On the sixth day of Christmas, my family gave to me: 6 BARBIES ROCKING......

On the seventh day of Christmas, my family gave to me: 7 TEDDY BEARS....

On the eighth day of Christmas, my family gave to me: 8 AMERICAN GIRL DOLLS....

On the ninth day of Christmas, my family gave to me: 9 BEANY BABIES.....

On the tenth day of Christmas, my family gave to me: 10 BREYER HORSES....

On the eleventh day of Christmas, my family gave to me: 11 FROGGIES LEAPING.....

On the twelfth day of Christmas, my family gave to me: 12 MORE DAMN BOOKS......

My daughters have been growing up with Christmas traditions that are slightly different than the ones I used to know. First off, there's "Froggie" my oldest daughter's stuffed frog from when she was a baby. Froggie has full membership benefits in our family and merits her own Christmas stocking. After Froggie, comes the 27 American Girl Dolls owned by the 3 girls. Each has their own wardrobe and Christmas Wish List. Then comes my wife's tradition of stringing up enough Christmas cards that they completely go around the living room, not just once, but twice! We keep permanent nails embedded in the molding just for this purpose.

Unfortunately, my wife is not in a good holiday mood until at least two walls are covered, whether she even gives me time to read them or not. I've noticed we purposely sent out a second batch of Christmas cards if it looks like we are cutting it close in Suzie's pursuit to twice encircle the room. Is this normal? How many other people hang up the Christmas cards from their Newsday delivery person? Suzie also finds it a special blessing that our insurance company sends extra-long length Christmas cards so they can help fill space.

We have a tradition of designing our own Christmas cards. Everyone fights over whose turn it is, but it invariably is my task to burn out the office Xerox machine running off the 1,350 copies we need each year. Suzie thinks the tradition of making our own family Christmas cards came from her former display artist boss, Jim Mulconry. Jim once showed us an entire album of personal family Christmas cards he had designed each year dating back to the 1950's. Not bad for a guy who's Jewish!! Suzie was impressed and started doing it the next year. Meanwhile, all I could think of was the year from my own childhood when my mother decided to have personal family photo Christmas cards sent. She told my very busy dad to order them, and he did, although a bit reluctantly. He even told her he got them all stamped and mailed out for her.

When my mother got her copy delivered in the mail, she promptly opened it, looked at it twice, then shrugged and put it on the table. When my sister and I got home from school, we noticed it right away. The card said "Hoppy Christmus from Mickey, Margorot, and kids". Dad had ordered them from a store in Chinatown, near where he worked. Mom admitted she was slightly upset her name, Margaret, was spelled wrong, but didn't want to waste any money sending the card back to be corrected. My sister and I were a bit more upset. The "kids" in the family photo weren't even us, but a couple of Chinese kids. Dad said something about it was cheaper to split the order with another family and besides the card didn't say the kids were Mickey and Margaret's, it just said "kids". I always wondered how the Chinese family felt about seeing their own kids with my mother and dad on the card.

I have simpler tastes. If it has a frog on it, I buy it and hang it on our Christmas tree. Our seven foot "Sears Best" plastic Christmas tree is covered with frog ornaments, frog lights, frog tinsel, and a frog tree topper. (As well as 4,000 other assorted frog ornaments and 6 Star Trek ornaments). Needless to say, our youngest daughter's favorite ornament was the Star Trek "Galileo" model which had Mr. Spock saying, "Happy Holidays, Live Long and Prosper". You simply have to have a Christmas tree whether you are Christian, Jewish, Muslim, or atheist. It's the American way.

After my wife's grandmother passed away, Suzie and I bought her grandfather a 3-foot artificial tree with 4 Snoopy ornaments on it. He set this up each year. After he died, the tree went to my mom and dad, with the same 4 ornaments, and the much-welcomed news, "Now you won't have to spend $5.00 on a Christmas tree each year." Over the years, it was a tradition to go over to their house, pull the tree out of the basement closet, pull off the garbage bag, and set it up on a table in the living room- already decorated. Wha-la!

Some traditions end before you want them too. In the fall of 1999, my sister passed away after a long-term battle with cancer. That Christmas was the toughest. Her husband was also by then in the hospital near the end of his life, and I was left to take care of my mother alone while the health aides were on a much-needed vacation. Still, I muddled through, and I showed up at my nephew's house at 2AM to sit by the fireplace for a few minutes and share thoughts and memories about my sister, family, and Christmas's past. Last year was slightly tougher, as I had to carry Grandma from the car to our house, when I realized she was too weak to walk anymore.

Thanks to assistance from Lenore, my wife's sister, Grandma joined us in an after-dinner game of cards. That was also the year I had to personally give the traditional $5 to everyone on her behalf. And it was the first time I didn't mind doing it. When Grandma said she was tired, I brought her back to her house. I stayed the night, only leaving for a short while after she was asleep so I could attend the midnight services at church even if I was alone. Grandma passed away the following month, and I'm sure my sister was there to welcome her to her new home in Heaven.

I am now the patriarch of the family. Grandma's tree was claimed by my middle daughter, and it stands contentedly in the corner of our living room with the same quarter-century old Snoopy ornaments. This year, the Christmas cards are once again winding their way around the living room, and again I've spent too much on gifts. To make up for the perpetual "5 Bucks from Grandma" however, we bought our youngest daughter a piccolo to go along with her flute. Our middle daughter is getting a new professional trumpet and can retire the worn out 35-year-old student model- (the one I used as a kid). I asked my oldest daughter, Ali, if there was something special that she might like from Grandma. She surprised me by saying she didn't need anything, and besides, wasn't I already helping pay for her college tuition? I replied that Ali should think

198

of something special from Grandma. She again replied, "I've already got some things from Grandma, a pile of $5.00 bills, some good memories,.... and my 'Dad'."

"Wow," I thought, "there's a mature, sweet, and loving daughter.... I think I'll keep her."   Merry Christmas.

CHAPTER 33

THE BIG '50" AND DADDYHOOD

The years seem to continue to fly quickly by faster each year and I seem more tired than I ever used to be. I've only been a Daddy for less than 2 decades, but with three daughters ages 18, 14, and 11, I've already had a total of 43 accumulative daddyhood years of experience. According to my wife and daughters, I'm still clueless and should go back to school for remedial studies of the "Rulebook for Perfect Daddyhood." In other words, times change but I haven't. Actually, I have changed noticeably-- both physically and mentally. And I've hit the dubious chronological milestone, the Big 50th birthday.

Actually, the Big 5-0 hit me hard. For the past several months I was actually looking forward to it as I read numerous e-mails from my high school classmates who were all reaching the half century mark during the last year. Back in the Dark Ages of history, I skipped 3rd grade and hence was a year younger than my classmates. Being a year younger had a bit of a social stigma during my high school days. I wasn't old enough to get a driver's license until nearly the end of my senior year in High School and none of the cheerleaders would date me since I was a "younger" boy. I guess they were following motherly advice to date older boys since men mature later, (not realizing that men never actually mature.) Anyway, the drawback of being younger when I was 17 helped me when I was 49 and I could observe my classmates' different reactions as they reached the 50-year milestone.

Some of my classmates were terribly upset with the realization that they were now firmly on the downward slope of life. Others were too busy with their lives to stop and notice they had gray hair. For a select few (who will remain nameless should they ever want to be Supreme Court Justices), reaching 50 was a good time to celebrate that the drugs they did in the 1960's didn't kill them after all. For many, it was a pleasant milestone to stop a bit and reflect on what happened during the half century of our life experiences.

I was part of the latter group until I received a totally unsolicited envelope in the mail. More dangerous than a potentially anthrax laced letter bomb, it was an invitation to join AARP!!! ARGH! My first thought was, "How the hell did they know my birthday, but they must have gotten the year wrong." Nope, AARP (formerly know as the American Association of Retired People) now accepts members on their 50th birthday, whether they are retired or not. I never considered joining AARP, since, based on my financial projections, I figured I could afford to retire when I was roughly 87. If 7-11 raised their coffee prices again, I wouldn't be able to retire until I reached triple digits. AARP's invitation announced it was providing me with a temporary membership card, a subscription to Modern Maturity, health tips, and lots of extra benefits befitting my newly acquired 'Senior' status. As I said, ARGH!

It's strange, but I really didn't feel impending "fiftyitis" until AARP threatened to send the Florida State Troopers to my home on Long Island to drag me down to a retirement community in Florida. Next in the offering were discounts for Viagra and Rogaine as well as a pair of large oversized wraparound sunglasses and a sudden craving for a 4:30 PM early bird special dinner at Denny's. This couldn't be happening to me! I've still got a full head of hair. Then, I looked in the mirror and saw my own dad-- wrinkles, gray hair, a small pot belly, and tired eyes. Ouch. Why do I suddenly miss Liberace now when I didn't even like his music for the past 49 years?

As I thought about living 50 years, I realized I had much more experience than merely 50 years of life. I've experienced nearly 25 years as a grandson, 48 years as a brother, 49 years as a son, 34 years as an employee, 5 days as a self-employed boss (that was a bad week), 27 years as a husband, 18 years as a Daddy, 17 years as a student, 20 years as a professional geologist, 10 years as a volunteer with the Village, 4 years with the Garden City Community Theater, and even 6 months waiting at red lights. Not to mention the nearly 40 years I spent as a clueless egg inside my mother before I was born. Oh no, that's nearly 300 years! No wonder I'm tired. I'm lucky to still be alive! I mentioned this astounding fact to my wife, and pointing out that by my calculations, she was nearly 450 experience years old. I thought this tidbit of information would make her day, but her steely reply was that I'd wasted all my 300 years being totally clueless.

Where did the years go? It's been a long time since I've turned around to look for my dad when someone calls me Mr. Alvey. In the mid 70's, my wife and I bought our first house. After the closing, we piled her younger brothers and sisters into a car, and all drove over to look at the "new home" we'd just bought at the age of 24. As we got out of the car, I realized I'd forgotten the house key, so we walked around the house peering in the windows until one of the neighbors called the cops. We were nearly arrested for trespassing since the cop couldn't believe that we scruffy looking "kids" had just bought a home. It took a call to my dad to straighten out the "misunderstanding." I always felt I'd be rich if I could ever pay off the whopping $30,000 mortgage on the 3 bedroom ranch house. I never suspected that nearly 30 years later I'd be taking out a mortgage for 5 times that amount, just to pay for a long needed new garage – and to repair all the things that have been worn out over the years.

This life experience stuff is amazing. I remember exactly where I was, sitting in 7th grade with Mr. Chiaravelli's English class in November 1963, when the school principal announced that President Kennedy had been shot. I vividly remember being at work when the Space Shuttle Challenger exploded in 1987 and thinking the crooked plume of smoke reminded me of Big Bird. I can vividly remember things that happened decades ago, even if I can't remember where I just put my eyeglasses.

I can remember many of the events in detail, but not quite what year they occurred-- the decades have slipped by too fast. I've lived through the precise time period to personally watch the World Trade Center being built, actually work there for several years, and many years later witness it come crashing down. I remember quitting my job in early 1982 and leaving the country to work in Saudi Arabia partially to avoid facing the fact I was turning 30. I also remember my sister throwing me a surprise belated 30th birthday party the following year when I returned.

When my dad died in 1985, my mother got out her street map of Brooklyn to show me directions to the family's cemetery plot. I stared at it awhile I but couldn't locate the Long Island Expressway. Mom looked at me as if I was stupid and pointed out Horace Harding Boulevard. She was still using a map from 1938 and simply said, "It works for me." I gave her a look (Wow, Mom, you're getting old!) that I never thought I'd see again. Fifteen years later I unfolded my map of Rochester, NY to find the small suburban town where my nephew now lived. It wasn't on the map! My nephew inspected the map and realized it was printed in 1979, long before the development was built. I started to say, "It works for me," but I got the same look from my nephew that I'd given my own mom…and I suddenly began to feel old.

As a Daddy, I've had plenty of opportunities to play games with my children as they've grown. We've progressed from simple blocks and Legos to Candyland and Shoots and Ladders to Scrabble and Monopoly. I've also finally mastered the art of vacuuming the den without sucking up more than 2 pairs of Barbie shoes or My Little Pony hair clips. Unfortunately, this talent is now wasted as Barbie and My Little Pony are now relegated to boxes in the attic for my daughter's future children.

I suppose as soon as I pass 50, I'll have to start playing more age-appropriate games than my recent favorites: a) Fantasy World - How to Afford College Without Selling Your Body Organs, b) Drive your Kids to Every Activity Imaginable, or c) How much Coffee can Daddy Spill on the Rug? Some of replacement games recommended by my "senior" classmates are a) Sag, You're it, b) Hide and go pee, and c) Musical recliners. I can't be "Old" yet. "Old" is when a sexy babe catches your fancy- and your pacemaker opens the garage door. "Old" is when you are cautioned to slow down by the doctor.... instead of by the police. "Old" is when an "all-nighter" means not getting up to pee. Old is when "getting a little action" means you don't need to take any fiber today.

Some of the physical changes on my body have been subtle. I now have more hair growing on my ears than my dad had on top of his head. Because of deteriorating spinal discs, I'm actually a full inch shorter now than I was 20 years ago. My ears are numb to the 568,357,429 (and counting) separate pieces of advice my wife has told me over the last 30+ years. My eyes have gone to legally blind status in seven states. I haven't actually gained much weight since I have osteoporosis which causes thinning of my bones, but I'm gradually taking on the general physique of an amoeba... with moles. I've now got so many moles, my daughter K.C. played connect the dots on my chest for 2 hours while I dozed at the community pool last summer.

Actually, I'm not exactly in bad physical shape, especially compared with my classmates who died of a heart attack in their 40's. I did sit-ups once in the 1970's, and my last physical showed I had the lungs of someone merely 110, not even half of my calculated 'experience age'! During the last half century, I've drunken at least 23 glasses of water and enough coffee to float a battleship, cruiser, and 3 destroyer escorts. I'm sure I've maintained my svelte figure due to my fondness for the four necessary basic food groups: coffee, beer, Snickers and Doritos. I've probably worked in my garden 25,000 times and have tracked dirt into the house 24,487 times (hey, nobody's perfect). I still have the leg strength to stand perfectly still, and watch people work at least 45 minutes a day, and I avoid the urge to eat more than 2 donuts an hour –unless I've been working for more than 45 minutes.

I didn't have a big party for my 50th birthday! My wife and I plan on having a joint "100 years" party next summer, which will be exactly between my 50th birthday and the 11th anniversary of her 39th birthday. My family did get me some great gifts, befitting my maturity. In addition to two sweaters and three nightshirts, my daughters made me a new handmade belt with a fossil buckle, a handmade clay figure of "Catbert" from the Dilbert cartoon series, 4 glass frogs and 1 glass turtle, a handmade Happy Birthday Daddy glass, and a set of HO scale railroad tracks so we could run my antique (1950's era) model trains around the Christmas tree. You never get too old to play with toys, you only become old when you stop playing with toys.

I remember when my generation's motto was *"Don't Trust Anyone Over 30"*. Now our motto is *"Don't Trust Anyone Under 40!"* I'm proud to be a member of the Baby Boomer generation – we can continue to rewrite the rules as we go along. Someday, '70' will be the new '50' and we'll start considering that the mid point of our lives. Still, I'm going to stand on the street corner, light my AARP membership card on fire and scream to the younger generation, "Hell no, I won't go!" Then, I'll get out my Jim Croce, Mama Cass, Harry Chapin, Liberace, and Beatles cassette tapes and play them really, really loud.... while I wait for a table at Denny's.

CHAPTER 34

DADDYHOOD AND THE ENERGY SUCKING SOFA

Time is passing ever more quickly, but lately I haven't been able to whittle down the "To-Do" list that my ever efficient wife, Suzie, keeps updating on a more regular basis than Bill Gates introduces new versions of Windows. For some reason, just like each version of the new and improved "Windows", I still keep crashing. I seem to have no energy anymore. Initially, I wondered if it was due to passing my 50th birthday, however, I finally discovered the real culprit why I can't get anything finished - it's our energy sucking sofa. And, therein begins another episode of "Tales From the Darkside of Daddyhood- *The Saga of the Sofa From Hell*."

When Suzie and I were first setting up house back in the dark, ancient days of the Prekideroic Geologic Time Period (before kids), our first living room sofa consisted of a not-so-colorful beige sectional sofa handed down from my Mother. Since my mom's other name was "SHE WHO MUST BE OBEYED", we kept the sofa, in spite of the fact that it wasn't very comfortable and was, frankly an ugly 1950's style that never even fit in with my parent's 1940's style furniture. Furthermore, neither my sister nor I had ever even been allowed to go into my parent's living room as children. The room was off limits, reserved only for company and

Christmas. To this day I can never understand why it was called a living room, when no one was allowed to actually live in it, even our family dog.

A few years later, it was the family dog that rescued Suzie and I from our first sofa hell. I was taking care of good old "Gypsy" for my parents while they wintered in Florida. One evening I came home from work to find Gypsy had finally gotten her revenge for being banished from the sofa - she chewed the cushions to death, and then "marked" it as her territory- as only a dog can. My first thought wasn't "OHMYGOD!", it was "What will SHE (Mother) say?" I quickly borrowed Suzie's sewing kit to fix the sofa, but her staple gun was out of staples and her glue stick was dried out. I debated running away from home, but remembered it was my own house, even if it was my mother's sofa. There was no way to repair the sofa, and I finally threw it out. (Only much later did I catch Suzie silently giving extra dog treats to Gypsy while pretending to scold her for being 'bad'. I think Suzie had been hiding dog treats inside the cushions, so we could toss the sofa without disobeying "She".)

We replaced the dog chewed sofa with a suite of beige, bargello print, Herculon-covered furniture, a sofa, love seat, and barrel shaped spinning rocker. This was the first time we had actually gone shopping for new furniture at a store other than my favorite home furnishing chains, "St. Vincent de Paul" or "Salvation Army". It was a new experience for Suzie and me. I was personally surprised that I couldn't just buy a new sofa at 7-11 with my daily coffee and paper. Suzie wanted something new, clean, and stylish, moderately priced, but compatible with our home decor. I wanted something to sit on. Suzie won, and we shopped for months. After shopping at twenty different furniture stores for the unique perfect furniture, Suzie found the perfect living room set, only to find out we bought the exact same set as two other couples in our group of friends.

This set served us well for the next twenty years. It was very comfortable - the sofa was long enough to sleep on, and the love seat was, well -- appropriately named. The barrel chair was my favorite, and I spent hours spinning around in circles pretending to be Captain James T. Kirk while watching "Star Trek". I remember how upset I was when my brother-in-law accidentally broke the chair. Rather than throw it out, I sadly buried it in the backyard, near the graves of my pet frogs, with a small stone marker. I may have also given it a 21-phaser gun salute.

Time passed and Suzie and I had our first daughter, Alexis, and moved to Garden City. The Herculon sofa set came with us, and I remember sitting on the sofa next to "Ali" for countless hours watching one of the best children's TV series ever, "Fraggle Rock". Next came Erin with more TV shows, as well as hours spent reading or bouncing her on my knee. Finally, there was K.C., and "Rugrats" or Disney videos while she sat on my lap. There were always at least 5 lost coins and a few kernels of popcorn to be discovered buried among the cushions. The sofa and loveseat continued to serve us well until the fateful day of "The Great St. Paul's School Garage Sale".

St. Paul's School was a landmark in Garden City, established in the late 19th Century as a boy's school. It closed in the late 1980's and the property was sold to Garden City. Prior to vacating the 4-story stone building, the Episcopal Church held the "Mother of All Garage Sales" to dispose of the furnishings. I had better explain that my wife is: 1) from Garden City, 2) is a garage sale fan, 3) is determined to preserve anything historic from Garden City, and 4) has no real understanding of the severely limited status of our checkbook.

The night before the St. Paul's garage sale, Suzie camped out by the front door to be able to be the first to get into the school and "get the good stuff", hopefully a new sofa. I showed up an hour before the start of the sale and saw a line of people stretched four deep around the block. It was going to be a popular event. There was Suzie, a mere 2nd in line at the front, (first in line was God, who also apparently liked garage sales and somehow had advance warning of this one.) Suzie was talking and giving advice on how to run a garage sale to some of the other garage sale patrons. (I think God was also taking notes.) The Bishop then opened the door and began saying a welcome to the crowd. Many people couldn't hear him from the back of the line, and he made a fatal error, by calling to the up-to-now polite crowd and telling everyone to gather in front of him for a blessing. The poor guy was crushed by the stampede that developed as everyone realized they had a perfect "God sent" excuse to cut in line! I thought I heard someone near the front door squeak out "Oh Dammit", but when I looked again there was only a small puff of smoke.

It was Episcopal pandemonium as the crowd surged through the door. Professional antique dealers began to plaster everything they saw with their custom made pre-prepared "Sold" stickers. They knew a bargain when they saw one, and also knew they could easily triple the price of a Tiffany style lamp once they got it out of the building and into their own store. Suzie was not to be deterred. She spotted a Victorian style sofa and grabbed the nearest thing she could to mark it reserved -- me. I was bodily thrown onto the sofa with firm instructions not to let anyone else claim it while she went to find a volunteer worker to pay for it.

I felt like a bleeding herring surrounded by hungry sharks, but I fought as instructed and I kicked away anyone who came near the Victorian sofa. As I preserved the sofa for Suzie, however, I felt several strands of the horsehair stuffing piercing my backside. By the time Suzie returned with the garage sale worker, I somewhat resembled a crucifixion victim, bleeding from several limbs, but the sofa was ours. And, Suzie happily informed me that it cost less than our mortgage payment, a real historic bargain! I shuddered to think how I was going to explain this to my mortgage company when I told them their next check would be a little delayed.

A real bargain. Well, the Victorian sofa was delivered home a few weeks later, and my comfortable Herculon sofa relegated to the den. The beloved loveseat, however, was first brought upstairs to Alexis's room, but was finally thrown out when we realized all of the cushions had worn out and it was only held together by a 20 year accumulation of dust. I missed the loveseat, and the Victorian sofa sat in the living room glaring at me. It was a real relic from the past, actually owned in the 1850's by the Stewart family - our town's founders. It was tufted, and hideous, and the horsehair stuffing continued to prick me whenever I sat in it. Notice I didn't say "on" it, as in truth, the bottom cushion was bowed from the bottoms of 150 years of students sitting on it. Later, I found out the only thing holding it together was 150 years of gum from the 150 years of students.

Still, the genuine Cordelia Stewart Victorian sofa was "historic", and I seemed to be the only person that did not fully appreciate the fact that there was no way to comfortably sit on it. Since I was not able to "sit and veg", however, over the next 8 years I accomplished quite a bit. I added an extension onto the house, rebuilt my garden, added a backyard pond, volunteered 10,000 hours, founded a community nature preserve and local bird sanctuary, helped a dozen scouts earn their Boy Scout Eagle badge, went camping with my daughters, raised turtles and frogs, wrote articles, began teaching college courses at a community college and helped my daughters grow. And, there were still nights when I snuck downstairs to sleep comfortably on "Old Herculon".

Time passed again. Recently, we realized the Victorian sofa was showing its age. Actually, I realized there were too many areas we had to place a crocheted doily to hide where the original material was missing. Suzie convinced me it was time to restore the sofa…and get rid of "Old Herculon." "What's wrong with Old Herculon?" I pleaded. Suzie pointed out the sofa only had three legs left and was balanced on the radiator to remain level. Suzie also pointed out it had no cushions remaining without at least 2 holes in each. I agreed but was as sad as if I found out a friend had been diagnosed with brain cancer. Besides, the holes were great hiding

211

spots for our current herd of pet gerbils. When Suzie pointed out that one of the 'threads' sticking out of the cushion was actually a gerbil tail, I agreed we'd need a replacement sofa in the living room while the "Vic" was being restored.

We spent the next few months shopping for a new sofa as well as looking at 3,000 swatches of sofa material and 50 different furniture restorers. It was as complicated (and expensive) as planning a Long Island wedding reception. Even the aspect of a new sofa was daunting. My only two demands were that the new sofa had to be comfortable, and long enough to sleep on.

After much searching, Suzie found a sofa that met my expectations. I named it "Big Softy", a large, ultra marshmallow-soft, black leather convertible sofa with big, mushy, soft cushions, and no absolutely back support whatsoever. I wasn't planning on sitting up much anyway. Big Softy caused another missed mortgage payment, but this time I didn't complain, it was just tooooo comfortable. Big Softy was delivered, and the Victorian picked up by the refinishing company, Hans and Franz ...with another hefty payment as their downpayment. Suzie kept in touch with Hans and Franz as they pumped up the bill and re-did Old Vic. Then, one day I came home and found New Vic in my living room - all redone, with new tufted flowerprint tapestry material, new stuffing, newly refinished wood, new fixtures, and new legs.

No more bowed bottom, but when I sat down, the sofa was just as uncomfortable as ever. I even felt another stab in my back, but instead of horsehair needles, we spent the next month pulling out leftover pins from the sofa. Suzie then informed me that Hans and Franz had some leftover material from refinishing the sofa so had taken two of our living room chairs to refinish them in matching material...and also took the equivalent of a mortgage and two car payments for the work. I retreated to the den and jumped onto Big Softy, and immediately cried myself to sleep.

212

Big Softy is comforting, but in a very devious way. It's an energy-sucking sofa, and every time I sit on it, I slump down and slowly lose all energy. I become not a mere couch potato, but Rip Van Winkle's long-lost cousin-- Rob Van Wrinkled. Big Softy is just too darn soft and comfortable to just sit on. No matter how hard I try, I invariably find myself slowly starting to sag, then slump, then I drift away. Suzie and the girls are amazed that I fall asleep in five minutes and can stay asleep for the entire weekend. My to-do list ain't done, and I've lost track of friends and classmates. I stay out of the living room at all costs, not daring to get New Vic dirty. When I'm asleep on Big Softy, I'm dreaming of the days long ago when I innocently spun myself in circles on my old beige Herculon Star Trek captain's barrel chair, asking Scotty to beam me up.

CHAPTER 35

PROFESSOR DADDY AND THE STARS

Einstein was right, time is relative but it sure flies by quickly. A few years ago, I formally became known as a "Professor" in addition to Daddy. I was now also Professor A. I accepted an offer to teach an Earth Science course at a nearby community college. The school wasn't exactly the "Harvard of Long Island", but it was a good opportunity to see if: 1) I actually knew any Earth Science, 2) could actually teach Earth Science, 3) earn some extra money from one college to eventually give to another college for my own children's education, and 4) get me out of the house on Saturdays so I would have a valid reason not to do my chores. To me, reasons 3 and 4 were about equal, and I figured I could "wing it" with reasons 1 and 2. Yes, I know I 'wing it' frequently. It somehow keeps me from the adult life of having to be prepared.

My first semester as Professor A was an eye-opener. The course is taught on Saturdays. Being a full four-credit science course, it includes a 2 hour lab period in addition to 3 full hours of lecture. There is usually a full complement of 30 students in the class, but many of the students are not what I anticipated. Many are older than the typical college sophomore, many are from immigrant families from a variety of countries, and some students have a graduate equivalency degree rather than a formal high school diploma. For some, it is also the only "science" class they need to take for an Associates Degree. I love a challenge, and the first challenge is to find a common ground where all of the students can start to add to their knowledge of the Earth and its environment.

The first day didn't begin well. I introduced myself, discussed the course, what text and lab book to buy, the basis of their grades, and began to lecture on the compositional and formational differences between metamorphic rocks. (Exciting, right??) I was halfway through the fascinating complexities of mafic formations when a hand went up. "Professor A? What's a rock??", someone asked. I looked around at the class. There were 10 blank faces, 9 glazed expressions, 8 sleeping students and a partridge in a pear tree.

Actually, the 'partridge' was "Larry", a 15-year-old gifted high school student who was taking a Saturday 4 credit college course--- in his spare time! "Larry" had already completed High School Earth Science (in 6th grade!!!) and was quickly appointed my lab assistant. When none of the other students could define what a "rock" was, (although I gave half credit to the two students who insisted "rock" was an old type of music) I knew I had to try a more simple or basic approach. "Welcome to Planet Earth, students!" I replied. "It's the third rock from the Sun! Repeat after me: MVEMJSUNP!"

The students sat in silence. Most of them began to practice the fundamental and basic art of studenting-- never, ever make eye contact with your teacher – especially if you don't know the answer to a question. "Evasive eye maneuvering 101" is an art I've perfected being the Daddy in a household of three daughters. This is especially true if they ask me for money or anything about sex. I just close my eyes or stare at the floor and tell them to go see their mommy because I've got a very important half gallon of milk to buy at 7-11.

Back at Earth Science class, I suddenly dropped to my knees to make eye contact with the students. "Gotcha! I said repeat after me: MVEMJSUNP! It stands to the order of the planets away from the Sun - Mercury, Venus, Earth, Mars, Jupiter, Saturn, Uranus, Neptune, and Pluto.

The easy way to remember the order is to remember the sentence, My Very Educated Mother Just Served Us Nine Pizzas." A few heads nodded, and I was pleased to that discover most of the students had IQ's somewhat higher than a plant. I then asked a tough question, "What's the fourth planet called?"

My star student Larry raised his hand, but I watched several others slowly counting on their fingers and called on Curly instead. I knew it would be a tough semester when Curly looked up from her fingers and answered, "The fourth planet is called Mother". Curly was one of my memorable students. She missed over half of the classes, but always e-mailed me the reasons, which included: 1) the unexpected death of 3 grandmothers and the homework which she had carefully completed had been accidentally cremated with the bodies, 2) she was injured in 2 different car accidents which also burned up the homework she had carefully completed, 3) she had to go into hiding for a week because the Immigration Service was after her and had confiscated the homework she had carefully completed, and 4) she may have been exposed to small pox and was in isolation, but the hospital burned the homework she had carefully completed. She badly flunked both the mid-term and final exams, but in a desperate attempt to pass, had submitted an assigned research paper on my favorite topic, 'Global Warming'. I had assigned this topic to her in an attempt to help her raise her grade to at least 2 digits instead of a meager and lonely single digit average.

I began to read what I anticipated would be an essay on the Earth's climate changes due to increased carbon dioxide emissions in the atmosphere, but the submitted essay was a bit unexpected. Curly, who apparently didn't hear me quite right, wrote her research paper on "Global Worming". It was subtitled "Our Amazing Little Friend, the Earthworm". She discussed how you can make a fortune with your own backyard earthworm farm, that earthworms eat dirt, that they are good for fish bait, and that you can cut them in half and both halves grow into new earthworms. She also asked the eternally troubling question, "Do earthworms yawn?" It was one paper I wish had caught on caught fire along with Curly's missing homeworks. I flunked her but I have kept the essay as a special tribute to the many earthworms who probably have a bigger brain than Curly.

Other students have been just as memorable and, thanks to e-mail, a few keep in touch even after they graduate. One student, "Moe", made Curly seem like a Harvard Professor in comparison, but he was in class every week with a loud friendly "Hi, Professor AAAAAy!" and handed in his homework each week, (although wrote his homework and research paper in crayon.) He had a limited grasp of science or math but drew very well. He was very enthusiastic when I brought a pet toad and turtle into the class to help explain the difference between amphibians and reptiles, but Moe interrupted me when I showed a picture of a dinosaur and began to lecture on the similarities between reptiles and dinosaurs. Moe called loudly, "Professor AAAAAy! Professor AAAAAy! That's not what a real dinosaur looks like! That picture doesn't look anything at all like Barney!!" He was a good-hearted young man, and still calls me on occasion. He even graduated from the community college and has gone on to study at cooking school-- where I hope he doesn't accidentally flambé Curly's next homework assignment.

I had one other student that was causing me a tremendous amount of heartache. She was a "special needs" student and needed a single science class to finally graduate after 6 years as a second-year student. Her homework was almost always wrong, (but at least she was making an effort.) She flunked most of the quizzes, but nearly passed the midterm when she was given a special time period and proctor to read her the questions and record her verbal answers. During class lectures, I noticed she always had the textbook open and appeared to be writing notes in the pages. As an incentive to get her to pass, I gave her a special research assignment and asked her to write a paper on Pluto. At the end of the semester, she turned in a lengthy, well illustrated paper on the history and characteristics of Mickey Mouse's dog, Pluto, and an essay on the eternal philosophical debate regarding what the heck kind of animal was Goofy? If Pluto was a dog and barked and acted like a dog, then how come Goofy could talk and act like a human? Why did Goofy wear clothes, but Pluto was naked? I asked what she intended to do when she completed the course and she told me she was going to Cartoon Illustration University. She showed me her textbook, which was covered in hundreds of doodled cartoons, and not a single note about Earth Science. I wished her luck, told her Goofy was actually originally named Dippy Dawg, but I gave her a passing grade (D---) feeling only a little goofy myself.

Some of my students work very hard to master Earth Science, and I send them to the Museum of Natural History or bring them out to a bird sanctuary I manage. I invite them to go to the beach a dark night when I know there will be a spectacular meteor shower. Many of my former students have done well. Some have gone on to Colombia University, Brooklyn College, NYU, and the NYC Police Academy. It is always a pleasure to get a note or e-mail from a former student asking when the next meteor shower will occur. One student even received a telescope from her family as a graduation gift and sent me pictures she had taken of Saturn (the 6th planet, not the car). I sometimes get small gifts at the end of the semester – frog neckties, rock paperweights, and even a bone. Yes, a real bone which the student assured me was a dinosaur fossil he had found in Brooklyn. I suspect the bone is actually a small remnant of the missing Teamster's President Jimmy Hoffa, but I'm not asking any questions.

I especially enjoyed Earth Science the year my daughter Erin was studying Earth Science in High School. That year, we studied together and shared homework assignments. I borrowed many of her labs for my own classes. My students appreciated the changes, and the fact that I actually knew how to do these labs (thanks to Erin). Erin aced her Regents Final exam, and I learned a lot- about Earth Science, as well as about Erin.

I found I really enjoyed talking about Earth science and the dinosaurs, climate change, volcanoes, and the planets. My own children were amazed to hear I could talk for 3 hours straight. I can't do this at home. Actually, I have trouble getting a word in edgewise, and frequently have to raise my hand. It's the result of being the only male living in a house with four females. The book, "*Men Are From Mars, Women Are From Venus*" by John Gray is not an Earth Science book, but a supposedly practical guide for improving communications at home. I read it and was startled to discover that I really was from Mars.

I have all of the attributes of a typical Martian male, including a cave where I can go and think alone. I like to fix things. I'm concerned if I run out of clean underwear. If someone asks me a "yes" or "no" question, I can (and usually do) answer in one word without even thinking. Erin assured me I will never have to worry about wearing out my thinking genes, but I was excited about the book since I'd lost my "Guidebook to Perfect Daddyhood" right after my first child was born. I read many of the passages from "Men are From Mars" to Erin and she helped me study.

My wife, on the other hand, is not only the goddess of mommyhood, but the Queen of the Venusians. She is the Empress of Advice and is worshiped on her home planet for her ability to answer "yes" or "no" questions in no less than four hours while thoroughly discussing all possible sides of the issue. She is concerned with everyone's feelings. She likes to make lists. She can instantly change her emotions for no apparent reason whatsoever and she remembers every particular time in the history of the Universe when I screwed up or didn't "respect her feelings".

That "respect" part was actually written in the book, and John Gray advised that to have a happier marriage, the husband should actually listen to his wife and sometimes respond, "I heard you. That is interesting and I respect your feelings on that. I love you." It is supposed to be the magical sentence Martian men never say, but what Venusian women want to hear when they talk to men. I tried it. Once. When my wife finished a long discussion on something (I really don't remember what she was actually talking about, but I'm a Martian), I looked her in the eyes and said, "I heard you. That is interesting and I respect your feelings on that. I love you".

My wife looked at me and replied, "What's wrong with you? Don't be so sarcastic." and walked away in a huff. I retreated back to my cave. Did I mention that John Gray was divorced?

CHAPTER 36

DRIVING AND DADDYHOOD

My three daughters have been growing up quickly. It seems it was only last year when I was still vacuuming 10,000 free-range Cheerios from the back seat of our minivan. Now I merely harvest the herd of hair brushes they abandon on all of the seats and storage compartments. I remember thinking I'd finally have enough extra money to fix the minor pipe leak in our basement when I didn't have to buy diapers for my babies anymore. Instead, no sooner had K.C. finally mastered the art of "potty", and I purchased my last case of Huggies, when lo and behold, I began to have to buy cases of Depends for my mother. Such is life for a Daddy in the 'between' generation. My kids kept getting older, and my mom kept acting younger. And, my hair kept getting grayer. The minor pipe leak never did get properly fixed. At least now, when I want to go swimming, all I have to do is go into our basement.

Another sign of the passing years is our refrigerator. Our refrigerator survived eighteen years as a pin-up board for magnetized school photographs dating from pre-nursery school through elementary school, middle school, and high school. There are rows and rows of wallet sized photos of each of our girls lining the fridge. In addition, there are photos of each of our nieces, and their cousins, my grandnephew and grandniece, and countless certificates and artwork plastered at least 4-inches deep all

221

around the fridge. The hinges on the door even sag a bit under the weight of handmade, Daisy Scout, kitchen magnets lovingly crafted out of tongue depressors. There is also a single black and white wallet sized photo of a cute high school junior dating back to 1969, a girl who was destined to become the Mommygoddess. It's there just to remind us that we were kids once ourselves. We finally had to buy a larger refrigerator, not to store food, but because we ran out of magnet space on the door.

All in all, being "The Daddy" has been a good experience. I figure I'm lucky in one respect– at least I didn't have to raise a child just like me. As an 11-year-old, I set off an entire matt of firecrackers in my bedroom because I lit them before realizing I couldn't get the window open. It was not a wise example of planning ahead. Grandpa, a Spanish American War veteran who had been taking a nap in the room next to mine, charged into my room to recreate his charge up San Juan Hill... using my head as the hill. For several years after this incident, I actually used the burn craters in the formerly green carpet as a realistic battlefield for my toy army men.

Alexis, on the other hand, was easy to raise throughout her childhood, just a lot more expensive. My activities as a child were simple-and inexpensive. Sunday school, watching TV, church youth choir, watching TV, scouts, watching TV, walking the dog, and getting home fast to watch TV. I can recite by memory the entire dialogue of all 78 episodes of 'Star Trek,' and all 196 episodes of the 'Outer Limits' and 'The Twilight Zone', as well as 'Combat 'and 'Gilligan's Island.'

Times changed by the time Alexis was born. Instead of TV - except for Jim Henson's 'Fraggle Rock', 'My Little Pony Cartoons', and 'The Simpsons', my daughters had art lessons, drawing lessons, trumpet lessons, flute lessons, gymnastics lessons, painting lessons, ballet lessons, photography lessons, macramé lessons, and ceramics lessons--, all at a mere $30 per half hour, which my wife says is reasonable until I pointed out I only earn that much for a full hour of work. My wife says I'm not being reasonable and that I really don't "work" for a living. She thinks that I just sit in a government provided office cubical reading e-mails, drinking coffee and nibbling cheese like the other office mice.

Our youngest daughter, K.C., will soon turn 13 and I am still tempted to leave home the night before her first "teenage" birthday. It was my vow never to live in a house with three teenage daughters lest I die of an overdose of female hormone poisoning. There are times I need a broom to sweep the hormones away from the sofa, and I've been known to wear my EPA 'Tyvek' health & safety protection gear (Level FH - female hormone resistant) when I go into the bathroom. I did promise to return home when our oldest, Alexis, turns 20 - fortunately this event takes place only 2 weeks after K.C.'s 13th birthday.

In actuality, Alexis has already "fledged" - she left the nest as all baby birdies eventually do. For Alexis, this event occurred the day she got her driver's license. She taken a drivers' education course, and it was my 'pleasure' to go for practice drives with her. Actually, I got 'volunteered' for this task by the goddess of mommyhood. It was her way of keeping our household chore duties "equal". I have already flunked all other household chores – other than taking the garbage out and buying milk at 7-11. Suzie knows I enjoy driving, so my doing the driving lesson chore would serve 2 purposes. First, I would be doing something constructive with my daughters other than getting them slimed whenever we went camping. Second, I would be getting out of the house so Suzie could get the chores done without me interfering. Do the girls drive Daddy crazy? Not really as much as Daddy drives Mommy crazy.

Our car was a perfect car for test driving. It was inherited from Grandma, a 1986 Oldsmobile Cutlass Sedan, which only had 35,000 miles on it although it was already 15 years old. It was the definitive "Little Old Lady" car, that Grandma only did use on Sundays to go back and forth to Church. It was also Battleship Gray– Grandma's favorite color. In spite of its age, it has not rusted to death (the car, not Grandma) and runs fine (the car, not Grandma). There is just a minor problem with only occasional heat or air conditioning and an interior headliner that droops down like a puffy quilt. Alexis used her artistic talents to pin up the headliner with hundreds of thumbtacks, decorated in the shapes of stars and moons.

I began reviewing the driver's education manual with Alexis. Her answers to a couple of the sample test questions surprised me:

Q: What are some points to remember when passing or being passed in a car?

A: Make eye contact and wave "hello" if he's cute.

Q: What is the difference between a flashing red traffic light and a flashing yellow traffic light?

A: The color.

I gave up on the manual and told Alexis some of the driving truisms I've learned over the years; 1) Under no circumstances should you leave a safe distance between you and the car in front of you, or the space will be filled in by somebody else putting you in an even more dangerous situation. 2) Speed limits are arbitrary figures, given only as suggestions and are apparently not enforceable during rush hour. 3) Never, ever come to a complete stop at a stop sign. No one expects it and it will inevitably result in you being rear ended. If you want your insurance company to pay for a new rear bumper, come to a complete stop at all stop signs. 4) If, at any time, you have witnessed a green light, it is okay to proceed through the intersection, regardless of the current color of the light. I figured if Alexis wrote answers similar to these on the written driver's exam, I wouldn't have to worry about her ever actually driving. Unfortunately, she passed the exam and got her learner's permit.

Our first afternoon, Alexis and I did very well with the practice drive. It only took 45 minutes for her to drive all the way across our lawn and into

224

the neighbor's bush. I remember my calming words, "That's OK, Princess, that neighbor's an invalid anyway, I'm sure she won't notice her forsythia bush is completely flat on our side. Besides, the tire ruts almost resemble lawn edging." After that we practiced driving in the empty parking lots of Nassau Community College or the former Mitchell Field Airforce Base, where the runways were almost wide enough to make a three-point turn with a B-52 bomber and there were less bushes to flatten. Ali improved a lot and soon took her driver's test, then camped out at the mailbox waiting for the results. Meanwhile, I drove Grandma's car on a daily basis a total of 3 whole blocks so I could park it in her driveway while I took the nearby train to work.

One afternoon, I got off the train and walked towards Grandma's house. I got my car keys out and bounced them up and down in my hand as I turned the corner towards her driveway. I suddenly stopped and stood looking at the empty driveway where I was almost certain I had parked Grandma's car that morning. The car was missing! Grandma's neighbor, Matt, happened to see me. Matt called over, "Hiya Rob! Looks like some-one got her driver's license in the mail today. I guess your daughter has 'fledged'."

Matt was right. I walked home, still nervously jangling the keys in my hand. Our first daughter had left the family nest, but I hadn't expected it to be with Grandma's car. I never saw much of either the car or Alexis after that, and if I did find the car in our driveway, it was mainly because there was less than a quarter of an ounce of gasoline left in the tank. My insurance company was delighted with the news of a new teenage driver in our household, and even sent me a personal congratulations note, along with an invoice for insurance that was larger than my mortgage. I decided to stop worrying about my teenage daughter's driving and take advantage of it. I got one of those bumper stickers that say, "How's my driving?" and put a 900 number on it. At 50 cents a call, I've been making $38 a week.

I missed the days when I was only concerned if my daughters wore a sturdy enough helmet while riding their bicycles. Our new family game was to play 'car stacking' in the driveway. Whoever left the house last had to use Grandma's car rather than the minivan. We are a typical suburban family that drives over 20,000 miles per year, yet never seems to actually go anywhere. We just shuttle the kids back and forth.

Our minivan was the "Grand" Voyager with an extended back to hold all of the luggage needed for our vacation trips. The girls all bring backpacks with them stuffed with schoolbooks and projects to keep them busy while we drive. Sometimes, I'm even able to complete backing down the driveway before one of them asks the question, "Are we there yet?" I found I really did need the roof racks when it came time to bring Alexis back and forth to college. I used them to hang myself when I found out how much college tuition really was.

The minivan was a leased vehicle, and when the kids were young, the budgeted 12,000 miles per year was sufficient for girl's soccer and camping. I hadn't planned on driving back and forth repeatedly across five states while Ali was a junior in High School. We were searching for the "perfect" college for our first child. It was no problem at all to drive from LI to Virginia on a Saturday with the entire family only to hear my daughter say, after five minutes on campus that the school was terrible because there were a lot of students walking around smoking tobacco. I didn't tell her of the other things smoked back in the 1960's, but got into the car and drove another 8 hours back to LI. We settled on one rule, all colleges had to be within a five-hour drive, but I forgot to include the words "at legal speed limits." Not mysteriously, my wife is recommending tons of local colleges for our other two children.

It was only a few months later when our entire family stood on the High School football field and watched Alexis receive her diploma and a trunk load of scholarships and awards. When she headed for college at Cornell University a few weeks later, it was the same day I received a photo in the mail of Alexis and me together at the High School Father-Daughter Dance. I looked at the picture of her mature and smiling face standing next to her proud Dad, and thought, "Cool, I've got Grandma's car back at last."

Unfortunately, time continues to fly by and as we recently left the local pizzeria and walked towards our car, Erin - our 15-year-old, asked for the car keys. She then ran ahead, opened the car door, and started it up more professionally than Dale Earnhardt. I only have a few more months until Erin officially begins driver's education, but I noticed Erin has already applied for NASCAR membership.

CHAPTER 37

A DIFFERENT YEAR FOR DADDYHOOD

Contrary to popular belief, I do not spend all of my time volunteering. I am just a poor, simple (emphasis on poor!) geologist employed by the Federal government. I try to set goals each year, but sometimes circumstances out of my control do not permit me to accomplish as much as I plan. One of the benefits of being with the Federal government is that employees rapidly accumulate vacation and sick time- (up to a limit) and can enjoy more "time off" to be with their families. Being the daddy to three growing girls, I enjoy being with each of them (except when they're teenagers!) knowing that all too soon they will fledge and leave my wife and me as empty nesters.

Unfortunately, being a government employee also means not earning anywhere as much as I did in private industry. The extra time off doesn't mean expensive exotic vacations overseas or to resorts. It usually means inexpensive entertainment for cheap budgets: camping at State parks, trips to local museums and art galleries, games of scrabble or puttering in the back yard or at my nine-acre bird sanctuary-- a community volunteer project I began several years ago. This year was a bit different.

Soon after the start of the year, I was summoned to jury duty. I missed two weeks at the office, but I got a valuable course in life. I was actually put on a case with eleven other jurors and listened to the trial of a young man accused of the robbery of a basketball jersey. It was interesting and made me feel blessed that my own children had the family, economic upbringing, and background to never even consider being placed in the same unfortunate circumstances as the accused. (Thank the Mommygoddess, not me!) The two weeks were also spent learning about our country's justice system as well as the lives and interests of my fellow jurors.

I returned to the office after the trial to find out my schedule was changed to a "flex time". I would be at the office nine hours per day for nine days and have every tenth day off in compensation. The program was established as an energy saving measure- to reduce commuting congestion a bit in NYC. Starting earlier in the morning meant I could no longer have breakfast each day with my family, but I looked forward to the extra twenty-six days home over the year. Unfortunately, my flex day frequently conflicted with my wife's busy schedule and we couldn't be together as much as I'd hoped. Instead, it became the day I'd go food shopping, volunteer at school programs, give lectures and talks about the environment and nature, do other chores, or work in the garden and bird sanctuary.

In addition to "flex time", as a senior geologist I was made a member of the government's Groundwater Forum - a great group of dedicated geologists from around the country that are experts on many aspects of groundwater contamination. Why was I made a member??? I think it had something to do with the group's decision to either reach out to the intellectually challenged or find a new member that was an expert on a previously unfilled but vital category-- beers of the world. I seemed to fit both criteria. Anyway, I participated in both of their week-long conferences, which reduced my office time even further.

There was also one other event that kept me away from office and home-- my youngest daughter, K.C.'s 13th birthday. Yup, my 'lapbunny' had at last become a teenager, and for a short period of time, I was actually the father of three teenage girls. For years, I've repeatedly vowed that I could not live in the same home as the father of three teenage girls. We only have 1 semi functional bathroom. The other bathroom became uninhabitable after the perfumes, hairspray, and cleaning lotions combined with a six-pound hairball in the bathtub drain and set off a new form of mutant life. No one uses that bathroom anymore. Anyway, as soon as K.C. blew out her 13 birthday candles, I arranged for an official Emergency Leave of Absence, and spent two weeks searching for a lost lizard species in Philadelphia until my oldest daughter turned twenty and I could return home.

During the Memorial Day weekend, I spent a lot of time moving some four hundred cobblestones across the bird sanctuary and lugged several weighty trees up and over the hill for planting. I also had to move tons of boxes around in our basement to make room for even more boxes. I had driven to Ithaca the previous weekend where I helped my oldest daughter, Alexis, pack her apartment and return back home after completing her sophomore year at Cornell. My back was also a bit sore from carrying her refrigerator up three flights of stairs to store in the attic.

On Memorial Day morning, I was taking a shower, and bent over to clean out a newly hatched hairball from the bathtub drain. When I stood up, I suddenly felt a sharp snap and instant pain in my lower back. The little hairball suddenly seemed to weigh six hundred pounds. The result of bending instead of squatting was that I'd fractured my spine. I had a 'lovely' ride in a bouncy ambulance and spent the next couple weeks flat on my back in the hospital until the vertebrae set.

I was then told to stay home for another couple of months until my back mended. I had a walker, an assortment of drugs, and my cable TV remote. I camped out on a fold-out bed in the den since I couldn't walk upstairs. I spent the next month watching out my den window. I watched it rain. I watched my poor cherry tree being attacked by squirrels and blue jays. They completely devoured my cherry crop - not that I was in any shape to climb the tree myself. Erin, my sixteen year old, finally climbed the tree and rescued the entire 2003 crop of five remaining cherries. The blueberry bushes didn't fare much better. I watched my grass grow from nice suburban lawn into an unkempt meadow, then a tall prairie and finally a dark jungle until my daughters and a good friend, Mike Lutz, used machetes, weed-whackers, and a D-9 John Deere Bulldozer to hack it back into control.

When I finally healed sufficiently to return to the office, I had another government surprise - "Use or Lose". It turned out that I'd accumulated more vacation time than I was permitted to stockpile. Even the Leave of Absence didn't count as a vacation since it was for official research purposes. Being out on sick leave didn't count towards vacation time either, so I did what any smart employee would do, I attempted to sell it back to the agency. I was denied. I did manage to donate some of it to a charity bank for employees with long-term medical problems, but rather than lose the rest, I wound up taking an unplanned three week vacation. I spent this time trying to catch up on three months of neglected maintenance at "Camp Bird"- my bird sanctuary project.

When I returned again to the office, I discovered I'd won an on-the-spot award for an innovative recommendation I'd made on a research project I shared with the US Geological Survey. My award? Another official "DAY OFF". I went home wondering if the government had subleased my office cubicle to another agency. My wife and kids were getting tired of seeing Daddy around the house.

The end of the Government's fiscal year is September 30, and I spent the last day of the year driving out to Suffolk County to inspect a cleaned up waste site, photograph surrounding properties, and wrote a brief report to fulfill requirements that all such sites undergo a five year review. It usually takes several months of effort to conduct these reviews, but I lucked out - I had been the original geologist on the site clean-up so I already knew all of the history and needed facts pertaining to the site. As a result, my report was able to be submitted in time to fulfill one of the department's annual goals.

The next week, when I received my paycheck, I noticed something odd- more money than I am used to receiving. Knowing that my agency isn't always infallible, and I might be responsible for such administrative mistakes (What the Government giveth, the IRS taketh away) I went to my branch chief and asked if he could explain where the extra money in my paycheck came from. I was shocked to hear that I'd received the bonus as a result of my "Outstanding Performance". I felt a bit embarrassed. I said that I really didn't feel I deserved the award since I'd been out so much. I said I felt a little uncomfortable being rewarded for outstanding work when I hadn't even been at work much during the year.

My branch chief looked at me quietly for a few seconds and then slowly said, "Rob, the award doesn't say anything about your work. It says you were an outstanding performer," and he left the room.

I cashed the check wondering what my bonus might have been if I hadn't shown up at all during the year.

CHAPTER 38

THE MASTER OF DADDYHOOD

Having three children of my own has given me many opportunities to be involved in more things than I ever expected. I spent hundreds of hours running next to two-wheeled bicycles trying to teach my young daughters to pedal and balance. My words of encouragement, "No, No, No!! Watch out for the Tree!!! That's OK, Princess, Daddy will heal...." didn't quite encourage or calm them. It did, however, give them the incentive to learn how to ride a bicycle from their friends. There always seems to be a miscommunication in Daddy-daughter conversations. Recently, my middle daughter, Erin, received her learners permit and asked me to take her driving. "Sure, sweetheart, that will be fun!" I confidently replied, knowing full well that even the bushes across the street were slowly trying to edge back from the curb in fear.

We did practice. She'd practice moving a mechanized 2,000 pound potential bush crusher along the road, while I'd practice screaming "No!! No!! Stop! Stop! Stop!" every time she failed to respond to another car coming in her direction. I thought my communication technique was perfectly clear when she accidentally closed the car's front door on my finger. I simply repeatedly screamed, "OPEN THE DOOR!! OPEN THE

233

DOOR!!" in a voice loud enough to cause the Concorde airplane overhead to make an emergency landing. Meanwhile, Erin stood by the rear of the car and cluelessly replied, "The back door is already open, Dad, what's your beef?" Fortunately, we both survived.

My voice is naturally loud. My bark is worse than my bite, but I sometimes don't realize that my bark can also cause damage, too. It was an asset when I was in the construction business, but not while playing My Little Pony with a six-year-old or calling, "I'M COMING" to my wife whenever she hails me from her studio to give me advice or a message. It is also an asset when I sing. I have a deep baritone voice and have no hesitation to use it to sing Christmas carols, Broadway songs, or old time rock and roll classics. As a kid, I enjoyed being out at clubs with my parents. My Dad seemed to know every classic by heart and could sing well. He loved piano bars where he could sit with a sweet daiquiri in one hand, a cigarette in the other and drown out the piano player in a chorus of "Shine on Shine, on Harvest Moon" – even if the piano player was actually playing "That Old Black Magic". Eventually, the piano players learned to just play what my Dad was singing.

I seem to be the only singer in my household. My wife, Suzie, barely lip-syncs the words in Church hymns on Sundays, and my oldest daughter, Alexis, used to routinely get up and walk out of her nursery school class whenever the teachers started to sing "The Wheels of the Bus Go Round and Round". The nursery school administrator even called my wife to let her know our 3-year-old future Cornell University Dean's List student was in mortal danger of flunking the mandatory nursery school music program. Suzie and Alexis took the news fairly well. They both just shrugged their shoulders, muttered "Big deal. Who cares?" and went back to their art lessons. Alexis never made much of a Lincoln Center quality impression with her 3rd grade kazoo either. (But note this mature perspective from her

Daddy-- Alexis won a ton of art prizes in the annual PTA art show, so Nah, Nah, Nya-Nya, Nah!)

Suzie, the Mommygoddess (*she who must give advice*), pre-empted any future negative reaction to singing after our next children were born. Erin and K.C. are both accomplished musicians. Erin is a fabulous trumpet player and K.C. is mastering both the flute and piccolo. Both girls get weekly music lessons, play in the school band, and enjoy playing. Unfortunately, unlike the piano or guitar, none of their instruments is the type you can easily sing along with while you play.

K.C. is our youngest and smallest, but also the one child that seems to have inherited her mommy's 'supersized' gene for talking. At dinner time, there are times I'm actually reluctant to ask K.C. how her day at school went. She gives me a continuous minute-by-minute account that lasts until my dinner is frozen and my ice cream is a melted puddle. I've actually had to stuff my napkin in my ears or in her mouth to get her to finish. If I ask Erin the same question, the response I typically get is "... OK..." or "I forget" which is a reminder that of all the children, she takes after me the most. K.C. also has a loud infectious laugh, and when she gets the giggles, the windows rattle. We're in the process of replacing all of the windows in the house.

K.C. is also the child that dragged me into the local Garden City Community Theatre several years ago. She wanted to be in one of their fantastic original musicals. I also joined the group and we've acted in a variety of plays under the encouraging direction of Brad and Ruby Gustavson and with other great people. There's only been one minor problem - auditions. There is a perpetual shortage of adult males that are not afraid of being labeled "nonmacho" if they sing and dance. Note- I do not imply that "adult" males are necessarily "mature", just that they are chronologically over the age of 15 whether or not they act like it. Being an adult male well over the chronological age of 15, I don't even have to audition. I just have to demonstrate I can breathe and have a somewhat regular heartbeat and I get a major part. K.C., on the other hand, must compete against what seems like the entire adolescent population of the Western Hemisphere to be chosen "bit player". Being an accomplished ballerina (as well as a member of the local church where the Community Theatre performs) helps give K.C. a slight edge over the competition. (So does having the Directors know that Daddy won't even consider being in the play unless his daughter is in it.)

Unfortunately, K.C. has a tendency to clam up under pressure and a bit of anxiety being asked to sing alone. This mystifies me. She certainly has no hesitation doing a solo on her flute or piccolo in front of hundreds of strangers. She's been on stage both in dance as well as band and the musicals. It seems it's the actual audition process for the Community Theatre that makes her act hesitant. She has to sing a short song alone, accompanied by the Community Theatre's music director on a piano. Three years ago, she had practiced a song at home, but since we don't have a piano, the key she learned the song in was not the same key as in the sheet music. When she began to sing at the audition, she became flustered when she realized this. She was eventually cast as "Kid #16". She was also "Pardner#3" and "Camper#5" in other productions, but K.C. and I had limited opportunities to actually be on stage together. As a Daddy, I've done my best to encourage her through the audition. My usual way is to simply yell at her to "Sing Louder!!", which I admit, doesn't seem to have the intended effect of encouraging her.

This year, I was not able to make it to the Garden City Community Theatre auditions. The evening they were scheduled, I was scheduled to travel with Erin to Rochester to hear her play her trumpet in a performance with the All-State Band concert. K.C. would have to be on her own. The question was, what would she sing, and could she do it without Daddy nearby to yell at...I mean encourage her, to do her best? I recommended a couple of Broadway songs for K.C. to select for her audition and told her to learn and practice them. Again, though, we were stumped without a piano. At church that Sunday, I mentioned this to George Bashian and asked if I could stop over his house to record him playing the songs on his piano so K.C. could practice in the right key. He readily agreed.

K.C., however, was not amused to find out I had made plans to record the songs for her and became upset when she found out George wanted her to join him when he played the songs. She was reluctant to sing and in my usual way, I managed to get her more upset by telling her she had to if she wanted to be in the play. I lead K.C. into George's home, and we leafed through a music book to suggest songs. K.C. weakly sang one song, and I guess George could tell something was wrong. He began to play the song again, only this time in a lower key. Then, he suggested I wander around the house a few minutes and look at his wife's baseball collection. I left George and K.C. together and puttered through the living room.

I've known George and his wife Susan for several years. They are a wonderful couple, and both regularly volunteer at church. Their own children have grown, but there were photos of them all over the piano. George and Susan have both acted with K.C. and me in the Community Theatre productions. Susan was cast as my wife in one play, and George and I sang the classic "A Little Tin Box" together. George is also "goofy" - and this is a compliment from a person who has a Master's Degree in "goofiness". George has also been the leader for many children's sermons and confirmation classes and is, in fact, a licensed minister (as well as having a law degree -note:"goofy" does not mean stupid). Anyway, George is also a person who cannot sit still for more than 30 seconds, is a Vietnam veteran, and is a lifetime ardent Yankee fan.

George and Susan are both baseball fans, and the collection consisted of autographed baseballs from a variety of Yankee and Brooklyn Dodger players. I spent time admiring the fading signatures of Mickey

Mantle, Pee Wee Reese, Carl Erskine, and Don Mattingly, Jackie Robinson and many other historic "masters of the game" as I listened to George and K.C. work together in the adjacent room. What I heard made me realize I was listening to a "master" of Daddyhood work his magic. George was calmly playing the piano and quietly encouraging and supporting K.C. as she sang. "That was nice. You've got a very pretty voice. You make me happy to hear you sing. You've got a nice smile, let people see it more."

Each of his comments were the exact warm and supportive type that only a 'master of Daddyhood' can say in a way that has lasting positive impact. I think even Mr. Rogers might have learned a few tips from George. George was an inspiration. He then quietly suggested changing the audition song to "You Gotta Have Heart" and helped show K.C. how to project more and vary her tone on particular words. As she continued to sing under George's guidance, I witnessed K.C.'s improvement unfolding and blossoming as her voice began to hit the notes with more and more confidence. Her singing began to have more heart. George noticed it too and told K.C. that is was similar to a musician making music with a score rather than just playing notes.

When they were done and the song had been recorded on our small cassette player, K.C. and I both said a sincere and deep felt thank-you to George. George then asked when the audition was scheduled for and said that although he was scheduled to be in the hospital for a test that afternoon, he would go to the audition and play for K.C. if she wanted him to. K.C. said thanks again, while I stood there wondering how many fathers wouldn't even leave work a few minutes early to watch their own child at a ballet recital while this "master" was willing to leave a hospital to help someone else's child.

As we drove home, I asked K.C. how the recording went with Mr. Bashian. K.C. said it went fine and proceeded to give me a minute by minute accounting of what she and George had done and said. She said it was fun and she learned a lot. Actually, so did I—and I didn't have to say anything. I'm still learning my part in the long running performance of 'how to be a Daddy'. If you want to know how K.C.'s audition worked out, go to the next Garden City Community Theatre production and find out. Thanks, George!

CHAPTER 39

DADDY'S NOT DONE AT 21

Last year I read an essay in the Long Island newspaper, *Newsday,* by Susan Cheever regarding her thoughts on the milestone of her daughter's 21st birthday. I was tempted to reply, sympathizing with her struggles and victories of being a single mom, but I was too busy working on my personal role of Daddyhood. I'm now 52 years old and have had 52 "Daddy" years' experience with daughters now ages 21, 17, and 14. It is a double milestone that the sum of my daughter's ages equals my own, and that my oldest daughter, Alexis has reached 21. That I am aging three times faster than them is a valid reason why even my wrinkles are starting to have wrinkles. Even though Alexis is now considered a responsible adult, by every legal definition however, my role as "Daddy" isn't over. It just continues to change. What a long, strange trip it's been.

On tax day in 1983, my wife Suzie gave birth to our first child—after a not so relaxing 30 plus hours of labor. Frankly, after the first 12 hours of labor had gone by, I became bored and was tempted to get on a plane to Florida and tell her to send me a postcard when she was finally done. My sole responsibility in this effort seemed to be to feed Suzie ice chips and tell her to breathe. I was more concerned about my wife's health than the impending new baby and didn't quite realize that I was actually saying goodbye and farewell to my high school sweetheart, girlfriend, and partner as she metamorphosed into the "Mommygoddess." We would no longer be a "couple", but a "family". Even in the recovery room, Suzie was already an expert 'Mommy' and was giving advice to the other new mommies and recommending books they should read to help raise their newborn. Her focus was on being Mommy- but at first, things weren't as smooth as she'd planned.

Our new baby girl couldn't keep food down, and within a short time had been placed in an incubator until the doctors could figure out the problem. Nourishment came from a tiny tube, and on top of the incubator I placed a small stuffed animal, "Froggie", to keep her company when we weren't there. We kept praying and wondering what we did wrong. Eventually, the problem was simply a milk intolerance - ironic because my wife was an avid milk drinker, and after switching diet and formula (as Dr. Rieger explained, "Stop drinking milk. After all, mommy cows don't drink milk") little Alexis stabilized and we were able to bring her home the next week. Suzie gave up drinking milk for the entire year so that she could breast feed our daughter. Much of that year is a blur from lack of sleep.

By that time, Alexis had bonded with "Froggie" much like a baby bird bonds with the first thing it sees. Froggie was a constant companion, with its leg held tightly by small fingers against my daughter's tiny nose. Eventually, "Froggie" had several identical sisters, and all of my daughters have their own collection of froggies, as gifts from daddy. Childhood passes by so quickly! There seemed to be an endless parade of newly outgrown clothes, books, and toys as Alexis matured, but Froggie has a special place.

I think her actual birth was the only difficult thing "Ali" (my personal nickname for her) ever encountered. We were very blessed to have a cute, intelligent, quiet, easy to raise, and artistic child. OK, I'm sure many parents feel the same way about their children, but my personal bias is justified. Alexis was a very pretty baby and remarkably complacent. She smiled easily and was soon trotted around NYC in a snuggli-sack doing modeling for catalogues and commercials. Her savings account (thanks to Mommygoddess) was larger than mine. Ali showed confidence early. When she began to walk, it wasn't with tentative hesitant steps, but with a wide open run downhill at a local park. Later, she spent years on gymnastics teams, balancing, tumbling, and playing catch me if you can. And rarely could anyone catch her.

I've always been somewhat in awe of Ali. Like all children, she did go through the "Terrible Two's", but the "TT's" only lasted about two weeks and were soon behind her. The much expected toddler tantrums were merely an unexpected, quiet "No" spoken for the first time. Quiet or not, it was still a shock. Each year brought something even more wonderful, whether it was a growing accomplishment in art, learning to read, or memorizing math tables. It seemed so easy to raise a child, we decided to have another one.

When Erin was born four years later, we had what we soon considered was "Demonbabyfromhell" and were looking for a reform school for toddlers. The weird part is that of all the girls, Erin is the one that has the personality most like mine. We were astonished when friends told us how wonderful Erin actually was. In retrospect, Erin, and her younger sister K.C. are great normal kids, we just hadn't had any experience with "normal" children before. While I still sometimes threaten to sell K.C. for medical research purposes, I'm proud to be "Daddy" to all of my girls.

Have I been a good or bad influence as a daddy to Alexis? It depends on whom you ask. If you ask Mommy, I've been good at getting Alexis dirty, and excellent at teaching her how to ignore Mommy's advice. OK, at least I contributed something. There are a few things I've learned too, such as if you want to be a parent, you have to know about what medicines to give your kids - Vodka is not a very good cough medicine for a

3- year- old. I've also learned what to write to the teachers to excuse your kids from school. You've got to make it sound good even if your family is just leaving early on their vacation to Florida. I guess my biggest influence has been "nature". My wife hates bugs, dirt, wild animals, being outside, and not being able to talk to people. My feeling is dirt is fine, being outside is great, wild animals and some bugs are cool, and listening to nature is a lot more enjoyable than listening to criticism or advice.

Alexis was not one of the super "popular" crowd in school, but by her own choice. The teachers loved her dedication and aptitude to learn, and she had a small circle of close friends. She is certainly gifted in art and has earned a ton of awards in both art and science. I felt bad when I had to give up helping her after 8th grade math - I just couldn't understand what she was studying. She has always been fiercely self-reliant and can stand on her own. She had no difficulty adjusting to being away from home at either gymnastics camp, at an Audubon Society school in Maine, or a summer art school, or summer internships in Washington DC inventorying trees, or above Lake Tahoe building mountain trails. I don't know who let go first, but I know there's no need to hold her hand anymore.

So, after 21 years of raising a daughter, was I able to celebrate her passage into the "adult world"? No. Actually, Alexis called me on her 21st birthday, from Mexico! I haven't even seen her in several months, and rarely hear from her. She's already a Senior at Cornell University and has spent the semester by the ocean in southern Baja California doing field research through the School of Field Studies. She's been out of cell phone range, has no internet access, and 'snail mail' takes over a month to reach her.

I can tell she's happy during her weekly telephone calls when she tells me how her boat got rocked by whales, or rescuing sea turtles, or studying kelp and seaweeds. Being stranded in the desert when her bike broke down, or playing soccer with fifty young native residents, or riding horseback along the shore or camping in the desert are the things I'd love to be doing myself. I tell her of my field work for the US Environmental Protection Agency at a Superfund Site Auburn, NY, of having venison stew by a drill rig, and finding some apple-scented perennial geraniums for a bird sanctuary I founded a decade ago. I don't know who is more amused by the fact that we've been accepted as co-authors of a technical presentation on dual uses of stormwater basins for community purposes, and I'm relieved to know she received the airline tickets I sent for her flight home.

We made a pact that we'll share a drink together at the nearby Dublin Pub to celebrate her 21st birthday when she comes home, and it brought back memories of my Dad sharing a late night meal at a local diner with me 20 years ago when I was working extra hard to refurbish a new home for my wife and new daughter. We didn't say much, but he told me kiddingly that I'd turned out "OK" even if I didn't play cards much anymore. I'm sure neither my own Dad nor I have ever read the long lost classic book "Rulebook for Perfect Daddyhood". He was there for support, not to give advice. He was over 80 at the time, and I was well past my 21st birthday, but the role of father and child continued then, much as it does now for the next generation. And, when I see our children, I have hope.

CHAPTER 40

DADDYHOOD AND THE CURSE OF THE FIVE BUCKS

There is a God, and *She* knows me well. In spite of a Christian upbringing, I'm convinced God is female. No "Guy" God could dream up 'humans' with all the varieties and foibles and "mistakes in the making" we are. If a "Guy" God were to create a perfect world, it would be populated only with dogs-- eternally faithful, and tale wagging whenever He appeared. A female God is why the world is so complicated. A "Gal" God must have created cats, crabgrass, women, and men, and then set in motion all the struggles' men face through eternity. Life itself is a struggle enough without added complications from some church particular programs.

Our family belongs to the local community church, and unlike many members of today's world, we actually go on a semi-regular basis (except during the summer when I understand churches are closed anyway). Our church is celebrating its 75th anniversary this year, and, of course, it needs money. This is not unusual. I'm sure there was supposed to be an 11th commandment in the Old Testament, "*Thou Shall Give to the Temple*". Even when Peter founded the church in Rome, I'm sure the first act was either a bake sale or the invention of the term "tithe". It's not unusual to be asked to give to the church. What was unusual was a couple of

Sundays ago when Reverend Jim announced that instead of the church passing around the collection plate, the deacons would actually be distributing money that week to all attendees! That actually woke me up from a sound nap!! Halleluiah!!!

I knew there had to be a catch somewhere. Rev. Jim explained that the church was challenging us. Each family would be given some "seed" money and trusted to do something with it over the next few weeks. At the end, we were all supposed to turn over our earnings from the seed money funds back to the church. Rev. Jim then gave a sermon about some master guy who went away and gave his servants his money or something to take care of while he was gone. Actually, since I had returned to my normal condition of dozing lightly, I'm not sure what Mr. Masterson actually lent his servants. It had something to do with "talents" and the master was really ticked off when he returned and found out one servant had merely stashed his 'talent' away for safe keeping, while the other two had doubled theirs. One servant even had 10,000 "talents", including juggling. Either the message was we were supposed to use our own "talents" to double the money, or we were supposed to become Catholic.

As the envelopes were passed around, the congregation became excited. I heard a few "Bingos" from prospective converts and tore open my envelope. It held a single five dollar bill. "Oh my God," I groaned, "It's the five bucks from Grandma!" I groaned again; the curse was back.... If you're confused, I better explain that "Grandma" was my mother–a lady that grew up during the Depression and was forever after known to be a bit "frugal", (which is of sort of like saying Hannibal Lecter has slightly exotic food preferences.) OK, she was tightfisted. It was hard for her to actually give away anything. She was also a churchgoer, (perhaps for the free grape juice and piece of bread every month) and religiously "gave" to the church...a dollar a week.

At Halloween I had to stop her from giving out packets of sugar that she's save from restaurants and diners. At Christmas or Birthday celebrations, she inevitably would give each of her grandkids five bucks. It was torture for her. The bills were so old, the picture of Lincoln didn't even have a beard yet. It was also torture for our kids, since their etiquette-conscientious Mommy still made the kids write a personalized thank-you note to Grandma for the "generous" gift. Even my wife and I got five bucks from Grandma. So did my nephew and his new wife on their wedding, but I think they had to split it.

I never could figure out what exactly to buy with my five bucks from Grandma. I was a little old for the My Little Ponies (only $4.99 with a ribbon and tiny comb for each one) that my daughters liked. (Actually, I think they worshiped the toys and were planning to start the 'Church of the My Little Pony', but that's another story.) The 'five buck fortune' used to burn a hole in my pocket before it mysteriously changed into a mere 'one' and then at last into three pennies before I knew it. How was I going to use the church's $5 "seed" money to grow? How was I going to use my "talent"? The other people in the congregation all seemed excited, especially when they found out one church had grown a starting amount of $3,000 all the way to $37,000!

I thought, "Well, maybe we can top that! I'll try something spectacular and get us $50,000,000!! After all, it's God's work!" So, I went and spent $2 on a Lotto ticket and waited for the winning numbers to come in.

Since I'm also a conservative person, I didn't blow the whole "bundle" on the Lotto but saved $3 for another venture. I'm glad I did. The next week, when the winning numbers were drawn (on TV between my favorite shows "Monster Garage and "Deep Sea Detectives"), none of the eight numbers called out or even the bonus number were on my card. I couldn't believe it-- an absolute ZERO, and no $50,000,000 payout. It ended my moral debate whether I would actually turn over the $50,000,000 I was sure I would win, or just call Rev. Jim-- from Tahiti, and let him know I was starting my own church, thank you very much. Maybe God (that clever Lady) knew me enough to keep me out of such temptation.

Anyway, I thought, perhaps I'd reached too far, so I planned to invest the next 2 bucks on a surer thing. A horserace! I've got the horse right here! His name is Paul Revere! And I want to make this very clear. Can do!! Can do!! This guy says the horse can do!!! I drove down to the local Off Track Betting and plunked down my bet on a sure winner. Did we win?? Well...let me put it this way: If the 18th Century Paul Revere road as fast as the 21st Century Paul Revere..., we'd still be British subjects. He didn't even show! And I was down to one last buck.

Meanwhile, the other people in the congregation were having fun and more success. One group bought lemonade mix and sold lemonade to earn funds. Another bought pumpkins and sold them. Yet another group designed a new church logo golf hat and jacket. There were bake sales, advertisements for mending, car washes, plumbing and electrical work, and even professional photography sessions. And I was down $4 and counting. What was I going to do with my "seed" money? Then, panic induced inspiration struck. I'd plant seeds! I'd grow cherry tomatoes, sell them, and earn money the good old fashioned way! I drove to Home Depot and found one remaining pack of super-sweet cherry tomato seeds, bought it with my last buck, sped home and dug out a row in my lawn to plant the seeds. I carefully spaded the soil, tenderly planted each tiny seed, watered the row, said a prayer, and then sat down and figured out how many super-sweet cherry tomatoes I'd harvest and how much money I'd earn for the church.

I was fantasizing about 40 gazillion tomatoes (and maybe a little about the actress Pamela Anderson, another nice tomato), when my daughter Erin came over and asked me what I was doing. I said I had just started growing tomatoes, (leaving Pamela Anderson out of it) and was going to sell them to raise money for church. Erin looked at me, then at the bare strip of dirt where our lawn used to be. "Dad, are you aware that it's mid October? In a couple of weeks there will be frost. You're not going to get any tomatoes this year."

I was crushed. I was also pureed and diced. No tomatoes and no more "seed" money. I'd failed. I called Rev. Jim and told him. Surprisingly, Rev. Jim said it was all right! "All right?", I asked, "How could that be? I lost the "seed" money!"

Rev. Jim just laughed in his usual John Denver imitation. He replied, "The reason the master got mad at the one servant was because he didn't even try to use his talent. You can't have any chance for success if you don't take a risk. Not everyone's talent can be doubled, but at least you tried and took a risk. Even my wife took a risk. She put her $5 on an office football pool!"

"Oh, then she lost her "seed" money too?" I asked.

"Not exactly," Rev. Jim replied, "She won $500. But, remember she gets her inspiration from a Higher Source, and doesn't nap through my sermons. Gotta love those Jets!"

CHAPTER 41

INSIGHT AND DADDYHOOD

As a typical male, I only have two eyes. Both of them are in the front of my head, just to the left and right of the top of my nose. For many years, my two eyes have been hidden behind thick, and usually smudged, lenses-- framed by wire band "John Lennon" style glasses. I can see, but only in three dimensions. Even with glasses, there have been innumerable things I've "seen", but not really noticed. It's a fault typical of most males, and a lot of daddies, but it doesn't fully explain why I keep calling my kids by their wrong name. They just change so fast, I don't always recognize them, and my wife wouldn't let me tattoo their names onto their foreheads.

My wife Suzie-- the Mommygoddess, has at least four eyes. One is on the back of her head. She uses this one to catch me in the act of trying to raid the cookie jar behind her back. "I see that! Don't you dare eat any more cookies before dinner!" (How does she do that; she's not even facing me. In fact, she's not even home!?!) She has kept me and our children on our toes trying to come up with new ways of not getting caught.... I mean, being on our best behavior. Unfortunately, it's no use trying to fool either Mother Nature or the Mommygoddess.

Suzie's fourth eye is the invisible one high on her forehead. This is the psychic eye she uses as the "Seeker of Truth" and as "She Who Knows

All". One look from this third eye, and I confess to having eaten the last bag of Doritos. (How did she know? Were my fingers stained orange again?) Even our kids find it disconcerting to never be able to surprise Mommy with anything. She already knows what they got on their report cards, who called and who is going to call, and even which child drank directly out of the milk carton (me. -- her 4th child).

She can even see through walls. I've stood in front of our pantry for thirty minutes staring carefully at each shelf trying to find the new bottle of ketchup. When I'm about to give up and switch to mustard instead, she suddenly reaches a long arm in from the kitchen and pops out a new bottle of ketchup without even looking. "Here, I assume you were looking for the ketchup." I swear I didn't see any bottle of ketchup on any of the shelves, and that she actually dragged it out from another dimension in the Twilight Zone.

My vision has never even been "average". For much of my adult life, I could see at 20 feet what a person with "normal" sight could see at 500 feet. I might be condemned to terminal cluelessness, but I don't even notice. Ever since I was a young boy, I've had to rely on eyeglasses to see anything further away than my elbow. I was nearsighted to the point of being legally blind. I even wore glasses when I slept, so at least my dreams could be clear. Alas, even my teenage dreams of dancing with Joey Heatherton were fuzzy. As a youngster, one of my biggest wishes was to be able to swim underwater and actually see clearly without my glasses floating off. Everything underwater always seemed disappointingly fuzzy and distorted. It was one of the reasons I gave up a potential career in oceanography and became a geologist instead. At least I had the eyes of a scientist– under coke-bottle lenses from reading a million books. And, the glasses were always smudged and dirty since I only washed them when I took a shower. (Once a month whether I needed to or not.)

As time went by, even my nearsightedness deserted me. I was now past 40 and I had to hold the newspaper farther and farther away to read it until I realized my arms had become dislocated from stretching. My astigmatism had also progressed until I no longer could see anything vertical. I tried using this as an excuse to lay flat on the sofa while watching TV, but it didn't prevent my 12 year-old from merely plunking down on the sofa without bothering to notice my stomach was not a cushion. I was fired from wallpapering our hallway after not realizing the striped pattern was supposed to be vertical, whereas my final project made it look like an explosion at a candy cane factory.

I was not a happy camper. My optometrist, however, was delighted to let me know I had now graduated not just to bifocal lenses, or trifocal lenses, but "vari-focus" lenses. This meant each section of eyeglass lens was properly ground to match the prescription I needed for different distances. It also meant I had to constantly bob my head up and down or back and forth until I found the precise spot where something was in focus. On top of that, the new prescription was $500.00.

For the next few years, I paid the annual $500 fee for each new stronger and stronger pair of glasses and bobbed my head. Then, one fateful evening, while 200 miles from home on a business trip, I decided to enjoy my hotel's special accommodations by using their special soap to wash my glasses. I scrubbed and rubbed and scoured and cleaned my $500.00 glasses with the hotel mini-bottle of rubbing cream soap. I soaked and stroked and wiped the glasses until they shined and gleamed…then realized that I'd completely glazed over the $500.00 plastic lenses with pumice stone, and they were absolutely ruined. This was literally $500 down the drain, and I had to pretend to see well enough to drive 200 miles home the next morning. That was a challenge.

Previously, I'd performed without my glasses in a community theatre play when I had been cast as a guardian angel. Why did I do this?

252

Because in my version of heaven, angels don't need glasses. I only fell off the stage once and banged into the curtain four times. I had better luck driving to home to Long Island from Albany without too many bang-ups because I had done it many times and "remembered" the way, although it did take me a long, long time, and I don't remember seeing the sign "Welcome to Ohio" on any of my other drives on the New York State Thruway. On top of that, when I finally got home, my wife scolded me for my successful deer hunt...which I hadn't noticed was draped on the hood of my car.

I was frustrated and shaken. I called my friendly eye doctor and instead of forking over another $500.00 for replacement glasses, I asked her whether I might be a candidate for the new laser surgery eye treatment. I was assured that for only $3,000 she could zap my eyes well enough that I could see stars. I said I wasn't as much interested in seeing stars as I was reading and maybe swimming without my glasses. Dr. "Eye" thought about my needs for a second, then realized she'd just booked a week skiing in Aspen, Colorado. "Easy enough," she said, "but it will cost you $5,000. Just let me make a phone call, then I'll schedule your procedure." And, I think she called her travel agent to book a 10-day ski vacation instead of a mere week now that she had found an additional source of funds.

My wife drove me to the office for the "procedure". Supposedly, I would not be in any condition to drive after it was over. We parked and walked into the office where I noticed a large TV showing what I thought was an old movie classic on the screen. "Oh look, honey, "The Crawling Eye"!! I remember that movie! It starred Forest Tucker! I don't remember it being in color, though."

My psychic wife hit me gently in the ribs. "That's not a movie. It's a closed circuit screen camera shot of the current patient having his eye laser surgery. Now sit down, you're next." I couldn't watch. The poor Eye! It kept trying to escape! It looked at me pleadingly! What was Eye going to do? It was clamped firmly in place. It couldn't even blink! What was I going to do? I thought of fleeing, but there was a sudden flash of light, and Eye was gone…and I was next.

I went in, and thirty minutes later walked out with freshly zapped eyes and wearing two large fly-like patches over my eyes. I could see, sort of, but the light was overpoweringly bright enough to make me wonder if I'd been turned into a vampire…I needed to hide in the dark. Suzie drove me home. I actually felt fine. I turned on my computer and proceeded to send friends e-mail messages about surviving my eye surgery but warning them to keep a look out for "Eye" if he crawled by.

What I didn't know was that I was temporarily too blind to notice that all of my messages were gibberish. I couldn't see enough to notice my fingers were misplaced on the keyboard by one row while I was typing. Instead of typing HELLO LENORE!!, my written message was Y#OO@ O#H($#!!

The next morning was better. I pulled off the patches and I COULD SEE!! I COULD SEE!! I was so happy, especially since I had to drive to Brooklyn to teach my earth science class at the community college. First, however, I had to go to an early morning appointment with Dr. Eye for a "post procedure follow-up". I got to her office, and as soon as I entered the waiting room, two other men pointed at me and gleefully shouted, "I see You! I see You! Ha, Ha, Ha!!"

The three of us had all had the laser treatment the day before and were giddy with delight that we could actually see something without glasses on our heads. We played Peek-a-boo for the next thirty minutes. The only drawback to the surgery was that we all kept stabbing ourselves. Yes, we'd each poke our own finger into the bridge of our nose, repeatedly trying to push our phantom eyeglasses back into place. A habit learned for 50 years is hard to break. I've learned to spot people who've recently had laser eye surgery. They all smile like idiots and say I can see you! They aren't wearing glasses, but they all have blood dripping from the bridge of their nose.

I was then checked out by Dr. Eye who professionally said: "This is my plane ticket to Aspen and my resort hotel reservation slip. Can you read the fine print?"

"No, but I can see you!!! Ha! Ha! Ha! Ha!"

"Good enough for me. Don't try to read for a few days. Visit again me in 10 days."

It was only after I had driven to the college, when I realized I really couldn't read…or even take attendance. Fortunately, I taught Earth Science, and was able to record who was actually absent versus who was merely asleep in class after I found a large magnifying lens in the Earth Science Lab room. Over the next few months, my eyes healed and my reading vision slowly improved. I'm just at the age where I don't bother with the fine print anymore. I guess the only real drawback was that after having my "day vision" corrected, I discovered how bad my "night vision" really was. I've passed the age where driving at night is possible.

At least I'm not the only Daddy that sees but doesn't notice things. When my father-in-law came to our house a few weeks after my eye surgery, my wife asked him to look at me and tell her what was different. (He's only known me since the 1960's.) He stared at me for about 3 full minutes in as much panic as if he had been unexpectedly asked to deliver an oral thesis to the college faculty while dressed only in whipped cream on a hot day. He was not a good test taker, but finally said, "Oh, you shaved off your mustache." Which was true...... three years earlier.

As far as my childhood dream of swimming underwater without glasses? I finally did that the next summer. I dove into the pool and swam all the way across the pool underwater with my eyes wide open. I was disappointed to find that everything was blurry. I started to mention this to my wife but before I could say anything she said, "Robert, no one sees clearly under water. It's natural. The water distorts things."

I paddled away in silence thinking, "How does she do that?"

CHAPTER 42

DADDYHOOD AND THE MIDDLE CHILD

My wife and I have three daughters. Erin Claire was our second child, born four years after Alexis. Her name is Erin, and it's merely a coincidence that I gave her a four-letter word for a name. Everyone we know refers to 'Ali' as the "*perfect*" one, and there is justification for that nickname. Alexis was not only a delightful and perfect baby, but an amazingly easy toddler and well behaved and wonderful preschooler. We wondered why other parents looked so haggard and stressed raising their children. Raising Alexis was easy. Even as a baby, she didn't stop us from going to nightclubs - we just stuffed her baby carrier under the bar. I rarely forgot to bring her home when we left, and it got easier when Suzie pinned our telephone number on her blanket.

Even taking a car trip up and down the California coast with her was no problem, we just packed her with our luggage. She slept through the night at 2 weeks. She learned to walk at 9 months, then potty trained herself a week later. Her entire "terrible twos" lasted only 7 minutes tops (she actually said "no"!!) She washed the dishes at 16 months, and even rinsed them better than I do. She had even earned over $10,000 in modeling fees before she was a year old. While other new parents complained about their

257

kids, my wife and I were convinced raising a child was easy. And then we did the most stupid thing a couple can possibly do...we had another child. Erin! ARGH!!!!

The only way to properly describe it is that if we had Erin first, we wouldn't have any children by now. Erin was even 'difficult' before she was born. After the first few months of pregnancy, my wife began to hemorrhage and was confined to bed lest she miscarry. We waited the full 9 months and began to make plans for delivery. Erin, however, declined to exert the energy needed to be born, resting comfortably inside Mommy's belly getting bigger and bigger, growing teeth and hair. Only on the way to the hospital after 10-1/2 months for a C-section, did "Last Minute Erin" decide to pop out and say her first words, "It's not fair. BWAAAAH!!" Meanwhile, I had spent most of my time in the basement trying to build a new art studio for my wife since her current one was being converted into a bedroom for the new baby. It is somehow fitting that even 18 years after Erin was born, I've never had the time to finish the remaining 4% of the art studio I'd started. I've been afraid to turn my back on her.

Erin started off with a different sense of time than most people. After waiting over a month extra before finally deciding to be born...while we were on the way to the hospital, she was delighted to wake us up at all hours of the night. Her "terrible twos" lasted five years. My wife refers to her as "Last Minute Erin", and there are innumerable times I've been asked to make a mad dash to 'Staples' at 8:59PM to Xerox a homework report for her, wondering if I can make it the 2 miles in less than the minute left before the store closes.

Last January 31, I came home from a hard day of work (which might seem odd since I work for the US Government) to announce the only thing I wanted to do was watch 'Jeopardy' on TV to see if the legendary contestant, Ken Jennings, was going to continue his epic winning streak. At promptly 6:59PM, exactly 1 minute before the 7PM show started, Erin came into the living room to tell me she'd finally finished her applications to two colleges, Boston University and the University of Maryland.

"Great!", I said as Alex Trebek began to introduce the two challengers, "I'll mail them tomorrow."

"Uh, Dad? they're, uh, due February 1." I shut off the TV....with my foot.

I looked at Erin as she smiled sweetly with the two applications in her hand. I asked, "They're due tomorrow? The day that starts about five hours from now. Great, should I drive to Boston first or Maryland? Or, how about you just plan on attending Adelphi or Nassau Community College."

I looked at Erin as she smiled sweetly and replied "Oh cool, Dad, I wouldn't mind living at home. You could even drive me to school for the classes." I thought about Erin living at home for the next four years for a few seconds and I began to frantically pack. No, I wasn't actually going to drive through ten states, but merely to the post office to send the applications via Express Mail. Her next surprise was to say, "Dad, before you mail them, I'll need copies made and Mom also needs another copy of my transcript."

Ok, the slight detour to Staples was expected, but it was only 7:20PM, not 8:59 so I didn't have to use my rocket-mobile instead of my car. I drove to Staples, wearing my trusty driving glasses, and started making the copies. Suddenly I cringed in realization my efforts might be futile, and this rush might not be necessary. It dawned on me that the Garden City Post Office had already closed at 6PM, and I'd have to drive to the Hicksville branch to mail the applications!! (This I know from my experience of driving to the Hicksville Post Office every April 15th at roughly 11:30 PM to mail my tax returns). It was now 7:55PM as I finished the last copies. Then I realized that even if I got to the Hicksville branch, it was

259

already past the deadline for Express Mail. Wait a minute...the Federal Express office wasn't too far away. I could ship from there!

I ran out of Staples, dove into my car, and sped to Federal Express. I screeched to a halt in their lot and ran up the ramp to the door and pulled... it was locked. "NOOOOO", I cried, and began banging on the door. "PLEASE LET ME IN!!"

Miraculously, an employee came to the door, unlocked it, and let me in, with the words, "You must be Erin's dad." Actually, he said "It's already 8PM so make it quick.", but I already knew that and within 2 minutes had filled out two forms, packaged and sealed the shipping envelopes, wiped out my last remaining credit line available on my Visa card, and was walking back to my car fumbling for my keys. It was only then that I realized I didn't have my trusty driving glasses. I turned to go back inside the Federal Express building just as the lights were turned off. It was 8:03PM. The door was locked. I crept home in a blurry haze wondering whether I had left my glasses in Staples or Federal Express or had accidentally mailed them to either Boston or Maryland. In any event, I never saw them again, and for that matter Erin never bothered to go to Boston or Maryland either. ARGH!!!

Erin and I have a good relationship. We both frequently wind up in the doghouse more often than any other members of the family. (It's not fair!) I'm still not allowed to do laundry after shrinking my wife's ABSOLUTE FAVORITE cashmere sweater into Barbie doll sized clothing. Come to think of it, my wife doesn't exactly have time to do the laundry. Sometimes I sneak downstairs at night and simply hose the laundry pile down with a can or Lysol or Raid. I think there is a den of lizards in the basement to control the fly population. (But that's another story.)

Mostly, I just wear old jeans and one of Erin's "Wheezer" t-shirts and ignore the laundry. Erin is another one that doesn't bother with laundry. She just wears the same t-shirt and Sears cargo shorts all year long.

Actually, she's been wearing the same pair for four years. She recently came up to me asking for duct-tape. When I asked why, she said her shorts needed repair. We both rolled our eyes, knowingly. The Mommygoddess only does mending once a year. If I lose a button off a favorite shirt, I just draw a pretend one on with a magic marker rather than put the shirt in the "mending pile". Otherwise, I'd never see it again. Instead of duct-tape, I showed Erin how to use Crazy Glue to mend most clothing....and we bonded. Literally.

Erin and I share the same sense of humor-- Weird, offbeat, and lots of 'Muppets.' We enjoy watching *'The Simpsons'* or *'South Park'* cartoons, and I keep a telephone message on my answering machine at work where 11 year old Erin apologizes for switching the milk and orange juice in the containers and really fooling Mommy on April Fool's Day. Mommy hadn't been pleased to have orange juice in her Cheerios, while I sat laughing milk out of my nose. Erin and I also share additional time together since it's my responsibility to drive her weekly to her trumpet lessons. This is usually a 40 minute drive, which means it takes me 30 since I have to drive like a maniac because Erin likes to dawdle before we go. During the drive, if she isn't trying to read her homework by flashlight, Erin and I actually "talk". She'll ask me what it was like when I was a child, or what music did I enjoy, or what was my father like. These drives and conversations have always been special for me.

This past year, Erin has been debating whether to major in art or music in college. It was a tough decision for the entire family since she is excellent at both. I'm not making this up. She's won numerous art and music awards and had her artwork in the US Capitol Building. She's also been an All-State trumpet player and received national ranking. Still, she couldn't decide which direction to concentrate in, and both *The Mommy* and I made recommendations. Last December, I drove her to Rochester for the All-State performance at the Eastman Theater. She actually wore long black pants and a cream blouse during the concert, but in the 3 minutes between the finale and when she met me at the stage door, had reverted back into her Sears shorts and a 1970's MASH t-shirt. I reminded her it was December in Rochester, but she was comfortable.

As we drove along the Thruway to return home, I told her Mommy had called and told us to visit a new college she'd been researching. Erin rolled her eyes but said nothing. I told her the college, Morrisville Community College, was a real "sleeper" - no one knew how it rated it academically, but it might be perfect for her, even if it was a little "out in the boondocks". Erin rolled her eyes but said nothing. The previous summer she had taken a music program at Colgate College in Hamilton, NY. Hamilton is not exactly a metropolis. Erin described it as, "What do you call 5 John Deer tractors circling a McDonalds? Prom night in Hamilton."

We exited the Thruway, and drove along winding back roads, passing fields of corn stalks and dairy farms. I felt a bit lost but kept following the directions. Finally, I stopped in a small one building Post Office - Wa-wa coffee shop - municipal Building and Library and asked where Morrisville Community College was. The village Mayor-Barber- Librarian-Clerk (I said it was a small hamlet) said, "Morrisville? Oh, you betcha, you're on the right road, but it's a bit in the boondocks." I said thanks, thinking I was already out, out, out in the boondocks, and returned to the car.

I told Erin more about Morrisville. "It's a great community school. You'll love it. Mommy said they just started their art program and are offering a neat work-scholarship...you get to teach cows how to paint. Remember, there is an elephant at the San Diego Zoo whose abstract painting fetch 6 figures!" Erin rolled her eyes but said nothing.

"Mommy also said Morrisville is expanding and is going to offer a new course in the art of tattooing. You could be a needle cleaner!" I said excitedly. Erin rolled her eyes but said nothing. "Don't worry," I continued, "They have music too. They want to start a Morrisville Marching

Band - and have all 11 of the music students already signed up. The costumes are great, they're made of actual cow hides by the fashion majors. Some even still have the tails and heads attached." Erin rolled her eyes, slunk a bit deeper in the seat, but said nothing."

I continued my sales pitch for Morrisville. "I'm sure you'd enjoy this college. It's not too far from Auburn Prison, and they have a special work release program with some of the less violent parolees. The school won't let them hold the needles, but they can be canvasses for the tattooing class, and also help out with the dairy. There's some debate about whether the college will let them join Marching Band, but they are starting a 4 credit course in kazoo just in case. Don't you think that would be fun??? Oh yummy, I wish I was going to college again!!" Erin said nothing but sunk underneath the seat.

At last, I turned into a frozen muddy driveway, and approached a large barn. I scraped Erin off of the floor of the car and happily said, "Let's go in and talk with some of the students." We walked through the barn door and saw a large ring with several students leading horses around. The students were all dressed as cowboys and cowgirls. Erin looked around but had the look slightly resembling a deer caught in the headlights. As we walked towards a group of students, I told Erin she might be able to take horseback riding as a course and would certainly be able to take the world famous Morrisville course in 'cavalry trumpet playing', even though when she gets to Iraq (did you know that there was an exchange program with the University of Bagdad) they frown on American women on horseback). Finally, I walked up behind a cute cowgirl and said, "HOWDY, y'all! This here's my big daughter ERIN". Erin cringed in complete embarrassment, then the cowgirl turned around. It was Alexis, our oldest daughter. "Hi Daddy and Erin!! Thanks for stopping by!"

263

Erin's jaw dropped. "Gotcha!" I said. "Mommy told me Alexis was competing today with the Cornell western riding team at Morrisville, and it would be nice to stop by to cheer her on."

Erin, looking only a bit relieved, answered" Thanks Dad. I can take a joke. You got me good. So there really isn't a kazoo band or cow painting course at Morrisville?"

"Nope," I laughed, "Just kidding."

"And there's no Auburn prison exchange program or cowhide marching band?"

"Nope," I laughed, "Just kidding."

"And there's no tattoo art class?"

"Nope," I laughed, "Just kidding."

"No tattoo class, that's 'tattoo' bad. Then I guess I really don't want to go to college here. But, Daddy, did you know Alexis has a tattoo?"

I stopped laughing, rolled my eyes, and said nothing. However, on the way home, I wondered if I should try to sell our youngest daughter, K.C. on E-Bay and cut my losses while I could.

CHAPTER 43

A DISTRACTING YEAR FOR DADDYHOOD

Last year was not one of the better years for me. It began with my annual physical at the US Environmental Protection Agency offices. One of the "minor" consequences of working on the Superfund Program, is I get the swell opportunity to work at a variety of toxic and hazardous sites. Most of the time (as a typical government employee) my assignment is to just stand around and watch other people work to clean-up the contamination, but I do have to walk back and forth to my car. One day, my work boots left a trail of pieces, dissolving and flaking apart as I left one of the sites. By the time I got to my car, I was listing a bit to the right with each step. I realized the entire heal had fallen off and the remaining sole was cracked in half which was allowing fluid to soak my foot. When I removed the boots, my socks and feet had turned green from melted boot lining. I washed and added a pair of socks and boots to the drum for disposal, not wondering what I'd been doused with, but wondering if I'd ever get the government to replace my work-boots. A typical day.

Since we do have a potential to get exposed to a lot of things, one of the benefits of this work is we get "medical monitoring', including an

265

annual physical. In January I had my physical. After being poked, sampled, weighed, and prodded, the doctor sat me down and gave me the news.

Doc Spock - "Well, Rob, the news isn't all that good. I'm afraid you're losing some of your hearing, and you have high blood pressure and high cholesterol."

Me - "Oh? What does that mean?"

Doc Spock - "It means you need to cut out the junk food, the smoking, the excess coffee and the drinking, and no more being a couch potato. But, from now on, you'll need to each a lot of green vegetables, like broccoli, and you've got to get out and run at least four times a week."

Me - "And if I do all that, what'll happen?"

Doc Spock - "You'll live many more years."

Me - "During which I can eat more broccoli and run even more?"

Doc Spock - "You bet!"

Me - "Can you just shoot me now?"

Doc Spock - "I'll ignore that, but I also am sorry to let you know you have a double hernia that should be corrected soon."

Me - "Can you just give me a last donut and shoot me now? "

Doc Spock gave me a referral and sent me on my way. I was not a happy camper. I went home, stopping on the way to buy a box of Hostess Twinkies, Slim Jims, Marlboro, Cheeze-in-a-can, a large coffee, and the food of the Gods- Doritos. I sat on the couch, put my bare (and still slightly green) feet on the cocktail table, and watched TV.

"Well, I thought, "a double hernia must be the result of 30 years of rough sex." Actually, I felt fine, had no discomfort whatsoever, and did not at all enjoy the prospect of surgery, especially anywhere in the vicinity of my own body. I can't even watch surgery on TV. I don't like blood, and mine in particular should stay inside my body. My wife, Suzie, and I have a deal. If the problem is spiders, I get to deal with it. If the problem is blood (or children or any combination of the two), she gets to deal with it.

Anyway, I wondered what I might have done to cause a double hernia anyway. It wasn't as if I was a professional weightlifter. Did I get a hernia moving the sofa into a better position to watch TV? Wishing the double hernia was really due to decades of wild and uninhibited sex, instead of just a general breakdown of my body with old age, I called my HMO for a referral for a hernia surgeon. I dialed the referral number and got the actual surgeon himself "Dick". I told Dr. "Dick" I had Standard Government HMO coverage, been diagnosed with a double hernia, asked how he would correct it, and whether there'd be any pain.

Dr. "Dick" was quite enthusiastic and replied, "Well, Robby, first I'd make sure all my tools were in good working order. Then I'd use my chain saw to slice open the trunk a bit above the weak area, excavate down to the 'loose parts' with a garden trowel or maybe a mattock, attach a hook and winch, yank the things back into place and anchor them with a bolt, and finally coat the whole area with tree wound paint. Actually, it won't hurt at all and if I'm in the area doin' work, I can stop by and get it yanked during lunch."

"Yank YOU!" I said as I hung up. I was very upset with the news. I couldn't imagine a doctor actually volunteering to make surgery a house call lunch break. I called back my Standard Government HMO and asked for another referral. As it turned out, the "specialists" for the Standard Government HMO program make annual bids for their services, and the selected specialists are listed in order by the lowest bid. The HMO representative stated that Dr. "Dick's" company, "Dick's Landscaping, Excavating, and Tree and Hernia Surgery, Inc." was the preferred specialist, but if I wanted someone else, I could appeal. I appealed and asked to be referred to a specialist from near the bottom of their list.

267

After meeting with the new specialist, Dr. "Cojones", I felt better, if still a bit uneasy, and scheduled the surgery after the summer season. Dr. "Cojones" advised me to take things a little easy until then. I figured maybe I'd get hit by a truck or a large meteor would destroy the Earth before then so I could avoid double hernia surgery altogether. In the interim, just in case the world or I really did "end", I planned on a camping trip with my daughters at our little heaven on earth, Mongaup Pond in the Catskills. It was an annual treat for my daughters and me for many years. Now that Alexis had graduated from college, and Erin was nearing graduation from High School, it might be our last time camping all together.

I bought all the necessary and absolutely critical camping supplies; a case of beer, hamburger meat, hamburger buns, cheese, Doritos, potato chips, ketchup, marshmallows, chocolate bars, a jar of instant coffee and two more cases of beer. Remembering what Dr. Spock advised about needing a more balanced diet (eat more greens), I added a jar of dill pickles and a six pack of ale. It was a great weekend, except for the rain, the snake, the leaky tent, and the mud. The girls and I played cards, went swamp-stomping, climbed a mountain, got dirty, inspected flowers and plants, and enjoyed a campfire and cooked marshmallows. I didn't think about my double hernia, but laughed and photographed Erin as she balanced beer bottle caps on her closed eyes (a great picture -- sort of like Little Orphan Annie, but Mommy didn't appreciate it.) We also ate our traditional breakfast meal at the Robin Hood Diner in the nearby town, -- a three-cheese omelet with eggs, bacon, ham, and sausages. The girls got inspired by the beauty of Mongaup Pond and we made an oath to rebuild our small backyard fishpond into Lake Froggy.

Erin, surprisingly, was scheduled to graduate from High School the next month, and we were planning to hold the graduation party in our yard. Since I was not really thinking straight at the time, it didn't deter me from agreeing to dig up our entire backyard to build Lake Froggy in time for her graduation party. After all, the girls all eagerly volunteered to help me. Even my normally sane wife liked the idea and gave me an IOU for Fathers Day towards a new pond fountain. So, when we returned home, I immediately began the project.

Two solid weeks of digging later, I realized I was still doing this alone. I'd come home from work, change my clothes (sometimes) and head out into the back yard with a wheelbarrow and shovel. The old, little pond was drained and discarded in no time, and the new hole kept getting deeper, wider, and longer. I began to run out of places to dump the wheelbarrow and built a medium sized bunker in the other corner of my property. I literally moved an estimated 6 tons of soil by myself and realized that might be one reason I'd developed a double hernia. I'd come into the house well after dark, dripping with sweat and covered with brown, slimy clay to find either K.C. or Erin sitting at the computer. They'd look at me and go, "Oh, hi Daddy. Did you want some help?" Each night, they seemed to forget I'd said, "Yes, dammit, I really, really, really, really would like some help digging." Finally, Erin came out to help, but only when I had a camera to record the progress. She had me take two photos of her standing in the bottom of the excavation holding a shovel, then went back in the house, figuring years later, when I'm fully senile, she could show me the photos of her building the pond for me.

Alexis was excused from the excavation project. She had a full time internship and volunteered to take care of my entire lawn, garden, and trees. She actually spent a lot of time weeding and planting things at my house, and even built a small rock garden and a planter which was promptly adopted by a family of baby bunnies.

The pond wasn't quite done by the time of Erin's graduation party, but I filled the liner with water and pretended it was anyway. Lake Froggy was now 21 feet long, 8 feet wide, and deep enough that I could hear echoes from China coming from the bottom. Meanwhile, I was also helping out planting trees, installing fencing, and building rock walls at the local Bird Sanctuary I'd started several years earlier. Yes, The Garden City Bird Sanctuary was another of many "things" I started during my life. It was also another "thing" that never quite got finished.

One "simple" project was to dig up a fifteen foot tree from a neighbor's house and replant it at the Bird Sanctuary. There were two reasons I was reluctant to do this myself, (a DOUBLE hernia) and also, I was also unable to get anyone else to volunteer.

I spent the rest of the summer digging fence post holes and lifting rocks. I also needed rocks to line Lake Froggy, and frequently loaded 500 pounds of rocks into the trunk of my car whenever I was "in the field" for the government. As luck would have it, one Superfund site was next door to a marble & granite counter manufacturer, and I'd spend lunch hours "dumpster diving" for broken pieces of granite slabs.

Eventually I built an entire wall at the Bird Sanctuary with colorful slabs of polished granite and marble pieces, thinking that some future Urban Archaeologist was going to make a unique discovery when they excavate the Bird Sanctuary 500 years from now. Even doing all the heavy lifting, I wasn't really concerned about getting a hernia. After all, I already had two and they didn't seem to bother me. On the other hand, I had already broken my back once, and didn't need or want to ever repeat that incident. It was the impending hernia surgery that bothered me. The main treatment for the broken back was bed-rest (which I got very good at) and lots of prescription drugs (which I got very good at.)

At the end of summer, Alexis left for graduate school (on a full research scholarship!), and we delivered Erin to Ithaca College for her freshman year. Even that trip was distracting. On the way to Ithaca, we joined my wife's family for a mini-reunion at a resort farm, suitably named Suit's Us Farm. The day was pleasant, but that evening we lit a campfire. As we added more wood to the fire, suddenly one of my nephews screamed. Then a niece yelled. Then I felt something on my eye, and as I brushed it away was stung by a hornet. We'd inadvertently thrown a hornet's nest filled log onto the fire, and the hornets were as mad as, well, hornets. We fled back to the cabin. Then, in the rush of running bodies, Erin and her younger cousin clunked heads, and Erin got her front teeth smacked in, which is not a good thing for a trumpet major to do. Suzie volunteered to clean up the blood, while I made sure there were no spiders in the room and wondered if the $30,000, I'd paid in trumpet lessons over the years was going to waste.

Erin eventually survived, but my bank account took another big hit. Finally, as things quieted down at home and the Bird Sanctuary, I scheduled the surgery for November 2. Suzie got me up early, and we met Dr. "Cojones" at the hospital at 6AM. I was worried. I don't know about you, but I am not really awake and functional until about 11:30, and I'm a morning person. Anyway, Dr. "Cojones" gave me a pill, a shot, and then it was 11:30 and I woke up. Holy cow!! I missed my own surgery!

In fact, I felt relaxed and ready to go home to sleep. I asked if he had really operated, and Dr. "Cojones" pointed out my new second belly button and the stitch. That was the extent of the incision. He gave me medication, told me to take it easy for a week, and see him before I went back to work. As Suzie drove me home, I pulled up my shirt and admired my pair of belly buttons. Cool! I wondered aloud if this would be a new fad that would catch on, and if I should get a matching set of belly button rings. How about a Kermit the Frog and a Miss Piggy matched set? Suzie wondered what drugs I was on, got me home, and into bed.

The next couple of days were a bit foggy, but by the third day I felt better. I saw Suzie sitting at our computer and she seemed to be having a bit of difficulty, so I asked her if she'd like some help. Usually, I do not have the patience to try to teach Suzie about anything mechanical or electrical. Instead, I pulled up a chair next to her and for the next two hours sat with her and mildly and politely answered her questions. I showed her simple tips on how to edit or arrange her files. I let her try to work through some of the instructions and only coached her when she asked. Finally, she looked up at me sweetly and said, "Robert. Do you know that you've just spent over two hours together with me, working on the computer, and not once did you even raise your voice? That's wonderful. I like you this way. Whatever it is that Dr. Cojones gave you, please stay on the drugs."

CHAPTER 44

PENGUINS AND DADDYHOOD

As a professional geologist, it is my scientific, personal opinion that the Earth was not created as a result of any Intelligent Design but evolved into the mess it is all by itself. Yes, there are forces much more powerful and mysterious than Man can ever hope to understand. I know this because I married one-- the Mommygoddess of our three daughters. It is SHE who has had to endure the constant struggle to raise our daughters, keep them healthy, and impart on them all of the wisdom and knowledge of the universe and art. I am merely here to do my Daddyhood duties – earn money to pay for all the lessons. I let her be the omnipotent and perfect Mommygoddess since I never was able to find my misplaced guidebook, the *"Rulebook for Perfect Daddyhood"*, and hence I have no clue what I'm supposed to actually do-- except take out the garbage.

I seem to screw this up on a regular basis too, since it's hard to keep track of the difference between garbage, rubbish, and recyclables. Two years ago, I merely tried throwing everything in my neighbor's mulch pile, but after three weeks I found out he didn't have a mulch pile, but he had a backyard fishpond which I had been filling up with newspapers, banana peels, and plastic bottles. He didn't notice, but thought the tide was bringing it in. Men really are stupid!

Last year, I actually tried to give my middle daughter, Erin, some advice. I encouraged her to pursue a music career by going to Ithaca College. I knew I was taking a risk actually opening my mouth to say something besides "Hi-de-Ho, I'm home! What should I nuke for dinner?" I felt safe with this advice since I'd already spent about 12 years and $200,000 on trumpet lessons, Erin was terrifically talented, and already owned not only a professional quality silver trumpet, but also hand-crafted baroque trumpet. She was even getting paid to play gigs!! And, she hated science. When the Mommygoddess found out that I had actually tried to influence Erin, she was not amused. In fact, she lectured me on the many, many, many reasons why I did not qualify to offer any advice to our children, (many of which I agreed with). Her final conclusion was that it really wasn't my fault, but I was literally as stupid as a penguin.

Was I *really* as stupid as a penguin? I had to think about that for awhile. I know I've been called the Village Bird Brain for many years, but I thought that was because I really did start a bird sanctuary in our Village. (That lengthy volunteer effort has enough stories collected for an entirely separate book, which I will title: *"NEVER VOLUNTEER!"*) I planned on doing some research on penguins when fortunately, a documentary movie was released, *"March of the Penguins"*, and I decided it was easier to see that than read a book. I saw the movie…and as I watched it, I had two thoughts. My first thought was I can't possibly be that stupid. These birds make Dodo birds seem like Einstein in comparison (and Dodos are extinct!). My second thought was, "Please, God, no matter how much I screw up in this life don't make me come back as a male Emperor penguin."

Male Emperor penguins must be the most stupid life form on the planet (besides 9 year old boys.) Each autumn, after fattening up on squid, Doritos, and herring all summer long, every Emperor penguin suddenly leaves the ocean and starts walking inland across 50 miles of ice. Why do they do this? The male penguins don't have a clue, they're just following the females who promised them a night of rough sex! Penguins can't fly and don't even walk too well, but guys of any species will do anything for sex, so they walk, waddle, and "bellyboard" up to 50 miles inland across the ice following the gals.

Finally, the females stop, and everyone spends the next week or so trying to decide if the penguin standing next to it is "cute" and a member of the opposite sex. It's hard to tell the difference, and accidents do happen. Finally, when the gals are ready, they signal and the couples...uh, "couple".

The male penguin gets on top of what he hopes is a female penguin and not just another guy who bent over at the wrong moment to pick his toes. Then they "mate" in wild passionate abandon for about 45 seconds. That's it! Over fifty miles of waddling across the ice for less than a minute's thrill and then the female stands up and it's over. I don't think she even asks for a cigarette. She just stands there. So do the male Emperor penguins, wondering if she's just waiting for him to catch his breath for more "coupling" or whether he'll get any compliments on his great "less-than-a-minute-waltz" prowess. I told you male penguins were stupid. This is just typical behavior for any male, but the stupid part comes next.

The penguins just stand there, doing absolutely nothing for the next two solid months! No cell phones, no radios, no Googling on the internet, no food, no nothing! The male and female pairs just stand by each other and wait as it slowly gets darker and colder during the Antarctic winter. They even miss all the sports scores!!!!! Why do the male Emperor penguins do this? Probably because the females say, "Wait, I have a surprise for you," and the males hope it's going to be another delightful 45 seconds of penguin sex. But nooooo, after two months of waiting, the female Emperor penguin suddenly lifts a flap of skin over her feet and behold, balanced on her feet is a single egg. "Surprise!!!" It's like she didn't even

275

know it was there. The Easter Bunny left them a gift. And now they were going to give the gift to the males.

The next activity is the only known Emperor Penguin sport, "*pass the egg*". The female carefully gets in front of the male and attempts to pass the egg from her feet onto his feet. This is not as easy as it sounds. Penguins have no hands, just flipper-like wings, and the egg is big, and penguins, especially ones that have stood around doing nothing for the past two months are a bit clumsy. If the egg slips off the male's feet during the pass, it will roll onto the 80-below- zero temperature frozen ice and freeze within a minute. "*March of the Penguins*" showed films of many couples who lost their egg during the pass and scenes of the penguins watching their egg quickly freeze. The females looked angry, and most of the males looked guilty, but I suspected at least some of them looked relieved because they had an inkling of what was going to happen next.

What happens next is that all of the female Emperor penguins then left the group and began a slow 70-mile waddle back to the ocean. Yes, 70 miles instead of the 50 they'd walked the first time. That's because another 20 miles of ocean had frozen while the waited for the egg. And, the females haven't eaten in 2 months. When they finally reach the ocean water, they have to dodge leopard seals who like to chomp penguin meat, but they have a chance to fatten up again and gossip with the other gals for the next two months. Why? Because all of the stupid male Emperor penguins are still standing in a group 70 miles away, balancing an egg on their feet, and probably wondering if the 45 seconds of penguin sex was really worth it after all. And, it's colder and darker than ever.

One simple fact. There are NO old male penguins. It's a social security plan President Bush would have loved. During the next two months of brutally cold and windy Antarctic winter, the older male Emperor penguins simply die. Every one of them! A few of the younger ones die too. I'm sure a few of them commit suicide when they remember they got fooled into doing this stupid egg babysitting the previous few years. It's completely dark almost 24 hours a day. The winds are up to 125 miles per hour. There is still no food, no beer, and they have to go almost four and a half months without eating. The females are gone. And, they have no idea if the Jets or Giants made the playoffs. I told you male Emperor penguins were stupid. As a matter of fact, I noticed that there were no females among the film crew that stayed in the Antarctic all winter filming the male penguins doing nothing. I guess the female film crews were smart enough to select the Hawaiian parrot film project while the males stupidly got stuck with the Antarctic Penguin project.

When Antarctic Spring finally comes, and the light begins to reappear for more than a couple of hours a day, the newly fattened female Emperor penguins seem to have a change of heart. They leave the ocean water and waddle back 50 or so miles to the males. As they approach, they call out "Hi guy, did you miss me?" or something like that in Penguinese language and the males respond. By now, most of them respond by saying, "Honey, you gained some weight, but you look good enough to eat", but some just lift up the flap of skin over their feet and say, "Holy mackerel!! What happened to the egg?"

What happened is that the egg hatched and standing on the toes of Daddy Emperor penguin was his new darling baby. Momma penguin comes waddling up to Junior and immediately bonds with the baby by throwing up on its head, totally ignoring the fact that Daddy penguin hasn't eaten in four solid months. The male Emperor penguin is then told to beat it and Mommy takes control of the babe. Not even a thank you. The males straggle away towards the ocean, some dropping dead of hunger along the way thinking, why didn't I just eat the damn egg as soon as She left and be done with it? Argh!!....

As I said, male penguins are the most stupid animal on Earth. If I survived my first year as a male Emperor penguin, you can be darned sure that as soon as I reached the ocean again, I'd start swimming toward Hawaii.

CHAPTER 45

DADDYHOOD AND THE OFFICIAL NASSAU COUNTY BIRD

Over the last couple of months, I've learned another lesson – "***Sometimes, simple little tasks become humongously complicated projects***." This is very, very true, and has been ever since the first ancient Egyptian decided to simply stack a few stones in the desert and started a 500 year-long pyramid building craze. The ancient Egyptians are still referred to as blockheads. Enough history. I'm talking about something just as spectacular as King Tut's Tomb – the saga of the "Official Nassau County Bird".

The saga began this past July, when I received a call from a young intern with the Nassau County Legislature Press Office. He introduced himself and asked me if I could recommend a bird for consideration as an "official" bird for Nassau County. Their supervisor, Judy Jacobs was interested in sponsoring the program. I was slightly taken aback and said, "Well I do like lots of birds. I like duck, turkey, goose, chicken, and an occasional Rock Cornish game hen. Why are you calling me? Is this some sort of radio contest? Do I win tickets to a "Byrds" concert? You're not really John Tesh from KJOY radio, are you?"

278

Give the kid some credit for persistence! He didn't hang up on me, even when I told him I was not a bird expert but actually a geologist and an enforcement officer with the US Environmental Protection Agency. He said he called me since I was known as "that bird guy" who founded the Garden City Bird Sanctuary at one of the Nassau County sumps. He also wanted to know whether I knew of other cities or counties that had designated an "official" bird and whether the public would support the concept. I stopped kidding and started to listen. Actually, I didn't know what to recommend and I told him I had to do a little research, but I liked the idea and would get back to him.

A "County Bird"? Well, it's not such a bird-brained idea. I already was familiar with the official New York State bird, the Eastern Bluebird, and knew that designating that particular endangered species as the Official State Bird helped bring attention to the plight of all birds and gave a boost to wildlife education and the environment. Everyone is also familiar with the American Bald Eagle as our country's symbol even though Ben Franklin advocated for the turkey instead. (I can imagine some of the other colonial Congressmen thumping their chests shouting, "We're turkeys!") Clearly, my recommendation had to be an intelligent one (so why did they ask me and not my wife, Suzie?)

Believe it or not, over 400 species of bird have been sighted on Long Island, and not all of them are Canada geese. There are even penguins!! (that's another story.) Our little island is smack in the middle of the Atlantic Flyway, a thousand- mile migration route for millions of birds flying back and forth from Canada to Central and South America. (except, of course, the Canada geese that stop off in Bethpage to play 30,000 rounds of golf.) Which species would best represent Nassau County? A shore bird? A field bird? A dodo? It couldn't represent all of Long Island – which already had adopted (but not officially) the duck! Why we even have a baseball team named the Ducks and there's a large, concrete 'Big Duck' farm stand in

Suffolk dating from the 1930's that been repeatedly relocated as our open space dwindles.

I crossed off many of the species that were considered nuisance birds, exotic alien species, the extinct ones, and ones that were already "claimed" as an "Official Bird" by any of the states, cities, or counties that had an "Official Bird". I inspected the list of over 80 species of birds that have been positively identified at our local bird sanctuary during the past ten years and thought the Tree Swallow an appropriate candidate since they do occasionally nest there and are distinctive enough to be remembered when seen. One neighborhood boy, Alex, even took a fantastic series of photos of the Tree Swallow that I'd mailed on his behalf to the Town of Hempstead calendar contest (only to lose to a photo of a duck). In spite of my fondness for the Tree Swallow, I decided to conduct a simple poll of suggestions with the Bird Sanctuary Directors and our email members group before making a final recommendation.

Well, I learned one thing. Politics and birds don't exactly mix. No sooner than I posted the poll, I got responses. The most popular responses were *"Get me off this mailing list"* and *"Drop my email address from your group or else"* followed by *"I guess you should drop my name too, that nut's going postal"*. Of the two-hundred email group members, I was down to 87 within 2 days. I then started getting serious suggestions, such as the Osprey, Goldfinch, House Finch, Tweety, Donald, Heckle and Jeckle, Roadrunner, and Big Bird. Next came a well thought out pitch for the Piping Plover.

"It is suggested that the Piping Plover be the official bird of Nassau County, as it is most representative of the County itself, especially its residents. Think of the similarities: The Piping Plover is on the Endangered Species List and is threatened with extinction from many outside forces.

The Piping Plover is drawn to the beautiful beaches of Long Island, which are the crown jewel of Nassau County.

The Piping Plover's continued existence is subject to layers and layers of government oversight and regulations, which while well-meaning, have caused the bird to become a symbol of a bureaucracy running amok.

While the Piping Plover likes beachfront real estate, powerful real estate interests try to deny it access to prized beachfront property, much like Nassau County residents who try to gain access to their own coastline.

The Piping Plover is also threatened by cats and dogs that harass it and threaten to overrun its homes, much like the ongoing disputes about undomesticated cats at Jones Beach.

The Piping Plover, like many Nassau County residents, winters primarily on the Atlantic Coast from North Carolina to Florida, although some migrate to the Bahamas and West Indies.

Like Nassau County traffic on the Long Island Expressway, it runs in short starts and stops.

Like the decline of Nassau County's population, the Piping Plover's current population decline is attributed to increased commercial and residential over development since the end of World War II.

Like the young residents of Nassau County, the Piping Plover is having difficulty finding places to live in the area. Much of the Piping Plover's continued existence will depend upon many different constituencies working together to ensure its survival, because without their help and outside assistance, it could become extinct. The Piping Plover is the perfect bird to be the symbol for Nassau County!

That message obviously came from a lawyer. Another message was from Joe G. an accountant, still buried in the office from tax season, who lamented, *"I guess I am truly the stereotypical monocular accountant. They look like sparrows to me :-) I have to get out more often, that whole*

281

widening your horizons...". Even an old buddy, 'King' Tony DiNonno, currently serving time as a guest of the Feds suggested a bird. *"How about the canary? Lots of my friends are here in the joint with me because some-one sang like a canary but it's still a nice bird. See you in another 6 years."*

I also got a good recommendation from my oldest daughter Alexis, currently a graduate student in Urban Forestry at Virginia Tech. She once had a summer intern position with the NYS Department of Environmental Conservation monitoring piping plover nesting areas and she suggested the American Oystercatcher as a Nassau County Bird. I had no clue what she was talking about. I'd never seen one. *"If you see one, you won't forget it! Besides, Oystercatcher – Oyster Bay, get the connection?"* I laughed, but she had a good suggestion and I later learned it was Legislator Judy Jacobs' personal favorite too.

I wrote the Nassau County Legislative Press Office a long reply letter with the findings of my research and suggested three possible candidates for "Official Bird". I suggested that they hold their own "vote" to select the winner. Somehow, this caught their attention. I then got a call saying that the Nassau County Legislature wanted to hold a press conference at the Garden City Bird Sanctuary (or, as my wife refers to it, *'Rob's Big Backyard')*. I reluctantly agreed. This was not due to whether or not I supported the concept, but because the Bird Sanctuary usually looked a bit droopy at the end of August, and there had been no rain the entire month, so most of the area was near death. I knew volunteering for this event meant a lot of work to spruce things up again.

During the two weeks preceding the Press Conference, I organized a group of volunteers and beat the Bird Sanctuary into shape (at least by the front gate). I had hoses watering the parched grass 24 hours a day, weeded, pruned, dug, and replanted to the tune of nearly $1,000 in expenditures. Finally, the day of the Nassau County Official Bird Press Conference came, and the Garden City Bird Sanctuary looked pretty good (at least by the front gate, but don't walk down the lower trail where I buried all the dead shrubs). I even filled all the bird feeders so we would be sure to have a few birds around for the event.

Presiding Supervisor Judy Jacobs came just as the sky opened up with teeming rain to the point that the camera and sound techs just grabbed all their equipment and dove back into their truck. After all that work, we had two short minutes holding umbrellas and hiding together under a tent and letting the County and press take 3 photos. The only "public" that showed up in the rain was a single woman who merely wanted to complain that the County wouldn't clean up the sump in her own neighborhood. Then they were all gone, leaving me wet and wondering how to pay for the $1,000 in expenses I shelled out on behalf of the Bird Sanctuary.

The next day, however, I heard from the Legislature Press Office. They thanked me for the work I'd done and wanted to let me know that the first day on on-line balloting had been a huge success. In fact, they had over 6,000 visits to their web site! The Press Secretary was literally giddy with delight. "Rob, do you realize that normally when a County legislator has a press conference or posts something on the web, they get maybe 100 responses and are happy with that number? This bird vote is drawing a heck of a lot of interest!"

By week's end, there were over 10,000 visits and the votes were increasing faster than the State primary elections. Since my phone number was in the press release, I also started getting phone messages such as: *"How come the House Finch isn't on the list, you Birdbrain!"* and *"My Osprey will eat your Tree Swallow's liver with fava beans for breakfast"*. There were also calls for copies of the ballot by people who didn't have an email address, requests for bird posters, requests to take a sick baby squirrel, offers to refinance my mortgage, and questions like "Where is the Garden City Bird Sanctuary?" I helped those I could and printed 1,500 ballots in our newsletter as well as another 1,000 for distribution. I was now out $2,500 in expenses and couldn't even afford a chicken for dinner.

The voting continued and the news of the voting started reaching many internet sites, including both Republican and Democratic Party "blog" sites. Everyone had their own nomination for County Bird including, "*Nassau Road Kill*", "*Democratic Dodo*", "*Republican Nuke Irano*". Community Action groups proposed the "*Nassau Taxasaurus*", a bird of prey that eats your retirement savings. And, one guy in Maryland who was still peeved I didn't recommend the House Finch. A '*New York Times*' reporter, Vinny M., called me, asking for a "sound bite" for a proposed article on the Nassau County Official Bird. I was impressed. Usually the '*NY Times*' only calls me to ask if I want home delivery, and I figured they'd never call me again after I ordered 300,000,000 subscriptions and told them to deliver them to my post office box in Antarctica. Vinny M. and I talked a bit about the voting, my role as the Village Bird-brain, attributes of each bird, County politics, my three daughters, my wife (the Mommygoddess) and he concluded that he had enough material to quit the Times and start a career in stand-up comedy. The '*Sunday NY Times*' was brief and well-written, but it gave away the news that the Osprey was is the lead! When will news organizations learn to wait until the polls close!!!!??? Now I know how stuff is leaked to the Press!

I stopped in at H. Frank Carey High School in Franklin Square to drop off a few copies of the ballot. As I got to the Assistant Principal's office, I saw a large poster on the wall "**VOTE FOR THE OSPREY! Seahawks Rule!**" This was one of many schools that had taken the Nassau County Official Bird vote to heart. Their school mascot is the "Seahawk", another name for the Osprey! Many of the teachers were wearing "Vote for Osprey" buttons, there was even an Osprey sighting contest going on, where a volunteer wearing the school's Osprey costume would go running up and down the halls. When the students saw him, they were supposed to write down where and when, and rush to the Student Activity Center for a prize, which they only got after they voted. Even the entire bank of school computers was set to the Nassau County Ballot web page. Any student that wanted to use the school computers had to vote first. Lorraine W., the Assistant Principal, was delighted that their bird, the Osprey, was going to win, and grabbed all 250 blank ballot sheets I had brought.

"I'll make sure these are all filled out and will personally deliver them to the County. That's another 250 votes for the Osprey," she laughed.

"Wait a minute," I asked, *"how do you know ALL of the votes are going to be for the Osprey?"*

"Because I'm Vice Principal. Need I say anything more?" she laughed. She said that October 28th was their Homecoming, and also the 50th Anniversary of their school. How great would it be if someone from the Nassau County Legislature came to congratulate their Osprey at half-time. I asked would they still feel OK if the Oystercatcher or Tree Swallow won. She laughed and replied, *"That would be fine, but our Osprey will eat both of them during the half time show instead."*

So much for the Democratic process. Then again, I wished H. Frank Carey School a lot of success, just as I wished Garden City High School students lots of luck when there was a last minute write-in campaign for their school mascot, the "Trojans". That would be an interesting Official Bird! Someone also wrote in my name as Official Bird, but I'm holding out for Garden City Mayor. That would ruffle some feathers!!!! I do qualify for Mayor, since one requirement is to be an idiot. However, I actually was cast as 'Mayor' in our Community Theatre play a few years ago, and there are enough idiots already.

The web ballot clearly states only one vote per email address. I was using the honor system on the paper ballots, and voters didn't have to write their names. However, I was still a Tree Swallow backer, and was tempted to get a rubber stamp and fill out 5,000 votes for the Tree Swallow myself.

Instead, I campaigned. I asked my wife and three daughters to please vote for the Tree Swallow and get their friends to. I found out that my wife had voted for the Osprey and my oldest voted 3 times for the Oystercatcher. I asked her how she had managed this subterfuge and she explained she was being fair. She used her family AOL account as well as her email addresses from her undergraduate school, Cornell, as well as her graduate school, Virginia Tech. Vote early, vote often. The secret of political success in a Republican County.

Election campaigns are cut-throat! Based on her wisdom, I immediately drove to work and voted using my USEPA email and then as the Bird Sanctuary President. It didn't help. Osprey continued to increase its lead after Lorraine W. from H. Frank Carey called a friend in Seattle, Washington and mentioned the vote to 75,000 Seattle Seahawks fans. I located a minor league hockey team in Maine, the Oystercatchers, but they weren't interested unless I bought a season ticket. Damn politics.

So, who will be the Nassau County Official Bird? Will it be selected in time for H. Frank Carey's Homecoming? Will their Osprey really eat an Oystercatcher? Will I eat Crow for nominating the Tree Swallow? Actually, the Tree Swallow is a good candidate with political considerations. The Tree Swallow is very territorial. It doesn't really get along with the Eastern Bluebird. The Tree Swallow actually competes with the Eastern Bluebird, and sometimes steals the bluebird's nesting sites. It's even been known to harass more powerful birds such as hawks and eagles. It's a perfect choice! Nassau versus New York State.

At the end, the Osprey was elected the official Nassau County Bird, and I received a nice copy of the sign advising it's the Nassau Bird, not my little tree swallow. H. Frank Carey High School won the day by adding 5,000 student votes from their computer laboratory and I ate crow for Sunday dinner. I hate politics.

CHAPTER 46

FLIGHT PLAN FOR DADDYHOOD

In addition to being the daddy to three fast-growing girls, during the last 10 years I've spent a good portion of my time as a geologist with the US Environmental Protection Agency (EPA) in New York. I do have to spend some of this time "on the road" but I enjoy seeing parts of the country that I wouldn't have an opportunity to see if I merely stayed in my cubicle. As a representative to the EPA Ground Water Forum, a diverse group of professional hydrogeologists from various EPA regions and State agencies, I also have the opportunity to attend technical meetings where we discuss the latest and greatest developments in many topics - investigative techniques, beer, research breakthroughs, beer and ale, environmental legislative matters, beer & lager, in-situ remedial technologies, and of course beer and brewing. I consider myself an expert on every one of the "other" topics discussed, especially micro-brews.

The 2005 Ground Water Forum conference was in Miami at the annual EPA National Association of Remedial Project Managers (NARPM) Conference, attended by about 500 professionals and one Long Island bird brain\geologist. When they announced that the 2006 conference would be in New Orleans, there were cheers and applause from all 501 attendees.

287

I had never been to New Orleans and looked forward to seeing the sites and hearing some jazz and continuing my extensive, long-term research on beer. I also thought it might actually be possible for me to arrange to bring my wife on the trip. Suzie has been the "Mommygoddess" for over 20 years and had a definite "hands on" relationship with the girls. This was a more than full time job as she spent 25 hours a day guiding their growth. By 2006, however, Alexis would be in graduate school, Erin would be finishing her first year in college, and K.C. had already demonstrated a good maturity and ability to survive without Mommy's constant presence. Suzie was enthusiastic about the trip, and I had more than enough frequent flyer mileage accumulated over the years to provide a free ticket for her.

Unfortunately, God didn't think much of our plans and hit New Orleans with Hurricane Katrina soon after the 2006 EPA conference was scheduled. Over the next several months, many EPA employees went to New Orleans to help with the massive clean-up, but the progress was very slow. Reluctantly, Suzie decided not to accompany me since so much of New Orleans was still uninhabitable. I had hoped to volunteer for some of the emergency field work, but got sidetracked by some surgery in the fall, as well as some surgery my wife needed the following spring. Instead, I volunteered to teach a basic "Introduction to Ground Water" training program at the 2006 NARPM conference. I thought this would be a nice way of putting my talents to good use.

Through the Ground Water Forum, several hydrogeologists planned a half day training session of presentations including an introduction to geology, ground water, and contamination. Everything was meticulously planned, including the graphics, timing, and content of each talk. I learned a lot- especially never to let a group of geologists prepare your talk. OK. Maybe they were right and using a Budweiser bottle label as the background for each of my slides wasn't setting the right mood, but I thought it looked cool. There were months of heavy discussions as to whether the manufacturer supplied "Ocean" or the "Wave" slide backgrounds were more appropriate and a verbal sparring match broke out when I suggested "Crayola" as an alternative. During this time, I "stole" as many introductory hydrogeology figures I could by using the friendly "Google" search engine and completed my technical presentation without much problem. I thought I was "done" until I got 35 pages of detailed editorial comments from the group...which I basically ignored for two reasons: 1), my wife's surgery recovery took up some of my time, and 2), I discovered that the age old question of whether to spell the word "groundwater" or "ground water" had never been resolved.

This was a serious issue! Is the term for water that is under the ground "two words" or "one word", and if two words, when was it correct to hyphenate it? This argument goes back to the days of James Hutton, the Father of Geology, in the 1800's. Apparently this argument has been the cause of war in the Middle East, which is ironic since there is so little groundwater (or ground water) there. That's why I prefer beer over water and can agree with both sides of the other eternal argument "Tastes Great!" or "Less Filling!" Anyway, the geologists and engineers have never agreed on the spelling convention. I have science degrees from an engineering school (Rensselaer Polytechnic Institute, which has a well-deserved motto, "Tute Sucks, Drink Beer") so I was more used to the term "groundwater", but I converted to using the term after reading the Official US Geological Survey Open Report -- "Ground Water and Death to All Engineers", which I suspect was written by a bunch of geologists after quaffing a few brewskies.

Thinking I was "done", I relaxed until I found out one of the other hydrogeologists wasn't going to attend NARPM in New Orleans. I suspected she got wet feet, but I volunteered to also teach on her behalf as a substitute. I was assigned the first presentation, "Introduction to Geology". After all, "geology" is always a one word term (unless you're George Bush) and I've been teaching "Introduction to Geology and Earth Science" for several years at local colleges. Since I hadn't actually prepared this presentation (carefully timed at 26 minutes and 45 seconds), I took advantage of a training course EPA was offering on presentation skills and public speaking. This course was being given at our EPA office in Philadelphia and I was looking forward to two relaxing days in the City of Brotherly Love.

Instead, I got swamped with work and couldn't make a copy of my "geology" presentation ahead of the Philadelphia training. I even had to drive to Binghamton and back to NYC (600 miles) before continuing down to Philly (150 miles) the night before the training started. The next morning, the class started early, and I was still sore from the ride and without my presentation. As part of the training, we were supposed to be videotaped as we gave a short version of our presentation to the group, then watch it and through constructive criticism, improve it for the next day. When I mentioned I didn't have my "slide show" with me, the trainer offered to download it from the EPA computer system for me.

Everything worked out fine, until I realized the EPA computer had downloaded someone else's presentation, so I basically "winged it". I grabbed a marker and doodled a lot of notes on a giant clip board as I talked. Ironically, I received a standing ovation for my talk, but whether it was due to my skill or the fact that I invited everyone out for a beer, I'll never know.

The government-sponsored trip to New Orleans was an experience. As a government employee, we've required to fly "GOV Airlines", not the airline of our choice, or even one of the many cheaper and more convenient flights that exist. It has something to do with government contracting and is why there is a $600 surcharge billed to our account if we need to use a toilet on the flight. GOV Airlines is also known to detour and make unexpected stops to discharge unwary passengers at Baghdad Airport.

The GOV Air flight was only 6 hours delayed, but my baggage never arrived. The only thing I had was a laptop, a DVD of the first season of the Muppet Show (compliments of a Fathers Day gift from my daughter), and an empty beer bottle. My lost luggage was later shown on TV in downtown Baghdad, being inspected for contraband. The GOV Airlines baggage clam service was horrendous.

The GOV baggage claim specialist said it was my own fault for not keeping my eye on the suitcase, and how could I prove I had any luggage in the first place. He charged my GOV account $50 for every form I filled out trying to locate my luggage. When I asked what I was going to do to get clothes for the conference, he replied that FEMA, the Federal Emergency Management Authority would take my name and process my emergency claim, after they deal with 300,000 other displaced and lost people and shoved me out the door.

New Orleans was rocked by Katrina, but not as badly as by FEMA. FEMA is a curse word in New Orleans for their mismanagement of the cleanup efforts, and I'm sure FEMA employees are then offered a job with GOV Airlines. I had no clothes, and almost all the department stores in New Orleans were still out of business. However, the souvenir shops were open 24 hours a day, and for the next four days I bought what limited assortment they had to sell. My wardrobe consisted of a pair of red hot chili sauce patterned boxer shorts, a French Quarter Jazz nightshirt, alligator head beach sandals, a T-shirt that said, "Katrina Beach Lifeguard - Closed, Save Yourself!" and an assortment of FEMA joke T-shirts. My favorite was "FEMA - Fix Everything My Ass".

The New Orleans people really, really must hate FEMA, and had a wide variety of T-shirt expressions using the four letters: "Federal Emergency Mismanagement Agency", "Fumbling Every Major Attack", "Failure to Evacuate and Manage Appropriately", "Federal Emergencies Managed Atrociously", "Funneling Everyone's Money Away", "Federal

Excuse-Making Agency", "Falsely Exaggerated Management of Accidents", "Finally Emergency Men Arrive", "Finally Evaluating Messy Aftermath", "Failure to Effectively Manage Anything", and a zillion slogans starting with F**k, such as "F**k Everything, Massive Anarchy!".

I looked everywhere for even one T-shirt that said something similar about GOV Airlines but wound up teaching "Introduction to Ground Water" to the EPA project managers while dressed in hot chili pepper shorts and a T-shirt that read "Forget Ever Managing Again". Surprisingly, I later was informed that I won an award from the EPA for my teaching. I think it was because of the way I was dressed, and I plan to wear nothing but chili pepper boxer shorts at all future conferences.

The last day of the conference I visited the French Quarter and went into a shop. I was only in there for about 5 minutes. When I came out there was a cop writing out a parking ticket. I looked at the car, then I went up to him and said, "Come on man, how about giving a government emergency worker a f***** break? After all, didn't FEMA help you?" He ignored me and continued writing the ticket. I called him a local New Orleans pig with no respect for FEMA. He glared at me and started writing another ticket for having worn tires. So, I called him a FEMA-head. He finished the second ticket and put it on the windshield with the first. Then he started writing a third ticket. This went on for about 20 minutes. The more I abused him, the more tickets he wrote. Personally, I didn't care. I came into town by bus.... and I had also noticed that the car's bumper sticker identified the owner as an employee of baggage claim services at GOV airlines. I figured this was a better reward than continuing to fight for frequent flyer miles.

I then took a Super Shuttle back to the airport, but not before mailing my alligator head souvenir suitcase and collection of FEMA T-shirts home via UPS. The GOV Airlines plane was only 5 hours late (so I had time to watch the entire 4 hour DVD of the Muppet Show on my laptop), but my suitcase made it home before I did. I'm looking forward to this year's conference, but I'm driving there myself.

CHAPTER 47

THANKSGIVING AND DADDYHOOD

As founder and President of the Garden City Bird Sanctuary, I'm frequently invited as a speaker for a number of clubs and charities. The groups like to hear my lecture about our community nature preserve and birds, and I usually consider myself to be entertaining. I don't accept money for this service, (although donations are accepted for the Bird Sanctuary) but sometimes they serve lunch. I never have a problem eating something someone else has cooked. I like birds. I like ducks. I like geese. I also like turkeys, chickens, and an occasional Rock Cornish game hen. Whether or not pigs can actually fly, I also eat pork. I'm not a vegetarian. I've spent close to 6 decades eating a variety of meat and fish-- even if my 3 primary food groups seem to be only caffeine, nicotine, and salt. I'll also throw in Doritos for dessert.

There's one primary reason I like Thanksgiving dinner. It is one of the few days that everyone in our family eats a meal together. We all actually sit down at the same table for a whopping 18 minutes. Well, maybe not at the same table, but at least in the same room since I have to squeeze an extra table into the dining room to fit all 14-18 of us. The number has gone up and down over the years as the family grew or shrunk depending

293

on a birth, death, marriage, or divorce. Originally, the Thanksgiving table included a highchair as the reserved place of honor for the new family baby. It was so cute to watch the babies eat ground-up turkey, mashed sweet potatoes, and strained peas, and then burping them out onto Grandpa.

A few years later, once the little ones were old enough to sit in a chair and hold a fork, they were relegated to a small table in the kitchen and could fend for themselves. During those years, I sat in the dining room next to Grandma, feeding her ground-up turkey, mashed sweet potatoes, and strained peas. It was a bit more difficult to throw Grandma over my shoulder trying to burp her, but I managed.

Grandma is now at the big "*Denny's in the sky*", probably having an early bird special turkey dinner with Grandpa. I used part of my inheritance to re-build our home and extended the dining room another 6 feet for our growing family. That Thanksgiving was a memorable one, since for the first time the entire family could actually fit in the dining room without spilling over into the living room. We thought we finally had a place for all our family members, but just like George Carlin's comedy monologue, the family quickly grew to fill the space for our stuff. The next year I volunteered to cook the turkey and began to eat in the kitchen myself.

This Thanksgiving, my wife received an ominous telephone call from our middle daughter Erin. She's either a Junior or Senior at Ithaca College (depending on how many tuition payments I'm behind) and became a vegetarian. This is odd since she hates vegetables. I think she's either a pasta-terian or a peanutbutter-arian, but more most likely just a tofu-brain. She and her cousin, Kate – a SUNY Binghamton student, announced that this year all the cousins would cook Thanksgiving dinner. This would be a special treat for Suzie, my wife. Suzie, however, was a bit skeptical of their offer. When pressed, Erin admitted that she and Kate thought that it was cruel to celebrate the slaughter of an innocent animal, and they were going to make a "Tofurky" (a Tofu soy based non-meat based 'turkey') instead.

On the list of life activities, my wife thinks "cooking" ranks somewhere slightly below "cleaning the turtle tanks" and "going to the dentist". She loves it when anyone else cooks. However, this Mommygoddess is also a smart lady. Yes, the girls could cook a Tofurky, but they were also going to cook and serve a real turkey for the family. People should have a choice. Suzie and Erin argued awhile, but they compromised on a "free range turkey", raised with love and tenderness and allowed the freedom to roam the fields and eat real natural food without preservatives and hormones and then gently and kindly "put to sleep" (preferably after prayers to the Great Spirit thanking "Her" for giving the world this turkey). And, a useful and additional word of advice from the Mommygoddess: the girls were NOT allowed to buy it upstate and leave it in the trunk of their car for a week or 2 to defrost. Had I known that advice was necessary to give, I would have become a "Doritos-and-beer-arian" and skipped Thanksgiving altogether.

Preparations for Thanksgiving Day dinner continued despite Suzie and my uneasiness. First, Erin arrived home from Ithaca and immediately disappeared, as usual. Second, earlier in the month I had spent nearly $300 on food that "earned" me coupons for 2 free turkeys at the local supermarket. Yes, "free" turkeys! Somehow receiving a "free" turkey makes shoppers feel better and not notice that their weekly food bills now exceed the annual budget of many developing countries. Third, I spent time consoling my oldest daughter, Alexis, who was not thrilled she'd been volunteered to prepare Thanksgiving dinner with everyone. It was understandable, as she'd been putting in 16-hour days at her job, and certainly puts in her share of help around the house. Fourth, I was told to postpone the annual family Christmas tree decorating until after Thanksgiving Day was over. This was a big sacrifice.

Macy's Thanksgiving Day parade brings back good memories. As a kid in the 1950's, my family went to NYC several times to see the parade, getting up at dawn to take the subway in and standing in the cold for hours. It was always very crowded, and as a short, nearsighted, chubby kid stuck in the crowd, I could never see the bands or marchers as they went by. The only thing I could see were the giant balloons floating overhead, but that was enough to please me, especially if my grandfather bought me a bag of roasted chestnuts as a treat. After Suzie and I had our own family, we stayed home to watch the parade on TV, and the tradition evolved to setting up and decorating our artificial Christmas tree while the parade was on.

So much for tradition. Mommygoddess decided we needed to postpone the tree decorating as there would be too many cousins in the house trying to prepare dinner and it would be distracting. They began to convene at 10AM – Matt, Brian, Emily, Kate, Alexis, Erin, and KC, plunking 400 pounds of assorted vegetables, spices, and mystery stuff from health food stores on our kitchen floor, dining room floor, and hallway. When I saw a small green box, labeled "*Tofurky*", I was a bit curious and opened it.

It looked like a fat, gray bologna or maybe an elephant dropping. The green box was a bit also disconcerting, as it reminded me of the climax of the 1960's science fiction horror movie where Charlton Heston yells out "*Soylent Green is **people!**" to the starving crowd. The Tofurky looked somewhat like a human bicep on steroids, or maybe a football. Alexis and I brought it outside and used it for a game of catch until the rest of the cousins arrived. We had fun. "Hey Alexis," I called, "why did the Tofurky cross the road??? To prove it wasn't chicken!"

It is true that Tofurky is advertised as America's number one turkey substitute. (What's the runner-up???) Tofurky sales have grown 37 percent this year from 2006. The company expects to sell 270,000 Tofurkys by the end of the holiday season, which translates to 438,000 pounds of tofu, wheat protein, canola oil and spices. Tofurky is supposedly very environmentally friendly. Choosing Tofurky over turkey means you're likely to come out ahead on the environmental scorecard. I think some people take "environmental scorecards" to extremes. One eco-advice I heard was if everyone would turn their ovens down from 350 to 345 degrees, it would be like taking 1 million cars off the road. I'd also heard that the President will pardon the National Thanksgiving Tofurky in a ceremony to be televised from the White House lawn. By pardoning the Tofurky the President hopes to demonstrate his commitment to the fight against global warming.

"Tofurkys are raised organically on free-range, solar-powered farms where they are able to reproduce naturally," said the President in a prepared statement. "There's less waste in producing a Tofurky and less waste in consuming one, and it's safer for Vice President Cheney to hunt than a real bird," continued the President. Following this year's ceremony, "Feathers", this year's National Thanksgiving Tofurky, will be sent to the Smithsonian Institute. There it will be polyurethaned and used as a doorstop.

Dinner preparations by the cousins went as well as I expected. Brian and Matt spent most of the time using the kitchen knives top act out their favorite scenes from "*Pirates of the Caribbean*" and made some sort of a cranberry-chutney that mysteriously used up an entire pound of red chili and cumin spice. Neither of the boys showed any appetite for the vegetarian Thanksgiving Day dinner, and they later asked their dad to take them out for another dinner at McDonalds on their way home. Alexis spent a lovely, peaceful, morning with me as we weeded and pruned our garden, but I found her in the dining room that afternoon fending off Pirate Brian. She used his confiscated knife to peel fifty pounds of squash and forcibly mash it into a senseless pulp. She pretended the squash was Erin and Kate who had 'volunteered' her.

I actually did help out. No-one knew how to cook the free range turkey. When I went into the kitchen, Kate was knitting a small quilt to try to keep the naked bird warm, while pleading with the bird to wake up and fly away. The rest of the cousins were afraid to touch it. Matt and Brian offered to hoist the turkey on the ship mast or yardarms, but I intervened since I didn't have any spare yardarms. I gave a demonstration of pulling out the gizzards, neck, and liver from the turkey's cavity, lecturing that these are the parts no-one knows what to do with, so the turkey gutting machines just stuff them back inside the bird for customers to play with. I set the oven for 350 degrees and told them when the temperature of the turkey thermometer reached 175, it's done. The Tofurky went into the oven an hour later.

Meanwhile, K.C. made sweet potato muffins, and redeemed herself in my eyes by tripling the amount of sugar in the recipe. Emily made an orzo casserole -- which I was afraid to eat after I remembered a friendly dog named Orzo that had disappeared. Kate made a pumpkin-corn-onion-pine tree-stew. Erin brought a frozen 'vegan" pumpkin pie (why the vegan froze is a mystery), and Kate brought hemp rolls. Yes, that kind of hemp, but natural, vegan hemp without any of the stuff that made hemp to charmingly attractive to 1960's college students. Erin also made something out of kale, mushrooms, cranberries, and Marsala wine, and argued with Alexis as to whether kale was actually edible or just a decorative plant. I tried burying my portion of the kale compote in our family mulch pile, but the squirrels dug it up and put it back on my porch with a threatening note.

A few hours later, I walked back into the kitchen and asked if the turkey was done yet. No one had checked, and they forgot about the 175 degree temperature notice. I looked in the oven, and the thermometer was glowing red, and registering 195 – the perfect temperature for a well-done pork roast. The Tofurky was also standing by the oven window begging to be released from hell. I ignored it and rescued the free range turkey (which cost $45 for an 11-pound bird, instead of our normally "free" frozen turkey from the supermarket). Surprisingly, the 267 pounds of potatoes and squash in the oven had insulated the bird, and it was still fine.

Dinner was served. The entire table was covered with vegetarian food and the 45-dollar "free" range turkey that glared at the Tofurky sitting on the adjacent plate. Before we ate, Kate gave a short talk on how wonderful it was that the family was together and could share in this natural dinner without harming eggs, meat, or dairy products, and enjoy the Tofurky. Erin gave a short talk that hemp rolls were really cool, and, by the way, she needed another $15,000 for next semester's tuition, and we should all take turns telling each other what we were thankful for. The response was pure silence. Finally, I said "I thank God that Erin is almost done with college and please pass the free range turkey and another hemp roll."

We ate a ton of vegetables and grasses to the point where I felt like it was a herd of cows grazing. I don't remember whether there was any stuffing, but the Tofurky was politely passed around, nibbled at, and then stacked back on a plate. It tasted like a rubbery mushroom. Suzie kept commenting on how proud she was of the girls and that the vegetables were really, really, really.... healthy, and please pass her another piece. My wife is a born martyr. I noticed Suzie ate an entire free range turkey leg and gravy in addition to drowning gravy on all the vegetable dishes. Later, she wrapped up 60 Tupperware containers of leftovers and gave them out to each of the cousins as they left. Around midnight, our doorbell rang. I went and answered it, but there was no-one there - just an abandoned Tupperware full of Tofurky. I buried it in my compost pile and said a prayer to the Vegan Soy God.

I wonder whether other Tofurkys will meet the same fate as ours but decided not to worry. It seems one of the tofu gutting machines at one of the nation's largest Tofurky plants recently malfunctioned, potentially contaminating millions of pounds of chunked, formed tofu product with deadly esoy.coli. Consumers who have purchased potentially tainted

Tofurky were urged to throw it in the street. "Nothing will eat it anyway", said a company spokesman. I'm hoping that next year, Thanksgiving dinner will include real turkey, although higher potency hemp rolls would also be welcomed.

CHAPTER 48

HAIR-RAISING TIMES FOR DADDYHOOD

One of the genetic traits I've inherited is an abundant head of hair. Actually, I have more hair growing out of my ears than some guys have on the top of their head. Unfortunately, quantity is not quality, and as time has passed, my locks of baby-fine blond hair slowly turned into the equivalent of crabgrass on my lawn. It's an uncontrollable stand of coarse, multicolored stalks...which match my eyebrows, much to the amusement of my daughters. I began to grow a mustache as a 16- year- old teenager. This was so I would look more mature and would help me persuade bartenders and 7-11 managers that, "Sure I'm 18 and can legally buy beer." The most common response I got was, "You look like a 16-year-old with a small yellow caterpillar on your lip.", but time passed, and my mustache stayed with me even as my hair slowly turned darker blond, then light brown, then sort of a salt and pepper. The gray hairs became as coarse as fir trees and occasionally I'd find a small nest or owl pellet buried in the mass.

Meanwhile, my wife and I had three daughters...all blondies with blue eyes, and each of them loved having very long hair to the point where Smitty, our local plumber, was on first name basis with everyone in our family since he had to come over frequently to unclog our sinks and

301

bathtub from long blond hairballs. Erin, in particular, has hair that exceeds 3 feet in length, and can go mountain climbing without a rope. She would hate it if I even tried to even off the uneven ends with a delicate trim. I'd have to show her the six strands that I cut, and she would take the hairs into the back yard to bury them next to the gerbils, frogs, newts, and other sorely missed house pets.

K.C. was born with basically no hair, just a few wisps of short cotton candy. It was fun to rub her head for luck, but many times I left a smear of Snickers or Cheetos yellow across her scalp. Eventually, her hair filled in, and she let it grow, and grow, and grow. She has donated a foot of hair on three separate occasions to "Locks of Love" -- a charity that makes wigs for cancer patients. Alexis's hair stays mysteriously blonder than would be expected naturally. She denied bleaching it, saying "It's the sun! I swear, it's just the sun! A giant sunspot jumped out of no-where and bleached the ends!" It doesn't matter, and she looks good with a Palomino blond ponytail and bangs. She even styles her boyfriend's hair, and he has gotten used to orange or blond streaks through his Mohawk. All the girls like playing stealth hairstylists. When the girls were little, I'd wake up from a nap to find hundreds of Barbie and My Little Pony barrettes glued to my head, but fortunately K.C. was the only one who had a friend play stylist with her and a pair of scissors.

My wife and I survived the "Big Hair" look of the 1970's, and her shade of red has remained Dark Auburn #2 unless I "accidentally" buy Strawberry Blond #6 or Copper Penny #3 from Clairol or Revlon. She used to have long, wavy waist length hair. It was her trademark. She cut it short while I was away for work in Saudi Arabia for several months. I didn't recognize her at the airport when I returned to Long Island. She didn't recognize me either since I had not gotten a haircut the entire 5 months, had lost 25 pounds, and my skin was 7 shades darker than before

I left. Sadly, her once extra-long red hair trademark never came back… She said it was too difficult to take care of long hair while raising the kids.

Men's hair styles have shifted back and forth from long to short, sideburns or no sideburns, all within a basic 4-inch length tolerance. For awhile I brushed it straight back, but somehow, the blown dry, brushed back look never made me look good in a polyester leisure suit…. especially with my trademark, small potbelly. From 16 through 50, my mustache was always there. It was something to chew on between snacks. In late 1999, shortly after my sister died, I shaved off my mustache. While my head hair was slightly salt and pepper, I'd realized that many of my mustache hairs were white or gray. Only a few holdouts were still "blondish", and I wasn't sure if it was merely coffee stains. So, I shaved it off. It didn't make me look any younger, and I still couldn't buy beer at 7-11 with or without it. Goodbye old mustache, old friend.

Working for the US Environmental Protection Agency during the last decade has had a significant effect on my lifestyle. The EPA is relaxed about what the employees wear to work. I used to be a white shirt, tie, and jacket regular, but the only ones who ever wear a tie and jacket at EPA are the defending attorneys of "Potentially Responsible Parties" who are hired to defend companies potentially facing multi-million dollar costs for cleaning up contaminated sites.

Apparently, the attorneys feel that they need $5,000 suits and $100 hairstyles to look "smart" and to justify their $1,000 per hour fees. So, if the attorneys have to wear a suit and tie to justify their $1,000 per hour consulting fees, they have my sympathies. The only other people who wear a suit and tie in the EPA offices are new people coming in for a job interview, and frankly, we don't see too many openings with today's Federal budgets. Meanwhile, I've saved a ton of money not having to buy suits or get haircuts on a regular basis.

Actually, I wear a tie to work on Mondays and Tuesdays. It's because I teach geology at a local college Monday and Tuesday nights, and I feel I need to give my students a reason to justify calling me Professor "A" in addition to paying over $1,000 for my course. My co-workers at EPA always comment when I'm wearing a tie. They wonder if I'm going to a job interview, and I've actually had a couple of co-workers wish me good luck or caution me that wearing a Kermit the Frog necktie and worn out jeans isn't exactly a corporate image many companies expect unless Ben and Jerry need a geologist. My response is that I have over 40 frog neckties, and if that isn't enough to get me hired by the Henson Company, I don't want to work there anyway. Besides, Ben and Jerry rejected my suggestion for Beer-nutty lager ice cream.

Last year, it seemed that many of my younger co-workers were favoring crew cuts. Short hair was very "in", as were tattoos. If I'd had one more beer at a conference in Philadelphia, I'd probably sport a Kermit the Frog tattoo. I stayed sober enough to decline to needle my arm with a space alien frog that the tattoo artist and my co-workers insisted would be a "cool" alternative. Instead, I went to my barber, Antonellas, in lower NYC and got a micro-crew cut in October. It was very military looking, which pleased my co-workers with the US Army Corps of Engineers. I was also surprised to note that I now actually had to shave my ears. For the first time in decades, I actually had to be careful of getting sunburn on my scalp. Still, it was "cool" and less permanent than a space frog tattoo. Hair grows, and mine seems to grow faster than bamboo in the tropics.

By Thanksgiving, my hair had grown back to its normal shaggy length, and by Christmas my wife advised me I needed a haircut. My ears had disappeared again, and the back of my neck was down well below my collar line. The day after Christmas, I accompanied Suzie and the girls to the Metropolitan Museum of Art. December 26 is my wife's birthday, and KC wanted to treat her to a special gift…an art tour at her favorite museum. It was a nice afternoon, but what I was most impressed by was seeing two separate men strongly resembling Santa Claus at the museum. Both men had long wavy white hair and full flowing white beards. Each Santa had a pot belly and was wearing a flannel shirt. They both looked tired, and it was clear that this was their first day off after a full, hectic Christmas season at some local department store.

They were relaxing and looking at the exhibits. Occasionally, a little kid would be dragged away by his parents, pointing at Santa, and either happy to see him, or upset that the rocket-launcher the kid wanted for Christmas didn't fire REAL rockets. The Santas didn't even seem to notice, but I had an epiphany. Next year, I'd get a third job as a Santa Claus. This would be a cool way of earning extra money. All I'd have to do is sit and occasionally ask, "What do you want little girl?" which I've had plenty of experience doing as the Daddy to three daughters.

The first part was easy. I simply stopped shaving and cancelled the haircut I'd planned at Antonellas. I began practicing "ho-ho-ho" at night, and developed excuses to my wife on why I didn't shave. A couple of weeks later, however, I realized I don't have a Santa Claus beard and never will. What I have is a Lincoln Beard, and there's not much demand for Christmas season Lincolns. Sadly, I shaved off the beard, but kept my slowly re-sprouting mustache.

What was personally worrisome was that my head hair had not only caught up with my graying facial hair but lapped it. During the last 9 years, mostly because these were my daughters "teen years", my hair was now basically salt and salt. Mostly white, some gray, and a few very defiant blond, brown, and black hairs holding out in the back. My wife keeps saying my white hair looks good, and makes my blue eyes stand out, but I notice she's still Dark Auburn #3.

I'm resigned to having whitish hair mainly because I have to laugh that there's a lot of it. Almost every new barber I've gone to has remarked,

305

"You've got a LOT of hair!" And then he would charge me double the normal price to re-style my head nest, while the bald guy next to me glared at me while getting the mole hair on his shoulder pinned to his ear and then carefully wrapped back and forth across his head in the comb-over to end all comb-overs. A few years ago, the graying color of my pate bothered me, and I tried coloring it. Yes, it made me look younger, but it was not natural looking and too much of a nuisance to maintain. The color and texture reminded me of a dead porcupine on my head (but at least a young-looking one!). However, as the hair grew out and the white roots showed, it looked like a dead porcupine floating on a glacier of ice.

By February, my fast-growing hair was taking a life of its own. One of my co-workers stopped me and said, "you know, you look like someone..." which I thought was odd, and replied, "Yes, Mike, I look just like Rob Alvey who's worked in to cubical next to you for the last 5 years."

"No," Mike answered, "You look like Samuel Clemens!"

"Mike, I'm Rob Alvey"

"No, you're.... Albert. Albert Einstein! Or Mark Twain.... Or Hal Holbrook!"

And so, it began. My mustache had filled in and spread well over my lips. My eyebrows were also becoming more Spock-like, and I was frequently picking small, dead birds out of my hair. Other co-workers began to call me Mark. My daughter Erin visited my office and thought I was starting to resemble an Albert Einstein poster I keep by my cubical. It was becoming fun to go to meetings and start the meeting by announcing I was growing my hair for "Locks of Love". The discussions that followed usually were regarding who I resembled more: Einstein or Twain. Or, possibly the OLD Kurt Vonnegut.

I didn't care but I was more worried that all the people that I was being referred to were all dead. In March, Erin took photos of me dressed

306

as all three, and made large black and white prints she sold on campus to raise money for the next semester's tuition at Ithaca College. The school graduated her early to avoid a mistaken copyright infringement lawsuit by the Twain estate. My own York College students also seemed a bit interested in the slow transformation for Professor A into Professor Einstein, especially when I occasionally began lecturing using a German accent. One of Erin's "Rob Einstein" prints showed up on the York College science wing hallway next to a biographical exhibit on Albert.

In April, I travelled to Philadelphia for an Army Corps of Engineers conference. I knew a lot of these folks from my work at EPA and we all wore a name tags, but people I've worked with for nearly 10 years kept coming up to introduce themselves to me. No one recognized me and one engineer even contacted Homeland Security to report that someone had stolen Rob Alvey's ID tag and was impersonating Mark Twain. Dean, one of the Corporate Lawyers with whom I deal with on an interestingly complex contamination case, also enjoyed discussing my hair at meetings, especially since he gets paid $1000 per hour for discussions. He is very smart, and I respect his knowledge, but the "Corporate" that hired him must think he's absolutely brilliant since he has the chutzpah to have the same thick mustache and exact duplicate hair style as George Armstrong Custer, a blondish ponytail. He also doesn't bother with $5,000 suits.

By June, my youngest daughter, K.C., was getting ready to graduate from High School, and worried that instead of having her Daddy take her to the traditional Father Daughter High School Dance, she'd be going with Albert Einstein. Alexis came to the rescue and dragged me into the bathroom where she sat me down and cut my hair. I mainly obeyed since she kept a pair of sewing scissors pointed 3 inches in front of my left eyeball and I prefer to be able to use both eyes. I did manage to keep my hand carefully protecting the top of my head, so the haircut massacre was only half successful. Instead of a comb-over, I had a comb-under, and my ears could disappear until the next stiff wind rose what looked like a kite sail on my head.

The Father-Daughter dance was a great evening, and the 3 pounds of hair gell on my head kept my hair style suitably presentable. And, I even wore a suit to the dance. A couple of weeks later, I tumbled into Antonellas Barber shop again and said to give me the usual. Georgi, the barber, spent a few minutes in the back room closet and came out holding a weed whacker. And a hard hat. And Safety glasses. His last words before pulling the starting cord were, "You've got fantastic hair…and I've *missed* it." VRUMMMMMM!!!!

I went from no haircut in 6 months to 2 haircuts in two weeks but having a "normal" cut just wasn't satisfying anymore. I finally asked Alexis to help, and she brought me out into the back yard, sat me on a lawn chair, and used scissors and shears to give me a new crew-cut. Sorry Locks-of Love, I can't hold out to grow a full ten inches of gray asparagus shoots. People sent me sympathy cards. One co-worker gave me a copy of a recent Time Magazine with a painting of Mark Twain on the cover. He was going to ask me to autograph it. I looked sadly at the cover. "Well," I thought, "what the heck, it's almost time to start another semester. Besides, with gasoline shooting past $4 a gallon, I'm not going to be able to afford too many more haircuts."

CHAPTER 49

BOXES AND DADDYHOOD

This year may have been a financial meltdown for many folks, and our family is not immune, but we've never had much of a financial to melt. Raising three children on Long Island is a tremendous monetary stress for many families, and our own bank account has been under strain for over 2 decades. The last time I looked, my checking account had a balance of $47-- and 2 cents. Financially, I have to frequently practice my magic act. I have many more bills to pay than my remaining $47 checking account balance can cover, but I'll keep the 2 cents for my own use. I earned it, although it came with a lot of advice attached to it. Getting kids through college isn't exactly easy. I tried to tap our family "found money bank" for some additional cash, but even that small, pewter container was empty.... with only an IOU and a receipt for milk inside. I looked at the empty coin container in our bedroom, and realized it was a child's bank, given to our oldest daughter, Alexis, nearly 25 years ago. Time goes by quickly whether you're having fun or not.

Actually, this was a good year. Our house is a little emptier, a bit quieter, and a lot more spacious. For the first time in 25 years, we have no children living "at home". Alexis, our firstborn, has taken the plunge and purchased a condominium in Suffolk County with her boyfriend. (Welcome to the land of eternal debt!). They packed up her room as well as her additional boxes from the basement and attic. We even emptied out the furniture she'd been storing in our garage since she returned from her graduate program at Virginia Tech.

I blessed Ali, and welcomed the temporary return of storage space in my garage until I had to buy 30 storage bins to hold the accumulated Halloween decorations and the prizes we keep for the Halloween Fests we run at our local bird sanctuary\community nature center. My basement even had some new room for me to be able to stand up straight among the cartons and shelves! Carrying out Ali's boxes was a delight, but her boyfriend had my sympathies as I carried box after box after box labeled "Alexis's shoes" and I shuddered to think of the "closet wars" they would eventually have when they unpacked.

Having Alexis move out was a bittersweet time. I had been storing a set of fine, gold trimmed Limoges dinnerware in my basement for over 30 years. It had been my grandparents set of fine china that my sister and I had inherited. It was a full, complete service for 12, with enough serving platters and bowls to feed an army of relatives. When my sister, Maureen, was dying several years ago, she gave me her half of the set, designated for Alexis. Maureen had four sons, and the fine Limoges china was her gift for the daughter she never had. I kept it carefully wrapped inside of old newspapers in boxes in the basement. My own household had only used the china once, a few years ago at Christmas. Now it would go to its new owner- so Alexis could store it in boxes for the next 30 years. She asked if she could sell the china. I told her only after I was dead, but she could look forward to possibly giving it to her own children someday so they could store it in their own house.

Not one week later, I came home to find a purchase receipt for a set of 12 more complete place settings of fine Limoges china. After getting up off the floor and dunking my head in the toilet, I asked my wife why and where she had decided to buy more fine china. I glanced at the price tag

310

and immediately met the floor again-- face first, and a bit harder than the first time. Apparently, Suzie was not merely feeling sorry for the empty shelves in our basement that no longer had the lifelong job to hold boxes of Limoges china. She was concerned that we were showing favoritism to Alexis, so felt it would only be fair to buy a set for Erin and K.C.

I reminded her that our checkbook balance was $47.00 (I withheld the extra 2 cents.) She then informed me that she was splitting the cost with her dad, but then clarified that he wasn't actually paying for half of it but was merely lending her half the deposit. And, the new set was such a bargain!!! Did I know the Limoges representative appraised our old set at many thousands of dollars??? It was only when I reminded Suzie that I had two more complete boxed sets of fine china in our basement and they were reserved for K.C. and Erin, that she reluctantly cancelled the order with Limoges and handed me my dinner… on a paper plate.

Our "babygirl", K.C., started college in September at Cornell University – planning on saving the world, the environment, and human-ity—with enough spare time to learn rock climbing, do some backpacking and hiking, tutor high school students, and serve food to the homeless. We packed her off with a full van of essentials: clothes, sheets, blankets, pillows, books, dishes, cooking utensils, camping equipment, stereo, com-puter, photo albums, suitcases, several storage boxes, a Christmas tree, an organ, a bicycle, and her collection of 178 My Little Ponies in boxes. A few weeks later she called and asked if we could bring up her winter coat and gloves, since it was now early October and the glaciers had already advanced onto Ithaca, and while we're coming, please bring 200 sand-wiches for the local soup kitchen. God bless K.C.. I could buy a lot of pea-nut butter and day-old bread with $47. The house is a little less cluttered.

Meanwhile, our middle daughter, Erin completed her undergradu-ate studies at Ithaca College earning a BS degree, and she began to think about what she wanted to do for the rest of her life. First, she lived in the woods awhile photographing birds and rattlesnakes, rescuing bear cubs, and collecting bones and ticks. (I do not make this stuff up!) Later she lived in Brooklyn with her Aunt Lenore studying art at Pratt Institute but found Brooklyn to be too 'wild' for her tastes. After her final exams, Erin left for Costa Rica with a backpack, tent, and camera to go rock climbing and volunteer at an "ecology center". She let us know this was a "well-planned" adventure that she had found on-line 2 days earlier. Erin likes to live "at risk". Living at risk is like jumping off a cliff and building your wings on the way down.

Before she left, an employee at the "ecology center" asked Erin if she could bring down a large box to Costa Rica for him. It arrived via UPS and sat in our foyer for a week before the flight. It was a crude, banged up cardboard box, weighing about 50 pounds. We wondered what was in it and how Erin would get it through customs. My wife was sure it was full of cocaine, but I reasoned that no one smuggles cocaine from the US into Costa Rica, but to make absolutely certain I volunteered to open the box and sniff what was inside. If it actually was cocaine, I planned to take several sniffs to be perfectly sure. Fortunately, or unfortunately, depending on who's sniffing around it wasn't cocaine or other assorted drugs, but pots and pans and underwear.

If I don't get a phone call from Costa Rica asking me to identify a long-haired, female body found at the base of a cliff, Erin plans to move back to Ithaca to live and do "something". I think Erin is merely avoiding being forced to actually clean up her room at our home. When she announced that she wasn't going to continue with her graduate degree studies, she expected me to explode. Instead, I suggested that we convert her bedroom into a new art studio for my wife, Suzie. Suzie liked the idea of finally being able to move out of the damp, dark, cricket cave, I mean basement studio, I had built for her. It was ironic that I'd started to build it over 21 years while Suzie was pregnant with Erin. I'd gotten about 92% done before Erin was born...and the other 8% never got finished (but it's on my list of things to do!!) All we had to do was clean out Erin's bedroom and move 30,000 pounds of Suzie's art and craft supplies up two flights of

312

stairs. (I'm exaggerating, it is only 28,935 pounds.) At least a lot of Suzie's supplies are already in boxes.

To accomplish this Herculean task, I had to buy some more boxes. Erin is as much of a packrat as the rest of the family but is box-challenged. Instead of putting her stuff neatly into boxes, labeling them carefully in Magic Marker, and storing everything neatly in the attic or basement, she merely dumps things into piles or stuffs everything into maddeningly thin cheap plastic food bags. I bought 12 new, heavy plastic, bright green, and brighter red storage containers from Home Depot (I'm starting to color code the boxes!) and dumped many of the plastic food bags into them, stacking up one corner of the room to the ceiling. That pile was just her grade school art projects.

There are still extra-large, framed photos of dead squirrels and dead frogs in the "art studio to be" that I can't fit into a box, and another 400 pounds of stuff that she volunteered to hold for a neighbor who no longer had storage space in his new apartment. Meanwhile, I'm trying to figure out how I can stretch a $47.02 checking account balance into buying the new paint and plaster we need to refinish Erin's former room after scrapping off a 15-year collection of comic strips and bumper stickers that Erin had glued to the walls. Or, where to put the 6 live turtles and 6-foot long turtle-tank that Erin had left behind for me to take care of.

I'll miss all three girls, but it won't prevent me from changing the front door lock. The oddest part was when my wife returned home from dropping Erin off at the airport. She saw me in the kitchen and was startled. She asked, "Who are you? What are you doing here?" I merely replied, "Remember me? I'm your husband. I've been hiding in a box in the basement the last 25 years waiting for the Mommygoddess to finish her work. What's for lunch?"

CHAPTER 50

DADDYHOOD GETS SET-UP, A CHRISTMAS STORY

This year, my #1 daughter- Alexis, began a blog as "Long Island's Garden Girl" about useful tips on landscaping and gardening. I've been following it on the Internet and suggest you also follow it on her website at: http://longislandsgardengirl.blogspot.com/2010/12/christmas-tree-conundrum.html#comments.

Her article for December 6th begins:

"December is always an eventful month, full of festivities, parties, and traditions. My family has always gotten a head start on the holiday season by setting up the family Christmas tree the day after Thanksgiving. My sisters and I would look forward to helping my dad haul up the artificial tree from the basement where it was stored for 11 months of the year, along with the boxes and boxes of Christmas ornaments. We seriously had enough ornaments for three or four trees. Each year we seemed to accumulate more and more – my mom could never part with the delightful, homemade ornaments my sisters and I made in grade school out of paper plates or glittery yarn, and my dad could never part with his beloved Peanuts or Star Trek ornaments. Secretly I couldn't really blame him for the Start

314

Trek ones – I mean who wouldn't want a miniature electronic Starship Enterprise ornament that could announce the arrival of Dr. Spock at the push of a button?

One year though, after noticing that the tree had begun leaning under the weight of all the ornaments, we decided to not put so many up, be more tasteful, and go with a themed Christmas tree. Unfortunately, my dad decided to go with a frog theme and "tastefully" displayed his entire collection of Kermit the Frog and Miss Piggy ornaments. This really brought about a good dose of teenage embarrassment when any of my high school friends came over to visit during the entire month of December and were able to witness the "Frog Tree" in person. But without an artificial tree, we would have never been able to set up the Christmas tree so early."

So, naturally, my first reaction as "Daddy" was, "Kermit rocks and so does Spock!", but actually I had a bit of remorse that I'd ever been a source of embarrassment to any of my daughters. I'm used to being a continual and everlasting, perpetual source of embarrassment to my wife, Suzie. (Note: Suzie reads and edits all of my writing to minimize any mention of things that might be a source of embarrassment to her. I, on the other hand, am mostly clueless that what I write might cause an embarrassment concern and my only rebuttal has been, "Well, it's all true isn't it??" and finding ways such as reducing the font size in the text to try to sneak something questionable past her. It never works.)

Besides, I'd already decided I was too tired to even bother putting up the Christmas tree this year. I'm slowly being retired from my role as "Daddyhood" since our former 'babies' and then 'teenagers' are now all in their twenties and assuming their proper and rightful place in society as mature adults (except Erin-- but that's another and much longer story! Besides, Erin takes after me the most.)

My family has always had a fondness for the Christmas season, and we don't include Black Friday as a special day. My wife likes to plan ahead and usually starts shopping in January. She considers it her goal to never, ever have to go near Roosevelt Field Shopping Mall after Thanksgiving, so tries to get her Christmas shopping done by July 4. What we also share is the annual setting up of Christmas lights, the Christmas tree (or trees), Manger, wreathes, ornaments, candles, my childhood model railroad set, petrified fruitcakes (I thought they were either Christmas decorations or heavy duty door-stops), and an ever-growing collection of other Christmas decorations. Set-up and take-down takes months.

With a crafty wife, a frugal mom, and three artistic daughters, we've also become accustomed to a tradition of creating our own hand made ornaments and decorations. The Christmas season doesn't get this attention all by itself, and our home was always a perpetual Macy's window display of Valentine's Day macaroni hearts, St Patrick's Day tissue paper shamrocks, Memorial Day crayon flags on toothpick sized flagpoles, and the annual Halloween lights, pumpkins, and frog-witches and frog zombies. All three daughters attended the same nursery school and as a result we even had three of each of the annual seasonal crafts projects they made, including 3 large colorful plastic tissue Christmas wreaths.

Therein lays one of the problems. To keep things equal and not show favoritism, I set up all three copies of their crafts projects. That is good. I also have to store all three copies of their crafts projects for 11 months a year. That is bad. I also have to find and locate the individual boxes that hold the seasonal decorations and crafts. They are somewhere in my basement, and that is very, very, bad. The basement is more than a wee bit cluttered (Times Square on New Year's Eve is just an empty, isolated desert in comparison). Also, I personally never met a label that had the courtesy to actually stay on a storage box. Sometimes I've used a heavy black Magic Marker to boldly print a description of what's in the storage box. That isn't effective since I repack boxes with different stuff each time. Erin, following my example, merely labeled her own boxes "Erin's junk" and nobody dares to look inside them.

It also doesn't help that my idea of cleaning up is to just stuff everything within my immediate reach into a box regardless of whether it was supposed to be in the box. (Anyone see my cup of coffee? It was here 5 minutes ago.) Some boxes haven't been opened for years, but I'm sure if I looked hard enough, I'd find the pet gerbil we misplaced in 1998. I'd probably try to make a Christmas ornament out of it. Those strands of Christmas lights are another problem. They actually aren't very expensive, but when one bulb burns out, the entire strand goes dark. I have to unplug each of the 50 lights on each of the 30 strands to find which bulb burned out.

Usually, I get frustrated and simply pull out all the bulbs and color coverings and put them in a bag as spares for the next year. I then drive over to my favorite shopping stores-- Home Depot or 7-11 and buy 5 more new strands of Christmas lights. I have a 32 gallon garbage bag in the basement filled with spare bulbs and colored covers and have learned that different manufacturers (or demonic Santa elves) make slightly different style bulbs purposely just to frustrate daddies everywhere.

It was always a tradition in our family to set up our Christmas tree on Thanksgiving Day during the Macy's Thanksgiving Day parade. Yes, we use an artificial tree, and it has served us well for many years. Our young girls were always delighted to observe me trying to set it up since it had about 200 individual branches that needed to be inserted in the correct holes and since I'd lost the instructions years ago, I invariably had branches left over. As a result, even though we used the same tree, it took on a different appearance each year with one or a dozen wayward branches sticking out at new spots. As our 1983 vintage TV showed Kermit the Frog, Snoopy, Spongebob and other giant balloons sailing along Manhattan streets, our tree slowly took shape and was filled with frogs, green lights, frogs, Star Trek ornaments, frogs, hand-made ornaments, frogs, photo ornaments of the girls, frogs, and a few more frogs. The rest of the house was also covered with Christmas frogs, Kermit, and Miss Piggy, and a few thousand handmade decorations. (Why should a house be limited to a single piece of mistletoe, when you could have 6 pieces and several 'mistle-toads' hanging from the ceiling?)

The Christmas set up also was a time for nostalgia, remembering my grandparents and other relatives who have passed on. My family was not financially well off. My mother's parents lived in a simple apartment in Brooklyn, and Pa Turban was a brewery mechanic. One decoration I inherited was a simple metal cookie tin that had been painted and had letters stamped out spelling "Merry Christmas" in a simple 1930's style with a light bulb wired inside. Another was a plastic Santa Claus, also lit with a red lightbulb, an ornament made of a simple seashell with a decal pasted on it, and a series of ornaments made from curtain rod rings my mother had crocheted with 'A' or a small wreath. For several years I also put up my set of childhood model trains at Christmas. This was the exact same set I used as a kid, until after thinking I was too old to play with them anymore, had given to my sister for her own boys to play with. A decade later she gave them back to me to use with my own children. Bless her!

There were also ornaments made from cookie dough, pinecones with sparkles glued, several ornaments with photos of our girls as babies and as they got bigger, even a cardboard ornament of an Elf I'd made a half century ago in elementary school. As our girls have grown and matured, the house, which used to be piled deep in My Little Ponies, Legos, and Barbies, now is merely stuffed to the rafters with papers that need filing. I even gave away our pet turtles (except for George, a psychotic red-eared slider that Erin had adopted.) No more Little Tykes oven remained in the den. I still remember when I found what looked like a flat, dried pancake in the Little Tykes oven many years ago. It turned out to be the dried out remains of one of our African water frogs that had mysteriously disappeared. Once we realized that it was not actually a piece of Little Tykes plastic beef jerky, we concluded it was the missing frog. It had apparently jumped out of its tank, hopped across the den rug, and into the toy oven without anyone realizing it.

As the Christmas spirit finally took hold of me and gave me a good, hard shake, I got the Christmas tree out of the basement. I also brought up another 3 boxes of a set of Grandma's best china (which hadn't been unwrapped since 1968- just after Grandpa Turban died), and trunks and boxes of all the decorations I could find. I brought a few over to the Garden City Bird Sanctuary, a local nature preserve I had founded years ago, and set them up on a tree donated in memory of Michael, one of my neighbors. I added a few garlands around three other small pines, and a couple of wreaths on the fence. These donations actually didn't make a dent in our collection. This year, I separated all of the home-made decorations and grouped them all in the dining room, covering the windows with handwritten notes to Santa. Some of these decorations were so cute, (usually the ones made by the 4 artists in our family), but others were a bit pathetic- the ones I made myself. Some even defied description. Deep inside one box I found one ornament that sort of resembled a furry reindeer – but the antlers must have broken off a long time ago and the legs didn't look right. No name was written on it, but it certainly looked home-made, so I stuck a hook in it and added it to the family collection on the tree.

I was actually proud of the way I'd assembled and set up the family collection and was eager to see what the girls thought. I hoped they wouldn't be embarrassed. A few days before Christmas, we had a great surprise. Erin came home to Long Island for a short visit. She had left home over a year ago to seek a career in Colorado....but only actually got there last month. (It's a long story and includes a few months on an uninhabited volcanic island in the Aleutian Islands and you can always go online to look at the pictures she took before her camera broke.) Anyway, she greeted us with a kiss and immediately went over to our Christmas tree and pressed the Star Trek shuttle Christmas ornament to hear Mr. Spock say, "Live long and prosper." Then, she counted the frogs. Then, she spotted the "family corner" in the dining room. She looked at the handprint wreaths made in nursery school, the clay snowmen, ice-cream stick snowflakes, and responded in a typical Erin manner, "Hey! How come you got more stuff from Alexis and K.C. hanging up than my stuff?"

I was ready to point out that at least the second grade photo ornament of Erin was actually centered in the middle of the grouping, when she suddenly went a bit pale and rigid. She looked at me and said, 'Daddy, you've got to get rid of that thing before K.C. comes home from college. That one ornament hanging by the handmade manger isn't a handmade reindeer. Look at it closely. Where did you find it?"

Erin was right. It wasn't a furry misshapen reindeer. It was K.C.'s missing gerbil from 1998. I hadn't recognized it when I set things up. Merry Christmas anyway.

CHAPTER 51

A MINOR DETAIL AND DADDYHOOD

The years certainly have flown by since the birth of our first daughter, Alexis, 28 years ago. I guess I've earned tenure in the Daddyhood profession, but I've switched careers a few times. By the close of 2010, I'd been working as a geologist in the US Environmental Protection Agency's "Superfund" division for almost 14 years. Its official name is the Emergency and Remedial Response Division. Some of the Superfund projects have lasted over 30 years, which is a reason the word "Emergency" in the name always puzzles me. Superfund sites are the highly toxic and hazardous waste sites that require a tremendous amount of effort to clean-up and restore. My responsibilities included primarily making sure the EPA's Remedial Project Managers (RPMs) had accurate information on the nature and extent of groundwater contamination so the right decisions could be made to protect human health and the environment.

Living in Nassau County, I'd frequently volunteered if the Superfund investigation was on Long Island. As a result, I became very familiar with such exotic, far off places as Franklin Square, Garden City Park, Garden City Village, Garden City South, Garden City East, Mineola, Hicksville, Glen Cove, Bethpage, and even the near- the- edge- of- the- world places like Hauppauge and Islip. There are a surprising amount of Federal and State Superfund sites within walking distance of my own home, and it kept me busy and challenged.

In addition to my "day" job, I also taught 3 evening classes each semester in Geology at York College in Queens, sometimes with over 120 students. I'm also the type of professor to give the students homework each week, so would stay up late to grade papers. I also spent a good amount of time on weekends and my days off as a volunteer to create a unique wildlife sanctuary at a 9-acre County owned stormwater basin near my home.

On top of that, I was always "Daddy" to our three daughters, Alexis (28), Erin (25), and K.C. (21). Adding it up, by now I've had a total of 74 years "Daddyhood" experience so far! With my youngest turning 21, however, I finally realized my "Daddy" job for the most part is over. Besides, none of them live here anymore. They've basically fledged. Alexis lives in Suffolk and works for the Cornell Cooperative Extension as a tree expert and is a certified arborist with a Master's degree in Urban Forestry. She's a published author, well respected among her peers, and even has a computer blog on gardening. She's a delight to talk with and visit, but certainly capable of taking care of herself.

Erin, our adventurous daughter, left Long Island after college a couple of years ago and went cross country to seek field work in environmental studies. I miss Erin the most since I never even know what state she's in, North Dakota? Missouri? She's a long, lean, blond, girl with distinctive 4-foot-long hair and a few scrapes and tattoos. Usually, she's in a state of happiness, as she calls to tell me "sky diving is super", or "I rescued a bear cub", or "I only broke my elbow, but falling off that cliff in California was an experience I'll never forget."

During the summer of 2010, Erin convinced me to go to Montana to visit her while she worked as a nature guide at Glacier National Park.

By the time I made plans and actually got there, she was already in the Aleutian Islands doing bird monitoring for an agency on an uninhabited volcano off the coast of Russia- far beyond cell phone range. She used a short wave radio once to tell me she was upset that an earthquake on the island had opened up a crevasse on the slope of the volcano and several bird nests had fallen in. After that assignment, she went to Vancouver, then Hawaii, then Colorado to find a new challenge.

K.C., meanwhile, is finishing her junior year at Cornell, and busy saving the world, so the only time I hear from her is when she reminds me that I haven't paid the tuition yet, or when she wants to hurriedly tell me about the latest environmental protest she organized. She's rushing everywhere – Cancun for the Climate Change Protests, Washington DC for Powershift protests, and Sustainability efforts. She talks faster than I can listen, and sometimes it takes a full day after our conversation until I realize she'd told me I was behind on the tuition payments. It's been a long, long time since I've had her on my lap and called her 'Velcro'.

When York College had budget problems, they cut back on the adjunct staff, and I lost two of my three classes for the Spring 2011 semester. I then saw an announcement on the EPA website…seeking candidates for a one year "detail" as an "special" assistant to the Regional Administrator for Region 2 – NY, NJ, Puerto Rico, and the Virgin Islands. I decided to apply. I figured, why not? It was something different, it seemed a new challenge, and besides, the timing was right since the kids were gone and the teaching's been cut back. I answered the questions honestly. One question seemed like a joke, so I wrote one back, saying the most difficult decision I've ever had to make was to try to answer honestly when my wife asked if a dress made her look fat. (Apparently, the review committee had a tough time figuring out whether my answer was appropriate, but they realized it is probably one of the toughest decisions all husbands eventually have to make at least once in their lives after the words "I do".)

The application also requested a sample of writing, so I included one of my older "Daddyhood" articles about volunteering. It may not have been the technical science writing sample they were looking for, but at least it had been published! Really, how interesting is it to sit and read a 30,000 word essay on the "*Natural Attenuation of Perchloroethylene in a Reducing Environment*"?? Could you do it without yawning? Me neither, and I was the scientist who wrote it. I'd much rather read "*Daddyhood Goes Swamp Stomping*" and not just because it's only 3,000 words either.

Well, there really must be a God, and God must have a sense of humor. In February 2011, the EPA's Regional Administrator announced that I was selected for the year detail. Her press announcement mentioned the years of volunteer work I'd done for my community and alluded to the essay I'd submitted as proof I was a considered as a candidate with unique qualifications and a different perspective than most people.

I spent the next two months getting ready for the new detail. One pressing matter was to be able to organize and hand off the responsibilities I'd had for over 40 Superfund sites to the other hydrogeologists in our branch...all of whom were overloaded with work already. I'd also been chairperson of the EPA's Ground Water Forum, a sort of in-house "expert think tank" and needed to finish up a work group and duties I'd had with them.

I changed my schedule so I wouldn't inconvenience the Regional Administrator – eliminating my "work at home days" and my "flex days" – a day off every two weeks in exchange for a nine hour daily work schedule. My schedule now coincided with the requirements of the new position. I was also committed to finishing a report and review of a complex, controversial groundwater project on Long Island and it was due the day my "detail" was scheduled to start. Also, I'd been working on a major project management program effort for the previous six years (in my "spare time") and needed to get that project completed so the EPA could train staff and implement it. Lastly, I had the toughest assignment imaginable; I had to clean up my desk. ARGH!!!! Details, details, details!

I am an admitted pack rat. When I watch the TV show, "Hoarders", I think the paper-cluttered people the show features are simply rank amateurs compared to a true professional like me. I've even bought boxes to store the boxes I store things in. (It's a family tradition). Each day I waded through one drawer at work sorting what wasn't needed, packing what was, and passing on to the other hydrogeologists "stuff" I'd saved regarding the projects they were now inheriting from me. I even had crates of rock core in my cubicle and finally had to borrow a government car to donate them to the geology department at Hofstra University. (No, they were not contaminated). Each week, an entire large blue dumpster was filled with my debris – all to be shredded and recycled. It finally dawned on me--- I was enjoying this, especially when I found the actual top surface of my desk for the first time in 10 years. Wow, Formica! Where did that come from?

Finally, the day of my new position as "Special Assistant" began. My wife dusted me off; made sure my socks matched and sent me off to work. I took the elevator up to the 26th floor – virgin territory for me and said hello. The first week is a complete blur. It turned out, the former "Special Assistant" wasn't leaving just yet, so I had no place to sit, and no computer or phone. I attended meetings (just to observe) and got introduced to 400 new people…. with no idea who was who, what their actual last name was, or what their position was. One lifesaver was Lisa – the Chief of Staff. She was very professional, obviously was devoted to her job, wanted to make absolutely sure I knew exactly what I was supposed to do, when to do it, how to do it… and never, ever, goof up.

I was given a "Blackberry", which I assume is an important communications tool rather than just a fruit. However, it wasn't programmed, there were no instructions provided, and I can't read the @!!$X tiny little numbers on it. Everyone else on the staff seems to keep their heads buried into their hands punching information into and out of their separate Blackberries. I swear some of them didn't realize they were text messaging the other people in the same room. (Or did they?) Anyway, I survived, moving each day to a new desk, crashing a new non-functional computer, and trying to keep up. But…I actually liked the new "gig". It was different, and I had never realized there were that many people at EPA who didn't work in the Superfund Division. Some worked on Clean Air issues, some on Clean Water, and there was almost daily interaction with Puerto Rico and the Virgin Islands, which somehow are considered in the NY and NJ territory. You can't make this stuff up!

Still, I was going through "Superfund withdrawal." I never realized I'd spent the longest tenure at EPA in that particular position as a geologist with the EPA's Technical Support Team. Old habits die hard, and I accidently kept getting off the elevator on the 18th floor and going to my old desk before realizing I didn't work there anymore. It was frustrating when a Superfund Project Manager emailed or called me to ask a site related question…and I couldn't remember which of the hydrogeologists had taken over that site. Worse yet was the comment from my former supervisor not to worry about my projects while I was gone for a year… "They'll still be exactly where they were when you left them…waiting for you to do something."

I now have a habit of dressing a bit better in respect for my new position at the EPA, especially as I now meet Senators, Congressmen and a host of other movers and shakers in the world. I wear a tie. OK, it's one of my many frog design ties, but only a few people have asked. I even met Miss America, and I was smart enough to tap her on the shoulder and politely ask if I could take a photo of her with the EPA's Regional Administrator who turned out to be a genuine Miss America fan. I'm getting good at taking photos, and my wife keeps busy using "Photoshop" to fix them up before I deliver them.

Erin also surprised me with a short, unexpected visit home. She helped me organize my collection of frog ties I was proudly wearing to the office. She mentioned I seemed to have a lot of newly found energy. She told me she'd just accepted a new job as a field biologist near the Mount Hood volcano in Oregon and would be in the woods for the next several months. I looked in her room in the early morning on the day she was scheduled to leave for Oregon but didn't have the heart to wake her to say goodbye. I ate breakfast alone, then picked up my briefcase and began walking down the block towards the train to work. Suddenly, the front door of our house banged open, and Erin came running out, still in her Kermit the Frog pajamas, yelling "Daddy, wait up!"

I stopped and turned. Erin ran up, threw her arms around me, and said "Knock 'em dead at work. I love you Daddy, "and then she ran back inside.

"Thanks be to God," I thought. "Good kid, I think I'll keep her." And I turned again and continued to the train with a little more energy than I thought I had left. Maybe we all still need to take care of each other. Some jobs are a pleasure.

CHAPTER 52

KERMIT THE FROG AND DADDYHOOD

This past year, 2011, has been a tough year – physically, financially, and emotionally. I still have three full time jobs which I put more effort into than most people devote to even one, but financially, our family continues to experience the uncertainties of a not so bright economic future. Physically, I've been sliding down a steeper incline on the road to our final destination. I've lost about 20 pounds, an unexpected amount of hair, increasing eye strain, and my reflexes have slowed noticeably. Emotionally- well, I'm still basically optimistic, but have been getting a continuous series of news, both good and bad, sent my way to the point where I want to cancel my phone, paper, and mail. I've been caught up in a daily routine of merely trying to get through each day without accumulating any more wounds.

Thanksgiving was a short and much needed break from work. My wife's family came to our house for dinner, and I let my wife chat while I cooked the turkey and food. Absent this year was our middle daughter, Erin. She had recently left Oregon and gotten a job in California. Alexis- our firstborn, was spending Thanksgiving with her boyfriend and his aunt in Connecticut. "Babygirl" K.C., however, had made it home

Thanksgiving morning from Cornell University and temporarily rejoined our family- with a pleasant reminder that I still owed some money for her tuition. (My chest began to tighten again.)

Around dinner time, I got a phone call from Alexis. She wanted to let us know she could come back to Long Island early on Friday…. and would I like to go with her to see the newly released Muppet Movie on Friday morning? I immediately said "Yes!! I'll try to buy tickets immediately. I'm sure it's going to be sold out!" Alexis calmly advised she didn't think we needed to reserve tickets and most likely we wouldn't have to stand in line at the theatre either, but I wasn't so sure.

K.C. was also interested in joining us. The Muppets haven't had a theatre released movie for over a decade, but the girls know I have always been a big Kermit the Frog fan since well before they were born. In fact, one of my favorite gifts was a DVD of the first season of the original Muppet Show, and I had a large collection of old VHS tapes of Muppet Shows I'd recorded off the TV…. besides almost all of the Fraggle Rock, Jim Henson Hour, Dinosaurs, and other movies and shows that had Kermit, Miss Piggy, and the other remarkable characters created by Jim Henson. My necktie collection of nearly 50 ties was all frog themed, and several were Muppet ties…which I still wore proudly to work. Unfortunately, time has marched on, and much of my Muppet memorabilia has been slowly collecting dust as life has passed it by.

Alexis, KC, and I arrived at the movie theatre a bit earlier than they wanted to, and I was surprised the parking lot was mostly empty. Alexis politely told me to relax, and that perhaps there would be more cars in another hour or two…when the theatre was scheduled to open. We waited, then went inside and bought our tickets. I was surprised they were only $6.00 each for the morning matinee! I would have thought scalpers would be selling tickets for $20 or $30 dollars. After all, this was a movie with Kermit the Frog and the Muppets!! Where were the crowds? Where were the mobs of fans? The girls escorted me in and sat beside me. The theatre was mostly empty. Then the lights went dim and the Muppet Movie began. What happened next was totally unforeseen.

The Muppet Movie began innocently enough with a new character, Walter. Walter was the younger brother of a real human, Jason and he lived in the real world with the rest of us humans. He didn't even know he was a Muppet, and none of the real humans seemed to notice either. Walter, for some reason, was a huge fan of Kermit the Frog and the Muppets. The Muppets had broken up years earlier, moved on to other activities, and were mostly forgotten. The rest of the movie was about Walter's efforts to convince the Muppets to get together again and put on a show.

As I watched the movie I felt as if I'd been hit and run over by an emotional steamroller. My eyes began to water as I watched Kermit the Frog meet Walter for the first time and explain why he was no longer interested in acting. Kermit explained that life had gone by. Seeing the abandoned and decrepit old Muppet Studio ready to be torn down and thrown out was hard for me to watch. To me, the typical lame jokes told by Fozzie Bear as he appeared in the movie with a Muppet knockoff group – the Moopets, were more than just lame, they were morbidly unfunny. Please don't misunderstand me. The Muppet Movie was well made, had very good reviews, and ended up on a positive note. It just brought back so many, many memories, it was difficult to personally watch and enjoy it. And I thank the girls for bringing me.

Kermit the Frog and I go way back. Nearly 50 years. Kermit was originally created in 1955 by Jim Henson along with many other Muppets. My dad and I both enjoyed seeing Muppet characters as they appeared on many TV shows. In 1969, Kermit was one of the featured characters on a new series, "Sesame Street" and I remembered babysitting my first little nephew, Paul, and watching Sesame Street with him. Paul's now in his forties. I remembered my 90-year-old grandfather, Ernest Alvey, laughing hysterically at the Muppet Ralph the Dog as we watched the Ed Sullivan Show at home. Pa passed away decades ago. So did my dad.

My family enjoyed watching the Muppet Show on television when it began in 1976. By then I was married to my high school sweetheart, Suzie, and already we were new homeowners in Hicksville. I'm sure I watched all 120 episodes. At least ten times. As the movie went on, I kept going back in time to all the experiences I'd had and the parts that Kermit the Frog and the Muppets played in my life.

Our first daughter, Alexis, was born in 1983. That was the year we finally got Cable TV so I could watch a new series, Fraggle Rock, which was being shown exclusively on cable. While the program was accessible to audiences of all ages, it used the Muppet fantasy creatures as an allegory to deal with serious issues such as prejudice, spirituality, personal identity, environment, and social conflict. My young daughter, Alexis, sat on my lap each week as we watched together. Red, Gobo, Boober, and Wembly all became part of our household. I later taped many of those simple shows, and we accumulated a whole herd of Fraggle characters and books.

Meanwhile, my home was turning more and more into a Kermit the Frog museum, with a growing collection of Kermit figures, Christmas ornaments, towels, sheets, pillowcases, posters, etc. I have to add that the house was also getting a wee bit crowded with other frog items, since I had also dabbled in clay sculpting and began creating hundreds of small frog-like figures of historic civilizations until we ran out of shelf space. We soon moved to a larger house in Garden City. But, that's another story and the Garden City home is where we raised our 3 kids.

The Muppet Movie progressed, but my mind continued to recess. I remembered the years my middle daughter Erin and I watched and shared the enjoyment of a later Jim Henson series, "Dinosaurs". Again, it had social and environmental themes in addition to silly humor. One year, when Suzie was ill, I made a Kermit the Frog Halloween costume for Erin, and we even had the opportunity to meet Jim Henson's daughter, Cheryl, at a store. Ms. Henson signed a stuffed Kermit figure for me, and I told her how much I had admired her father. I had Kermit the Frog watches, ties, and enjoyed going to the Muppet Stuff store in Manhattan during my lunch breaks from work. I remembered getting a Kermit the Frog lunchbox from my nephew J.J, who was surprised that I used it almost every day for the next decade.

I remembered impersonating Kermit the Frog's voice for our telephone answering machine, and that many people called back two or three times just to listen and laugh at the greeting. I remembered inheriting a Kermit the Frog coffee mug after my sister, Maureen, passed away and that a stained glass Kermit the Frog Tiffany style lamp is still standing proudly in my den, while the Kermit the Frog phone we used for many years finally broke and is now collecting dust in the basement.

I remembered when Jim Henson suddenly and unexpectedly died. And that a little part of me died too. And life went on. I remembered when a gift I received from the girls was a hand- made recording of Muppet Show songs on a cassette and playing it constantly as we drove up to Mongaup Pond for our yearly Daddy/daughter camping trips. I wondered where that tape wound up.

My youngest daughter K.C. grew up with the Harry Potter generation, and I can understand the positive influence those characters have had on her life. For me, the Muppets were funnier and also inspirational. They have been a part of my life. I hope the Harry Potter stories don't fade away for her. Maybe there will eventually be a Dumbledore balloon at the Macy's Thanksgiving Day Parade, but there sure was a Kermit the Frog Balloon. As I watched the Muppet Movie, I remembered taking a day off from work and going uptown to stand for three hours with a crowd watching the giant Kermit balloon being unrolled and filled with Helium, and I have pictures of the entire process. Hat's off to Kermit. I remembered a business trip to Philadelphia where I almost got a Kermit tattoo but fortunately, was just sober enough to know it would be a bad example for my kids.

In one short scene during the Muppet Movie, the voice of Bob Hope was heard in the background from a broadcast recording of the original series. It brought back memories of being delayed at the New Orleans airport and having a crowd of people around me as I played a DVD of the Muppet Show on my laptop computer. In another scene from the movie, a character looks at his watch, and both Alexis and K.C. poked me to let me know that I had the exact same Kermit the Frog wristwatch. I remembered being a Daddy and when a little girl's problems could be solved by simply giving a hug and a kiss. And that those times have passed away forever. It's not easy being green…. or an adult.

The movie ended and we went home. Later that afternoon I was still trying to collect my thoughts. I started humming an unlikely radio hit, "The Rainbow Connection", which Kermit the Frog sang in the Muppet Movie with all the dreamy wistfulness of a short green Judy Garland. I've read and believe the "Rainbow Connection" serves the same purpose in The Muppet Movie that "Over the Rainbow" serves in The Wizard of Oz, with nearly equal effectiveness: an opening establishment of the characters' driving urge for something more in life. I was missing something in my life. I went into my bedroom, found what I'd almost forgotten I had. I picked it out of the drawer and went to a store. Shortly afterward, I returned home with a new watchband, battery, and a now working Kermit the Frog watch back on my wrist where it belonged. I felt a lot better. Kermit lives.

CHAPTER 53

DADDYHOOD, THE CAR, AND THE CAT

I keep trying to be optimistic, but this year has thrown a lot of "stuff" at Mommy and Daddy. I still work as a geologist for the EPA Superfund, which is a good thing considering the economy and current conservative political viewpoints. My detail as Special Assistant to the Regional Administrator was cut short when two of the other six geologists left the Agency and another transferred out of Superfund. I resumed my former duties, but got assigned a whole slew of new, unfamiliar sites with new faces and problems rather than any of the ones I had considerable experience on during the previous 15 years at the Agency. I also have kept busy coping with politics and a tremendously complicated groundwater contamination issue on Long Island. It's not strictly a Superfund issue but I volunteered and am a willing participant to help as I can.

The "homefront" is where it gets more complicated. My wife's dad passed away after several years of declining health. For the past year, my wife has been the designated driver for his routine and 'not so routine' doctor and hospital visits. We'd been down to one car, and I needed that on Saturdays, Mondays, and Tuesdays to drive to York College where I teach geology at night. Apparently the one car household was a major inconvenience to my wife's family when Suzie couldn't get to her father on demand, as they invariably forgot a simple rule not to schedule Doctor visits on Mondays or Tuesdays when Suzie had no car.

Last fall I got a call from my wife's sister asking me if the reason we had only one car was because I couldn't afford extra insurance. I replied that I could pay additional insurance but didn't want to take on another car loan. (College loans for three daughters was already a stretch.) They then called Suzie and gave her "wonderful" news. Three of her siblings had chipped in and were GIVING her a car. Suzie was so happy she began to cry. Tears of joy. She thought it was such a loving and wonderful gesture from her family. It was the only time her family had given her such a big gift. I suspected it was only to ensure that Suzie would have no excuse to miss driving her dad whenever he wanted, but Suzie was more than willing to drive her dad whenever he asked. She called me a couple of days later and told me she was going to pick up the car from her brother's junk yard (there's a clue) and I should tell the insurance company to put it on our policy. I asked a logical question, "Honey, what type of car is it?" and the only information I got was that it was maroon.

Eventually, I found out it was a maroon Oldsmobile... a 1990 Olds '98 about 20 feet long, with leather seats, tons of chrome, about 100,000 miles, a broken radio and only the slight scent of someone's dead grand-mother in the back seat. It weighed about 8,000 pounds, got maybe 7 miles a gallon, and her brother paid maybe $600 for it. The title was clean, and we named it the "Boat". Suzie was so happy to have a car in her own name. She washed it every day, and even had me take photos of it with her smil-ing face, then wrote everyone thank-you cards. Her father liked the car. He probably loved cars more than his kids and could name each and every single car he and every one of his friends had their entire lives. The family photo albums included all the cars. Suzie drove him a lot...but he never forgave her for having his own driver's license taken away when his health had deteriorated to the point it was unsafe to let him behind the wheel.

Meanwhile, I had to hand over $100 every time the Boat needed gas... which seemed a daily feeding. Suzie used it as a big limo to drive a couple to their wedding, and she only got charged for two parking spaces by the valet parking attendant. It made my Chrysler minivan look like a mini-Cooper in comparison. The Boat had a certain style, but at least my van had a radio...and triple the gas mileage.

Then Suzie's Dad died. We spent the next couple weeks making arrangements and beginning the sad, but necessary task, of planning to clean out the house of a half century of accumulated car photos, car decals, car models, books and "collectibles". Then the Boat died. Actually, Suzie noticed the brakes were making noise and I brought it to my service station to inspect. He called me the next day and asked me to come over to look. Apparently, the former Boat owner never bothered to replace the brakes in 22 years and all the wheels needed to be rebuilt...at a cost slightly exceeding my mortgage payment. I talked with Suzie and told the mechanic not to fix it. We'd donate it to a charity. With her dad gone, we really didn't need it, and I wasn't about to start the never-ending process of keeping an old, tired car on the road.

When Suzie mentioned to her brother, Perry, about donating the car to charity, he was at our house within fifteen minutes, took the keys and the car and said he needed it instead of a charity. It took me another week to chase him down to get the plates so I could cancel the insurance. He re-registered the Boat, telling Motor Vehicles it was a gift, then must have found a spare brake in the junk yard and slapped one in so the car would at least have a chance to stop if it needed to.

We're still dealing with cleaning up the "estate", but meanwhile, our oldest daughter, Alexis, received an excellent job offer with Colorado Cooperative Extension in Denver and quit her position with the Cornell

Cooperative Extension in Riverhead. Mommy was heartbroken, but Ali said she could live a lot easier in Denver than LI and I simply said, Don't stay on LI just to be near your family." I'd made the family commitment decades ago, and I truly didn't want my own daughters to give up their own dreams and chances for success just to be able to visit Mommy and me on weekends. Alexis and I had one last Father's Day weekend in June, camping and hiking together by ourselves at Mongaup Pond Campgrounds in the Catskills. We'd been doing this together for over 20 years, and it is the best part of my life. Each year brings something new, and this was the year we saw and photographed a black bear by the lake.

We helped Alexis pack a truck as she headed cross country by herself. There were just two small things that complicated this. First, she knew she needed a new car in Denver, and would have to sell her prized 1998 Mitsubishi Eclipse. I solved that by offering her what she asked for the car. Not that I needed a "chick car", but I knew Suzie was depressed and thought it would be something she could enjoy. The second small complication was Kiwi, Alexis's cat. That was a bigger problem, especially since Suzie is allergic to cats...and I don't actually like them.

Alexis bought Kiwi as a kitten nearly three years ago. It was an indoor cat and woke her up purring every morning. Kiwi had a ton of cat toys and its own Facebook page. Alexis was concerned that Kiwi wouldn't tolerate being in a truck for five days and asked if Suzie could carry Kiwi to Denver when she flew there as soon as Alexis arrived. Suzie was pleased to be able to help Ali settle into her new apartment but was worried about traveling with a cat. Alexis advised she'd pay for the ticket for Kiwi and had a new lightweight carry case and a couple of tranquilizers from a Veterinarian so Kiwi shouldn't be a problem during the flight.

We took Kiwi home in her new carry case and I let her out in the small room I've been planning to convert to my home office. Kiwi jumped out of the bag and hid behind a bookcase, hissing and refusing to come out. For the next three days, I kept her in that room with her kitty litter box, fresh food, water, and cat toy. The former perky house cat turned into a cross between a bobcat and a Tyrannosaurus Rex. It actually roared in addition to growls. It did eat, but regularly attacked and scratched Suzie and me whenever we went into the room. It was not a happy cat.

I told Suzie not to feed it the night before the flight, and I'd stuff the pill into its food when I got home. Kiwi knew something was up as soon as I went into the room with a fresh supply of food. She wouldn't eat the pill and hissed and clawed at me. I retreated, put on a heavy coat and two pairs of gloves, reentered the room, and tried to grab her to put the leash on her collar so I could get Kiwi into the carry case. I thought I'd planned this OK but spent fifteen minutes chasing her around the 8-10 foot closed room. Fur flew everywhere and I learned cats can actually climb smooth glass windows.

I grabbed her but I found out it is very hard to manipulate a snarling, clawing cat with one hand while wearing two pairs of gloves and it's nearly impossible to lever a Barbie sized chain fastener open to slip it onto a cat collar. After the first 6 rounds of the heavyweight championship fight, I managed to slip the leash on her collar. Kiwi immediately clawed me then bolted, and her collar snapped off in my hand. I didn't know it had a safety release built into it. Round 6 to Kiwi. I retreated again, went and got my long fish net and reentered the room. After another 8 rounds, I finally netted her and bundled her up, wiggled the carry case into the net, dumped her in and managed to zip it closed.

Kiwi was still banging into the soft sides of the carry case as I staggered downstairs and showed her to my wife. I took off the gloves, goggles, and coat, wiped the small blood stain from my cheek, and said, "Here. Mission accomplished. Don't open the bag. In fact, if the Airport Security officers insist on opening the bag, stand back, tell them to all draw their guns and get ready to shoot, because if they hesitate this cat will kill them and the nearest ten passengers."

Suzie was worried. She was wondering how Kiwi, or she, would handle the flight to Denver. She asked me if I could somehow just open Kiwi's mouth and stuff a tranquilizer into it. I declined saying I'd rather keep all my fingers and I'm used to having two arms and went upstairs to change out of my sweat soaked clothes. I also wondered if I should take the cat tranquilizers myself to try to calm down, but decided it wasn't a smart idea. I might choke up a hairball. Suzie was packed (including two American Girl Dolls that Alexis had somehow left behind at our house) so I placed carry-cased Kiwi into the car, added Suzie, her luggage and off we went. The cat glared at us through the carry case screen...making evil plans for revenge if it ever got out. So, I did what any husband would do. I dropped Suzie, her luggage and Kiwi off at passenger drop-off, said "Have a nice trip" and sped away as fast as I could.

Suzie called the next morning. The flight was fine, and Kiwi survived. In fact, by lucky chance, Suzie sat next to a cat lover, and Kiwi only growled when Suzie got up to use the restroom on the flight. When they landed, Suzie handed Kiwi in the carry case to Ali. The cat stayed quiet. As they drove from the airport to her new apartment, Ali began to unzip the case. Suzie warned Alexis not to, but Ali's hand was already in the case. No, it didn't bite or scratch. Kiwi sat there and let her head be rubbed. It knew Alexis and knew it was safe. By the next day, Kiwi was comfortable in the new apartment and even let Suzie pet her. The only time it hissed was when Alexis asked if they should telephone me. I swear I actually felt that "hiss" in my bones, even though I was 2,000 miles away. It know this makes no sense, but I locked the bedroom door in my house and slept with the net. Just to be on the safe side, I "unfriended" Kiwi on Facebook.

CHAPTER 54

THE ENDING OF DADDYHOOD

I've managed to hit another milestone in my journey on this Earth. I'm now Sixty! I've accomplished six full decades of being "alive" -- whatever that is supposed to mean. I'll remind you all that I wrote a previous chapter in this book about personally turning 50. All right, all right, all right! A bit more than half of my semi-geological period of life has been as a "Daddy" species. The "Daddyhood" period, however, has ended as surely as the giant meteor which crashed into the planet and ended the Cretaceous Period of the geologic calendar...along with all the dinosaurs. I assume some of the Tyrannosaurs were also "Daddies". They even may have had time to acknowledge that their role as Daddy and dominant life form on Earth was ending before they got hit on the head by a large, fast moving space rock. My end of Daddyhood sort of crept up on me at a slower pace- -- although faster than a glacier moves. A milestone birthday is sort of like a glacier. It's hard to ignore these milestones when you are constantly reminded of the former (birthdays) or when you finally realize there is a 1000-foot-high wall of ice looming right in front of you (glaciers). It's hard to get around a birthday or a glacier.

My wife Suzie, the eternal "Mommygoddess", and I (mostly her) have raised three daughters, Alexis, Erin, and K.C.. Suzie and I were originally high school sweethearts. Our adventure together started way back in 1969. I worked as a weekend gas jockey at a local service station. In February 1969, while riding my bicycle home after work during a snowstorm, I was hit by a truck. Ouch. I don't actually remember this, but the hospital emergency doctor told me what happened.

As a result of getting clunked by a passing truck and bounced along the street, I was wheelchair bound for awhile. Suzie, the girlfriend of a friend, volunteered to help me get around at school by pushing my wheelchair while I carried her books. She talked. (That's a "given" if you know her.) I listened and surprised myself by actually talking too. (I was a science "geek" and not very good at conversation.) Something clicked and I asked her out on a date as soon as I could walk again. Our relationship continued through high school, including the prom, and on through college. We were married in 1975, bought a home (in Hicksville!!) in 1976, and both of us worked and made plans together.

There is an old prophetic axiom, "Life happens while you're busy making plans". As a couple, we both worked at our jobs. Suzie's job was as a display artist for Franklin Simon, A&S, and J.C. Penny. I was a geological scientist for Ebasco Services - a major utility engineering/construction company. We planned, vaguely, to eventually stop whatever we were doing, sell the house and go across the country for a year. See America! Someday. That trip never happened.

In 1982, I accepted a new challenge as a geotechnical engineer in Saudi Arabia. My wife joined me (after a frustrating 5 month delay.) When we met again at JFK Airport, we didn't even recognize each other. She'd cut her long red hair short, and I'd lost 30 pounds and was burnt a deep brown by the desert sun. There's not much entertainment in Saudi Arabia.

So, we made our own... and our first child was born right after our return to America in 1983.

My role as the "Daddy" began. Alexis, named after a favorite and adventurous aunt, changed our lives. I nicknamed her "Ali" after my Saudi experience. Alexis had complications right after birth and spent some time in an incubator. Ali stayed in the hospital and was monitored to find out what was wrong, while a few doctors scratched their heads. I bought Ali a simple stuffed frog and it stayed on top of her hospital incubator the entire time--- watching her when I couldn't be there myself. She eventually began to thrive and was released to come home. Alexis and "froggie" bonded and that little stuffed animal went everywhere with us the next 2 decades.

Suzie knew I had not planned on being a 'daddy', and she bought me every book on parenting. I never read any. Somewhere, I'm sure there is a copy of "*The Rulebook for Perfect Daddyhood*", but it may be in one of the boxes in our attic. I guess I didn't need it. Alexis was literally the perfect child, healthy (after the rough start), intelligent, calm, and cute. We moved back to Garden City, into a small, cheap, rundown house. It was three times the cost of the house we had in Hicksville. It was fixer-upper, near our parents' homes, and we have spent the last 28 plus years still trying to fix-up our own house.

We were the youngest family on the block. The new Mommy and Daddy. Mommy began to take Alexis modeling, and Ali got roles in TV commercials with residuals that lasted for years, and she had a healthier bank account that I did. I loved Alexis, and was always in happy wonder of the things she did, the things she said, and playing with her or going for walks, or watching the Muppets or Fraggle Rock, My Little Ponies, gymnastic lessons, art lessons, dance lessons, etc. Even Halloween was a treat as we both could dress up and go trick or treating. When my own Dad died on a rainy Halloween morning, I took some time during that sad day to dress Ali up in a hand-made pumpkin costume and take her around the block trick-or-treating. For the next two decades, I took Halloween off from work as a sign of respect and love for my dad's spirit, and for an opportunity to be with my girls.

Alexis could also run easily, and we used to play "chase". I rarely caught her, and she went on to join the high school cross country team and even does marathons today. Ali always called me 'Daddy." I was there when she said her first word. And, I loved hearing that. When Ali was eight, we began a tradition of going camping by ourselves for a weekend and taking walks among the trees. Mongaup Pond in the Catskills became a special place for us. Ali was artistic as well as a science kid and had an easy temperament – except for harrumphing or rolling her eyes. And I was her very own and personal Daddy. It was easy.

It was too easy. When Alexis was four, Suzie and I had another child, Erin. Her real name should have been Beelzebub – demon baby from hell. She had a unique temperament. Her first word was NO. Her first sentence was "It's not fair!" She was also intelligent, cute, and talented in many ways – just a bit more independent and not a calm type of child. Suzie and I wondered what we were doing wrong. Why did the simple lessons we could teach Alexis be rolled up into a ball by Erin and thrown back at us? I'm not complaining – she too called me "Daddy", had her own froggie collection, and toys. She was interested in watching Teenage Mutant Ninja Turtles or Jim Henson's Dinosaurs with me and enjoyed our walks. She too had her weekends with Daddy on camping trips, and trips to the museums, and art lessons, music lessons, soccer lessons, etc.

Erin liked the outdoors, and many years later backpacked across many States, and even lived on an active, uninhabited volcano in the far western Aleutian Islands. She called one day to let us know she was OK, but a bit upset that an earthquake on the volcano had caused a fissure in the ground to open and many of the nesting birds she was monitoring were killed. Erin is hard to catch. She called me from Montana asking me to visit her and see how beautiful the Big Sky country was. By the time I arranged a vacation and trip, she was already gone. Erin also has a huge natural smile... just like her Mommy, and she called me daddy and I loved her.

My last attempt to put the mythic "*Rulebook for Perfect Daddyhood*" guidebook to use was when Kathleen Carolyn (K.C.) was born. Third time's the charm. K.C.'s nickname was Velcro. She also bonded with her own stuffed "froggie" but glued herself to Mommy's (and my own) hip for nearly 4 years. She loved to be held or lay across our lap. Fortunately, K.C. was petite. She was also intelligent, talkative, artistic, talkative, cute, talkative, and made friends easily.

Did I mention K.C. likes to talk? She also had more toys than China since she instantly inherited every toy her sisters outgrew, as well as much of Alexis's wardrobe. Dresses had to bypass Erin, or she would scream or cringe, so they went directly to K.C. Her first word was "Mommy", but she called me "Daddy" and I loved her. It was also easy to throw her into the child seat on my bicycle and ride around with her.

K.C. became a Pokemon addict and had the good fortune to be the perfect age to love the Harry Potter series of books and movies, which she shared by reading them to mommy and me while we did the dishes...or tried to sleep. I once took all three girls to Sea Cliff to watch a 4th of July fireworks display. It was super crowded and nearly a mile long walk to the fireworks. After the event ended, K.C. was too tired to walk anymore. I carried her on my back, uphill the whole way, the entire mile to the car with her sisters. K.C. held my neck tightly, leaned over my head, and said, "I love you, Daddy", then fell asleep. I never forgot that, and what hearing those simple words meant to me.

K.C. also got me involved in something I'd never planned - acting. Our church had started a simple community theatre, and she was interested in auditioning for a part in their original musical comedies. I had merely planned to drive her to church but wound up the next ten years performing on stage, mostly as the lead idiot. K.C. and I even had a few short scenes together. It was fun. Erin used to practice lines with me and helped me make up extra jokes. K.C. was a bit more anxious about messing up on stage, and always perfectly remembered her token line in the play, while I got used to just winging it and making dialogue up during a performance. I'm still wondering what stage fright is supposed to be, and I can't sing or dance or follow a script, but it was an enjoyable "run" as a part of daddy-hood. And K. C. called me "Daddy", and I loved her.

Our home grew and our family grew. The first extension was a master bedroom and a den. Later, the dining room was expanded so we could actually get all the relatives in the same room for Thanksgiving dinner without an overflow to the living room. This didn't come cheaply, and I eventually had two jobs to help keep finances under control. Suzie was mostly a full time mommy, and her art career took a necessary backseat to a full time mommy career. I like gardening and spent a lot of free time outside the home adding plants and flowers and fruit trees to our property. Blueberry bushes were a big success. All the girls and their friends helped me pick the tart, ripe fruit each year. The years passed, and I somehow got involved in creating another "garden".

This "garden" is 9-acres and is actually a community bird sanctuary, nature preserve, environmental center, and arboretum, initially known as the Garden City Bird Sanctuary. I built it using about 25,000 hours of my own labor and a few thousand volunteers. All the girls helped tremendously. It's something they shared with me. And they called me "Daddy" and I loved them. At our own home, I planted a small European Larch tree in the back yard with Alexis in 1985. It's now 40-feet tall. There's another one planted a few years later, for Erin. That one is about 30-feet tall. There is also an American Larch planted almost 15 years ago by our driveway. It reminds me of K.C. It does not surprise me at all that my girls all share a love of trees with me. There's even an "Alvey Arboretum"

345

at the community nature preserve. I named it for Alexis. She earned a master's degree in Urban Forestry and is a certified arborist. Alexis, however, insists the arboretum is named after me, and she drew the logo showing a man on his knees planting a small tree.

Time goes by. When she was a teenager, Ali asked if she could start calling me "Dad" instead of "Daddy". She was maturing and no longer felt comfortable among her friends referring to me as "Daddy". I was a bit puzzled until she asked if I remembered when I began calling my own father "Dad" instead of "Daddy". She was right, and my name changed, and my "Dad" role was introduced. Erin insisted on sticking with calling me "Daddy", mainly because she wanted to be different than Alexis, but I knew that she too, was maturing quickly. K.C. adopted "Dad" without a discussion. Then came college and another decline in the role of "Daddyhood".

Each of the girls attended college in Ithaca, away from home. Each girl started with a good number of college credits from high school, a bunch of scholarships, and each graduated early. Not surprisingly, each girl has chosen a career in the environment. (The acorn doesn't fall far from the tree.) I think our camping trips together may have had something to do with that decision. It has been a financial hurdle, and there are still a lot of college loans to pay off. It's not a role of "Daddyhood", but it's a role a Dad has to take on to help the next generation. The girls have grown, matured, and no longer live at home. The toys have been picked up, packed away, donated, or sold. We call and talk when we can, or email, or Facebook, or send pictures. Daddyhood is over, and I'm a bit worn out, tired and grey haired. I like my current role as Dad-- there's less daily stress, less driving to lessons, and certainly a lot less "poop" or crying. They have grown up well and we will always love each other. Still, when I write to them, I often sign the letters "Dad(dy)". Just as a reminder.

It's been an interesting life.

CHAPTER 55

WEATHERING THE STORM AND DADDYHOOD

Living on Long Island gives you a different perspective of the world. It's a large island, over 100 miles long and filled with over 6 million people (although many people don't realize that Queens and Brooklyn are actually parts of geographical Long Island.) It's nice being surrounded by ocean water. I just don't want any flowing through my home and I'm not talking about mere pinhole leaks in our water lines. My family understands what a hurricane is from decades of experience. Historically, the "Big One" was back in 1938, before hurricanes were even named and most of Long Island was rural. We've had our share of wind and rain damage, and even 2011's Tropical Storm Irene caused a large oak tree to come down on top of my mom's former home a few blocks away from us. The most recent hurricane, "Sandy" which hit us on October 29, 2012, gave me a few additional lessons in life, whether I wanted them or not.

The last weekend before Halloween is the annual Halloween Fest and Haunted Hikes at the local nature center which I founded many years ago. Back then I had my three daughters to help me make "sump-thing" in our community. I volunteered them, whether they were originally interested or not. It was just something for them to work with their Daddy on.

347

They've all grown up and moved on to new adventures. Each has chosen to continue an environmental career choice and donates a lot of time.

I, however, am a creature of habit and somehow enjoy the challenge of lassoing new Halloween Fest volunteers and getting them to help me set up the half mile of trails, lights, decorations and ghosts, goblins and scary zombies needed to make the haunted hikes a memorable and fun experience for all. It is supposed to be a fund raiser for our nonprofit organization that manages the 9-acre site, but my wife and I somehow plow all the revenue back into new goody bags, prizes, and silky spider webs for the next year.

This year, we expanded the Halloween Haunted hikes to three nights- Friday, Saturday, and Sunday, and the Halloween Fest was scheduled for Saturday afternoon October 27th. Unfortunately, the timing of our Halloween event coincided with the impending arrival of "Frankenstorm", a real monster according to the Climate Channel and news. In fact, I no sooner got home from work on that Friday when I received a telephone call from my office at the USEPA asking me if I could take one of the government cars home for the weekend. They were afraid of flooding and damage to our Manhattan office and were looking for places to park the cars safely. Since a trip I'd planned to New Jersey for Oct. 30th had just been cancelled (due to the arriving storm), I didn't need the car.

Friday and Saturday night attendance at the nature center Haunted Hikes was a bit sparse as many families were shopping for emergency supplies. People were calling to ask if we were going to postpone it due to the coming storm, but I held out as long as I could. The Saturday afternoon Halloween Fest brought out a good number of little children and volunteers and several boxes of prizes were given away, but even before the evening hikes ended, I announced that the Sunday hikes were going to be cancelled because of the hurricane.

On Sunday morning, I grabbed a couple of volunteers and went over to the site. We spent the next three hours tearing all of the decorations down and throwing them into my van. We also returned the two generators we'd borrowed from neighbors, and they certainly were relieved to see them back with full cans of gasoline. By the time we were done, my entire den, living room and dining room were stacked with decorations to the point where it looked like a hurricane had hit us inside the house. A new item that had decorated the trails for 2012 were dozens of battery operated candles, made from paper towel rolls covered in Elmer's glue and white paint. The candles had been hung by invisible lines along the trails, so they floated ala Harry Potter's Hogwarts Castle.

I next did preparations for the storm (and noticed the winds were getting a bit stronger each hour). I filled my van with gas and drove my other car to the shop for repairs…cleverly getting it out of the way if a tree came down during the storm. After that I bought emergency food supplies-7 bags of Doritos, several Snickers, a box of donuts, coffee, and a jar of peanuts. I had all the batteries and flashlights an army of volunteers could use since I just did have an army of flashlight armed volunteers giving hikes at the nature center. I also had over 50 candles at our home since we were ready for a candle ceremony scheduled for January. I'd charged our cell phones and had just bought a cell phone charger that could be used in the car. Most importantly, I had 2 full cases of wine, stored in the basement.

My wife, Suzie, and I were all set with no kids in the house any-more. She dutifully called each one to let them know we were prepared and that we loved them. I realized that I still had all of my office phone calls automatically forwarded to my cell phone as I'd neglected to change the setting before I'd left work. Over the next two weeks I probably had 500 phone calls at my EPA phone forwarded to my cell phone. There were additional calls each day from my cell service provider reminding me I was going well over my monthly budget of minutes.

As it got dark in the late afternoon, Suzie and I decided to have some fun. We got out many of the floating Halloween candles and strung them up in the house, on plants, doors, and cabinets. Our own home looked sort of romantic. We cooked a dinner and when expected power failure came, I elegantly lit candelabras with some of our wax candle collection. "Let's have some wine, and relax," I said. I went into the kitchen, got the corkscrew, grabbed a bottle of wine, and began to open it. A few seconds later I felt a sharp pain in my hand and as I directed the flashlight onto my thumb saw blood gushing from a new deep cut…with a piece of twist-off metal wine bottle cap sticking out. In the dark I didn't realize the wine bottle didn't have a cork. I'd cut myself badly, then fumbled in the dark to find a band-aid in our medicine cabinet. It wasn't a nice start for a romantic candlelight and wine evening.

I returned to the kitchen where Suzie had finished dinner by herself and was standing at the sink washing the plates in the candlelight. I tucked my heavy-duty flashlight under one arm and stood next to her to help with the dishes. She had moved several candles from the dining room into the kitchen as well as half a dozen flashlights. As I reached across her to take a dish, I noticed my thumb was still bleeding, and then the heavy-duty flashlight slipped out from under my arm and landed…directly on the top of her bare foot. It was not a pretty sight. Suzie screamed in pain, and I had to quickly get her over to a chair to sit down. Within minutes, her foot was swollen to the size of Sasquatch-Big Foot. Later, it turned purple, particularly when I gave her what I thought was an ice pack from the freezer. It turned out to be a bag of my frozen blueberries. She did not want to go to the hospital, but she could not walk. I got her upstairs while the wind still howled. Sandy had already claimed one victim- our romantic, candle-lit evening.

The next morning was a clear day. The wind still blew, but it was very quiet in our neighborhood. No electricity, no train noise, no planes, and few cars. My wife works as a freelance reporter and photographer. She still couldn't walk on the foot, but as soon as we ate breakfast, she grabbed her camera and I got her into our van. I spent much of the day driving slowly around town while she took photos of downed trees, bashed cars, more downed trees, damaged houses, and still more downed trees. Our famous "Tree City" was gone, replaced by "Stump City". Suzie interviewed quite a number of people and we saw one house that was nothing but an empty burnt out basement. The house had been hit by a falling tree which ruptured the gas line, and the entire house blew up and burned. Only ashes and a hole remained.

Surprisingly, the local Seventh Street shopping block in Garden City seemed to be the only place that still had electricity. Suzie and I arranged to meet the newspaper editor at Dunkin Donuts to transfer the photos and story notes to the editor's laptop. I dropped Suzie off in the front of Dunkin Donuts store and parked. When I returned, the line up inside was incredible. There were almost 200 people in the small shop, many sitting patiently charging cell phones or using their laptop computers. Others were on the line buying what might be their last cup of coffee until their own electricity was restored. The editor and Suzie sat at a small table and shared the pictures and news. I know I cringed when I saw that one of the pictures was of an oak tree that had fallen and hit the house on Clinch Avenue that I grew up in. I remembered that it had a fireplace and during occasional storms when we'd lost power (including the Big Blackout in the 1960's that extended across several states). My mother would light the fireplace in the library, and we'd cook hotdogs and marshmallows.

As I waited, I got several more cell phone calls. Some were from EPA- a general announcement that our Manhattan office building was without power and closed. Non-essential employees were not required to report for duty. Three of the call were from our daughters. Each just wanted to hear my voice and let them know everything was okay. I didn't offer up that I'd broken their mom's foot within 45 minutes of losing electric power.

Over the next few days, Suzie and I became part time residents at the Garden City Public Library. They had not lost power either and had heat and computers available. Suzie continued to write and email her stories in. She liked the warmth of the library. She also spent a good amount of time in our sunny den painting a picture of a snow covered Garden City Bird Sanctuary meadow. Meanwhile, I spent much of the time cleaning up branches and debris in my own back yard and the bird sanctuary. I was warm from heavy physical the work, and rarely noticed my wife was wearing four sweaters, a sweatshirt, a scarf, and gloves while I was only wearing a T-shirt.

I enjoy working outdoors and slowly our home garden and the nature center began to show improvement as every day there was another 20 foot long pile of debris stored along the curb. Besides, I did have a bit of help from Mike, a young man who was doing community service. I got to know Mike a bit and liked him. He also didn't mind working outdoors. We made progress and dumped piles of debris on the curb. The Village removed the piles fairly quickly as they contracted with several tree crews, and our local firehouse was even used as a bed and breakfast by tree crews from Florida and North Carolina. Suzie interviewed them and pretty soon was involved with coordinating donations of supplies for the workers. We also invited a few neighbors over for candle-lit dinners and it was nice to be able to simply sit and chat in person without the distractions of TV, PCs, I-Pads, and cell phones.

With our power out for several days, I didn't want to buy a lot of food for our refrigerator. Each day I went to a nearby King Kullen food store and bought enough for the day. I usually pay by check. The second day, I learned something when my check was denied. The store monitors each check and has a policy against allowing check payments on consecutive days. This is to prevent fraud from a series of bounced checks. I explained the manager that I'd been shopping at this store weekly for over a decade and if they checked their records, they might notice my usual weekly food purchases were about $250 (for our family of 5) and I didn't think a $35 check was going to bankrupt them. The check restriction was waived, but I had to go through the same process each day...and our freezer was slowly defrosting in spite of adding bags of ice.

After a few more days of no electricity, I noticed the 40 containers of frozen raspberries and blueberries I had stored in my freezer from last summer's backyard harvest were slowly melting. Our backyard contains about 20 blueberry bushes and a productive raspberry patch. We harvest them on a regular basis, and I freeze a lot for use during the winter. Picking berries one by one takes a lot of time, and I used to be helped by my daughters until they moved away.

I didn't want to lose the 2012 crop, so purchased a few cases of canning jars, a ton of sugar, and some pectin. I spent a full day making raspberry jelly and blueberry jam on our stove. The bubbling fruit and sugar concoction added a nice scent to our home and the heat from the large simmering pot kept our kitchen warm to the point that the box of chocolate donuts (my emergency food supply) on top of our refrigerator had melted from the heat. This Christmas, I gave friends and co-workers jars of my homemade jam as gifts and have a growing reputation as a jelly maker.

The electricity to our home was finally restored November 7th. Rejoice! Rejoice!! Suzie was thrilled. Several other neighbors were still out, so we passed out remaining candles and flashlight batteries. I took down the Harry Potter floating candle-lights and packed them away for the next year's haunted hikes. We invited Mike the volunteer, over for dinner as a way to celebrate. He brought dessert. It was snowing lightly. That evening, as we barely finished dinner, the lights began to flicker and suddenly went out again. It was snowing harder, and the wind was picking up. After Mike left, Suzie and I sat at our dining room window and watched wave after wave of blue flashes in the sky as transformers blew and more lights in the area went out. Then, we simply went to bed in the dark.

The next morning, there was still no electricity. (The electric utility, LIPA, reported another 200,000 people lost power). It was very quiet outside and when we looked out, the ground was covered by about a half foot of heavy, wet snow. It was pretty. Every branch of the remaining trees was completely covered with thick snow. Then I noticed that every shrub and small tree was completely flattened. The snow was so thick and heavy, it bent and broke many branches. I spent the rest of the day with a broom gently trying to brush the snow off the thin branches. This "northeaster" did more damage to our property than Sandy. Our Japanese Maple split from the weight of the snow as did many branches of the memorial trees planted at the nature center over the last 15 years. The trails were again blocked by fallen and snapped trees. Suzie and I again took a drive around town, and she photographed the beautiful snow-covered Village, but we had to be careful as branches kept snapping and breaking onto the streets. It was pretty and disheartening at the same time.

By the next week, power had been restored to almost everyone in Garden City. My office was again open, the trains and subways were up and running and a more normal life resumed. The Village continued to remove downed trees and make repairs. I did the same at the nature center each weekend. Suzie's foot eventually healed too, and she was happy to at last be able to wear her own shoes again. I had an idea to make a memorial to Hurricane Sandy at the nature center, and the Village was able to save a slab cross section of a large, downed oak tree for me. I stacked a layer of paving stones at the site and the truck slid the entire 500 pound slab onto the pavers. We'll sand it flat and smooth, coat it with shellac, and carve onto it "In Memory of Hurricane Sandy - 2012". The 80 year old tree slab can be used as an educational tool at the nature center's arboretum. It can also be used as a seat where I plan to occasionally sit drinking a cup of coffee and reflecting on our lives during Hurricane Sandy.

CHAPTER 56

FURLOUGHED AND DADDYHOOD

The year 2013 was unusual. I learned the meaning of the word 'furlough.' I had an intimate, personal experience with being furloughed and why it may be different for people who work for the Federal government than for "normal" civilians. My children fledged a couple of years ago, so I no longer have "daddyhood" experiences of endless drives to lessons, or home based interactions with our girls. We did attend a family reunion in March, flying out to California with our youngest daughter KC, for a week's visit with Erin and her boyfriend Jack. Alexis drove from Denver and met us in San Luis Obispo along the California coast. The girls and I hiked daily, visited museums and art galleries with Suzie, drank ourselves silly in the vineyards, and had a great time that week. However, there was a bit of an uncertainty for all of us. Daddy was being "furloughed".

The Federal Budget for Fiscal Year 2013 cut budgets across a lot of the government, and we were required to take several days of unpaid leave. At first, no one knew exactly how many days we would lose, so I spread my furlough days out so that I wouldn't lose more than 1 day of pay per pay period. I could schedule the days, and so I used my unpaid leave to attend a local technical conference, drive up to the Catskills to visit a plant nursery, and work with volunteers at a community bird sanctuary I had founded about 20 years ago. I took another furlough day to go camping at Mongaup Pond in the Catskills with Erin and KC during the summer, and another day to go hiking with a few fellow EPA scientists. All in all, I lost about 2 weeks of salary, but was able to keep up with our bills and other obligations. I also enjoyed the alternate activities.

Then Fiscal Year 2014 hit, and on October 1, 2013, I was completely out of work in a government shutdown. I work for the EPA in the Superfund Division, and my job requires me to spend a lot of time at toxic and hazardous waste dumps (besides the one where Erin's bedroom used to be). My wife, Suzie, did her part to help wean me away from my work. The first day, she brought me out to the Merrick Landfill, which was officially "closed" as a municipal dump site and has been converted into a nature preserve. I walked the trails while she painted scenes of the surrounding wetlands and beaches. I have to admit, it was a good day. There was even a pond on the landfill, birds, a dock for fishing and a park ranger who rode me around the site as my personal tour guide.

The next day, Suzie brought me with her again, this time to model for her art class. I'm sure that she meant well, and figured I'd enjoy getting some pay to simply sit still in a chair and do nothing for a few hours. I hated it. I cannot sit still and do nothing, and the women at the art gallery were talking constantly and knocking into each other. I was curious to see how I was being painted, and after 3 hours, took a look at one of the artist's work. She had been feverishly painting, using a ton of brown paint. When I looked at the painting, she had meticulously painted a detailed brown wall and in the shadow was an outline of a ghost sitting on a bench. It turned out she wasn't that interested in painting me. I then found out Suzie had scheduled for me to be there as an art model the next three weeks! I apologized and told them I had unexpectedly been re-assigned to an emergency hazardous group in Afghanistan and wouldn't be able to return until there was peace in the world.

I had no idea how long I'd be unemployed, but I was not about to spend the time as my wife's art model. (Or start doing the backlogged household chores.) The next morning, I got up at dawn and headed over to the local bird sanctuary I'd started in the community almost 20 years earlier. I left my cell phone at home, and left a note on the breakfast table, "Have a nice day, I'm out gardening". I left home at 5:30 am and came home about 7 pm. Suzie took one look at me and saw I was completely filthy. I'd spent the full day weeding, cutting down branches and digging out dead plants. She didn't have to ask where I'd been, she simply made me throw my clothes downstairs to for washing, and then marched me upstairs to shower.

I followed the same routine the next two weeks. Up and out of the house at dawn, over to the bird sanctuary, or even just in the backyard, and overhauled the landscaping. Each night, I went back inside dirty, filthy, cut up, bruised and tired, but somehow content. I mentioned this to a couple of co-workers I knew who had also been furloughed from EPA, and soon they also volunteered their time to come over to the sanctuary and help (which also happily prevented them from being 'volunteered' as art models or doing chores). We removed the last downed trees from Hurricane Sandy, installed post and rail fencing, and set up the trails with a zillion Halloween decorations. I usually left the gate unlocked while I was over there and found the sanctuary to be a magnet for the housewives and neighbors as a place to jog in the mornings for exercise.

Suzie was also busy with her art, her photography, and her volunteer work with the local historical society and as the official Village Historian for Garden City. She was also on a few church committees taking photos and writing articles on the many church functions. We left each other napkin notes on the breakfast table as a way of communicating. I began to wonder if this was what I could expect if I ever could retire.

Retirement isn't something I'm looking forward to. During FY 2013, a lot of experienced EPA employees had retired, and the agency's work force was dwindling. It turns out they had invested enough years to retire comfortably and weren't happy with the budget cutbacks and forecasts of things to come. Also, while salaries have now been frozen the last several years, pension benefits included cost of living increases, so those that qualified to retire were losing more money if they didn't.

I took one of the pre-retirement planning courses. I only started work with the EPA about 15 years ago and am under a different "plan" than those who'd started years earlier. I need a minimum of 5 more years to get any pension, so the earliest I could retire is at age 67. I was also a bit surprised that I'd need to be 77 before full pension benefits kick in and was majorly surprised to learn I was supposed to be saving for retirement out of my own salary. Since my government salary barely covers the mortgage alone, at the rate I'd saved, I could plan on retiring at roughly 97. Instead, I helped put three girls through college in hopes one of them will eventually take Mommy in when I finally drop dead commuting on the LIRR and subway at age 86 as I still will be working and paying off a zillion dollars in college loans.

The pre-retirement instructor for EPA was great. He was 75 and still working AFTER he retired from the Feds. He said he had enough saved but had gotten bored sitting home after 2 weeks with nothing to do but write napkin notes to his wife, so he started a consulting company and went back to work. The pre-retirement class was very informative. I learned that many Federal retirees make the mistake of moving from New York to Florida as soon as they retire.

Florida has a good state tax system and is a lot warmer in the winter than NY. Many new retirees sell their Long Island home, and immediately move to Florida to save money. This is a mistake. Since many retirees have kids and grandkids, it turns out retirees can't simply buy a one bedroom condo and bank the saving from their LI home. They have to buy a 3 bedroom condo so there are extra rooms for the kids and grandkids to stay in when they visit. Next, they have to get super cable service and internet connections, so the grandkids won't feel deprived and buy an extra refrigerator and bathroom to accommodate the company.

Since you're in Florida, the kids, grandkids, cousins, and former neighbors are all going to bless you with extensive visits at your condo and will invariably want you to take them to Disney World, Sea World, Universal Studios, and sailing. You'll also have to buy an extra car since the extended family will need local transportation too. This means a lot more has to be budgeted than you ever planned for in retirement.

Instead of Florida, retire to Wyoming! Although it's a bit chillier in winter than Florida, the tax structure is about the same and you'll save big time. You won't have to buy a 3 bedroom condo with an extra bathroom since no one you know ever wants to visit Wyoming. You won't even need cable or satellite TV since there are no TV stations in Wyoming and, best of all, your kids are going to miss you so much they'll send you a prepaid round trip ticket to visit Long Island every Christmas. You'll save a ton of money and can go fishing and hunting all you want!

CHAPTER 57

LUCKY PENNY AND ME

There is an old Greek saying that a person is never truly dead as long as someone remembers their name. When you think about it, that makes sense. There are certainly enough historic figures who live on through history books and writing and tales of their lives. Julius Caesar, born over 2,000 years ago, is still a vital force and his presence is still here, even though he was stabbed to death centuries ago. Samuel Clemens died over 100 years ago, but as Mark Twain, he will live forever through his writings and humor. When a person thinks back fondly about their deceased grandma or grandfather, those memories bring those loved ones alive again in our hearts and minds. Even if they've been gone for decades, they are still with us. Discussing long gone relatives is like a having family reunion. Many people pass on stories about their "funny" aunts or "crazy" uncles or even great grandpa's brother who was killed in the Civil War. The lives and personalities of those people are kept alive for the next generation to share and enjoy.

I think the Greek saying also extends to dogs. At least it should extend to dogs. A dog is often called Man's best friend. There's a reason for that. The dog was the first animal domesticated by Man and has been sharing our experiences on the journey through life for thousands of years. They have served a variety of invaluable purposes for people, providing protection, herding, rescue, and companionship. Through the many generations of people, a great variety of dogs has been bred and developed. Dogs come in all sorts of sizes and shapes, from Great Danes to tiny Chihuahuas. Some dogs even have a "lineage" and their own family histories are documented to show the quality of that particular breed.

Dogs provide companionship. You are never alone when you have your dog. Dogs like to be with you as much as you like being with them. They are loyal. Their needs are very simple, just some food and water daily. And shelter- if it's available, and a place to walk or run. Dogs can sleep anywhere but the shelter of a home is as welcome to a dog as it is a person. For the most part, and unlike people, dogs don't complain.

A 'family' dog is a part of the family. It's a special relationship. We name our dogs. Some are complicated names so people can proudly show off the dog's lineage. I like simple names such as Gypsy, Patsy, Lady, Hunter, Brownie, or Penny. Naming a dog is a way of recognizing the value of that dog in our own life. The dogs know this too and will come to you when you call their name. Mostly.

Dogs talk with us in a language we learn from them...if we take the time to listen. A family dog will let you know if it's hungry. The dog will tell you it needs to go "out" or whether someone is coming to the door, or if there's a danger to you. Or if it wants to play or is happy or sad. The dog will also sometimes come up to you and simply ask if you are OK, then rub its head into you and nuzzle to help make you feel better. They share our lives, watching us grow and watching us eat. For most people... and dogs alike, the bond is strong and positive. I have no tolerance for people who abuse dogs or neglect them or who are too self- centered to offer back the simple care for a dog. Those people never learned responsibility, and I suspect their attitude towards other people is the same as it is toward their dog.

A child who grows up with a dog learns some responsibility. Dogs need to be fed and walked regularly. A family dog likes to be shown affection and welcomes a pet or friendly rub. A child with a dog is never alone. Dogs like to play and run. A child with a dog always has a friend to play with. A child can talk to a dog and tell it many concerns or secrets and knows that the dog will never tell anyone else or tease you or think you are stupid. A child with a dog always has someone they can trust. A child can share a small snack with a dog, and magically the food tastes better than eating it alone. A child with a dog has someone they can easily love, and who will always love them back. A child with a dog can train that dog to do a simple trick and learns that he or she has the ability to teach. A child with a dog can experiences how a dog uses its keen senses of sight, hearing, and smell to observe things in our world that we can't even see. A child with a dog learns to learn and to be curious and observe. Dogs are great companions and teachers.

There's only one problem. Dogs age faster than humans. In a dozen short years, while a young child simply grows and matures into a young adult, a newborn and frisky playful puppy transforms into a mature adult, then into an old and gray and slower senior citizen... and then dies. A child with a dog learns that every life ends. Someday, whether you want it to or not. Life is simply a journey. For some, the journey is all too short. Especially for dogs.

I've been on my own journey for many decades. It's been interesting and I've seen and learned a lot. It's also been a bit tiring. Sometimes the path is straight, and you can see far and wide into the distance. Sometimes the path curves sharply and you can't see what's up ahead or its dark and hard to find your way forward. There are also a number of intersections and crossroads on the path and choices you have to make as to which path to take. Sometimes the path turns uphill at a steep angle and it's hard to keep going. Sometimes you can trip on a hidden object, but you get up again for some reason, and continue on.

There's always something to see along the path, and you meet a great number of people along the way. Some walk with you, some give helpful hints to ease your way along the path, and some block the path ahead. Some companions walk along the path with you a long distance, and many just cross your path a few minutes on their own journey on another path. You never know where or when the journey will end. Sometimes...well, you never even get a chance to know it is ending. And you can't ever walk back along the path…. only forward. The journey is one you have to make by yourself. Having a dog makes it a little easier. The right dog makes that part of the journey more fun. They just want to walk with you, and help you see more than you would alone.

My Dad liked dogs his whole life. There's an old framed black & white photograph in my home of a little long haired chubby young boy with a large, white dog. That was my Dad...the photo taken over a hundred years ago when he was three. I remember, long ago, when he told me the dog's name was Patsy and it was his first dog, and that Patsy was 'special'. It was many years later when I realized that my Dad had no father around by the time he was three. Maybe that was why Patsy was special. Dad had no brothers or sisters. The family was simply him, his young mom, and their dog. There's another small black and white photo of my adult Dad sitting on some porch, holding a small dog on his lap. And smiling. It wasn't Patsy, but by looking at the photo, I knew the value Patsy had given to my Dad while he was young.

I was born and raised in New York, but my dad was originally from Michigan. When I was young, we used to visit his mother and stepfather on holidays. They had a dog, Princey - a white, gentle, old collie. My grandparents were also old and gentle. Grandpa had been retired for many years, and he spent much of his time walking Princey, or sitting on a rocker on their porch, drinking a bottle of beer and rubbing Princey's head. One year, we heard that Princey had died, and the next time we went out to Michigan visit, my older sister went to an animal shelter with my dad and bought a puppy for Grandpa. It was a black and white Sheltie collie. Grandpa named her Gypsy and took her for a walk.

And, just like that, Gypsy became part of the family. About 10 years later, Grandma died, and Grandpa and Gypsy moved to NY to live with us. I was attending a nearby college by then and lived at home. My Dad had recently retired, and he and my mother spent the winter in Florida, leaving me to take care of Grandpa... and Gypsy. Both were easy to take care of. They came as a team, and even at 90, Grandpa spent a good part of his day outside walking Gypsy through the neighborhood. At night, Grandpa, Gypsy, and I sat in the den watching TV. We took turns rubbing Gypsy's back. Life was simple.

A few short years later I graduated from college and married. That year Grandpa joined my parents in Florida for the winter, and Gypsy stayed with my young wife and me at our house. I'd take Gypsy for a walk, and my wife was later surprised to learn that I knew many of the neighbors. It was simply because walking Gypsy helped me meet the other dog owners in the neighborhood and it was easy to say hello to them as our dogs said hello to each other. I knew the names of the other neighborhood dogs better than I knew the names of the neighbors. Then Grandpa's journey ended. He went peacefully and quietly. A year later, Gypsy's journey also ended. It was with her passing that I felt the true impact of the loss of Grandpa. Gypsy was the link to the time I had with shared with him.

My own family dog story is quite simple, (or maybe not so simple). I grew up with a dog. She was my dog. My Dad got married "late" in life. The family originally consisted of Dad, Mom, my big sister, me, and Tippy, a beagle. I was only 3-years-old when Tippy's journey ended. I was too young to understand but knew that everyone was sad that Tippy was gone. A few weeks later we visited my grandparents in Michigan, and when we returned to Queens, on the steps of our bungalow style was a small puppy. My sister was the first one out of the car and while I stopped to pick up a penny I'd just seen in the driveway, she saw the puppy and picked it up. My Dad and Mom were puzzled about why and where and how this little puppy showed up at our house. We brought it inside and got an old blanket, and Tippy's wooden sleep box, and placed the puppy by the fireplace. Dad checked the puppy to see if it was hurt, then fed it a bit of milk and beef.

Dad and Mom talked together a bit, and then looked at my sister and me and said, "I think we have a new family dog. It's a female. Do either of you have a name you want to give her?" I said to name her Penny, because we found her the same day that I found a penny. It's a lucky day. And that was how Penny became part of our family.

She was a simple mutt, but mostly a wire haired terrier, black and white patches on a small 18" high frame, with clear brown eyes and a few whiskers on her chin. She was about 8 weeks old when she showed up and was smart. She quickly learned to be paper trained, and then housebroken. Penny quickly learned to sit near my Dad at the dinner table, because he could give her a small bit of food without being scolded by my mother. My sister and I had to sneak the food to Penny without letting our mother catch us. She wouldn't scold us, but we'd get served an extra portion of lima beans at the next dinner.

A few weeks after Penny arrived, my Dad brought her to the vet. They returned home later that afternoon, but Penny was in bandages. I asked my dad why? He said she had been "fixed" and since she was a terrier, the Doctor had also docked her tail and trimmed her ears. I was horrified. I didn't know what "fixed" meant but asked why her tail had been cut off. Dad simply told me that was the "rules". "People are supposed to follow the rules. Some dogs are supposed to have their ears trimmed so they stand up pointed like, and get their tails shortened to about 3" so they don't get them caught in doors." I couldn't argue with my Dad.

I learned something that day. He was just following rules, but sometimes the rules aren't the right thing to follow simply because they're rules. Sometimes, it's right to question the rules and decide what to do or not to do yourself-- especially if following the rules leads to someone else getting hurt. Regardless, Penny healed quickly and looked more like what people expected a wire haired terrier to look like. She was still my dog. I was never embarrassed about how she "looked" to other people.

Penny grew out of puppyhood quickly, but always was a happy ball of energy. We were constant companions and spent two years solidly in each other's company. My mother told me how sad and quiet Penny had seemed the first day I went to kindergarten. When I got home, Penny charged to the door and nearly bowled me over as I came in. She jumped and wagged her stumpy little tail and barked and ran in circles. I spent the next hour rubbing her head and telling her that I was going to school every day but would always come home for her. And I think she understood.

Penny helped me succeed at school. As I learned to read, I'd spent the evenings reading to Penny. My first written letters weren't my own name, but the word PENNY. My teacher just smiled, and taught me other words to share with Penny-- dog, food, walk, etc. When I was eight, my family moved from Queens to Garden City. I missed my old friends, but Penny helped me make new friends quickly as I walked her around the neighborhood. She attracted the boys and girls and adults whenever I walked her, and it helped start conversations. She easily adjusted to her new sleeping area in the basement, still using Tippy's old wooden fruit crate as a bed. I slept in my own room on the main floor, but I would sometimes go down to the basement at night to make sure Penny was all right.

My mother's father, Pa Turban, then got sick, and moved in with us. Since he couldn't walk too well, Pa Turban was given my bedroom to sleep in, and my mother apologized to me that I had to sleep in the basement on a guest bed cot. I didn't complain...and I don't think my mother ever realized what a gift she had given me. For the next two years I slept in the basement and had Penny right next to me at the edge of the bed. I would spend part of the night rubbing her belly with my foot while telling her of my day at school and of the things I wanted to do when I grew up.

Pa Turban ended his own life's journey quietly one night. Penny may have been the only one that noticed, because she woke me up and was upset. She seemed to want me to do something. I couldn't figure out what she was trying to tell me, but I calmed her down and we both went back to sleep. A few days later, I moved back upstairs into my former bedroom. Maybe that's why Penny was upset. But she didn't complain and accepted it.

A couple of years later we moved again, only a few blocks away, to a smaller house. My sister had already gotten married and moved away. I had the second floor of our new house to myself, and Penny had a new sleeping spot in yet another basement. We explored the new neighborhood together and watched TV at night while I rubbed her head. She was a bit slower by now and her eyes weren't the bright clear brown they'd been when she was young. Her fur was no longer distinct patches of pure white and black but blurred with gray. It was only in the Springtime, when I'd bring her to get her annual haircut for the hot summer, that the black areas revealed themselves again. Somehow, Penny would be young again- for just little while, and she would run with me through the grass in the back yard. And I rubbed her back and we both felt happy.

A couple of more years passed. Suddenly, I was finished with High School and accepted to an engineering university. I left in early September, saying goodbye to my Mother and Dad, my sister, girlfriend, and Penny. Penny understood but seemed to be a lot slower and somewhat more tired than she'd been even that summer. I rubbed her head and told her not to worry, I'd see her at Thanksgiving.

In late October, my parents headed off for a vacation in Florida, and my sister volunteered to visit their house and take care of Penny while they were gone. I was worried about Penny being alone, but my sister said she'd be OK. Two weeks later, I made an unannounced trip home anyway...just to check. I got back to Garden City in the early evening. I opened the door to the house, but there was no friendly bark. It was quiet. Too quiet. On the kitchen table was Penny's leash, Penny's collar...and her blanket. On the floor was a simple wooden fruit crate, empty and old looking. Penny was gone.

My sister told me Penny had simply died in her sleep. She said Penny had lived a lot longer than most dogs do, but she was an old dog. Besides, she was lucky. She'd had a long and good life. I told her we were the ones who were lucky. We were the ones who had Penny. Lucky Penny. Lucky us.

CHAPTER 58

THE LAST OF MONGAUP POND AND DADDYHOOD

Over the years, I've written well over 50 stories about my experience as the 'Daddy' of my family. One of the recurring themes of my many *"Daddyhood"* stories has been about camping, hiking, and exploring nature at Mongaup Pond in northeastern Sullivan County within the NY Catskills. Briefly, this is a New York State Department of Environmental Conservation Campground. It was initially preserved in 1960 as an addition to the Catskill Forest Preserve. 1,310 acres of land, including Mongaup Pond were acquired and campground construction began in 1964. In 1966, with 65 initial campsites, the campground opened to the public. By 1968 most of the current 163 sites making up the present day campground were completed. Mongaup Pond, at 120 acres, is the largest body of water within Catskill Park, and there is a small weir or dam at the southern end where water feeds into Mongaup Creek. The state campground, three miles north of DeBruce in Sullivan County—but far from "town"—is located in the 14,800-acre Willowemoc Wild Forest, in the southwest corner of the overall Catskill Park.

Reservations for a NYS campsite are relatively easy and inexpensive to make, and Mongaup is popular-- even though it is a bit hard to get to if you are unfamiliar with the area. It's on Mongaup Road and can be found several miles off the NY Route 17 exit at Livingston Manor. (Head towards DeBruce - another small hamlet you may never have heard of.) Cell phone coverage is dismal so don't try to use a GPS download to guide you. It is only about three miles away from the Catskill Fish Hatchery on the same road, and I'd advise you to bring as much food, drink, ice, and mosquito spray as possible since it's a very long way to a food store in Livingston Manor. However, it's also worth a trek to Livingston Manor to eat at the Robin Hood Diner. My daughters and I enjoyed the tradition of eating at least one meal there each camping adventure, and the waitresses are invariably generous enough to refill my coffee thermos for me. One year, my daughters even bought me a souvenir Robin Hood Diner coffee mug.

I'll credit my sister-in-law, Claire, for suggesting Mongaup Pond as a place to go camping with my daughter, Alexis. Ali was around seven years old at the time and the eldest of our three girls. I enjoyed camping as a kid when I was a Boy Scout and I have a natural tendency to acquire dirt faster than the "Peanuts" character Pig-Pen-- who was always drawn traveling in his own dust storm. I enjoy simplicity and don't need a ton of gadgets. Claire's husband, Jim even gave me our first tent, and I still had my old Boy Scout sleeping bag and cooking gear in the basement. Camping with my daughter was reluctantly approved of by my wife, Suzie, although she quickly declined to join us. She enjoys the wildlife she can see at the Museum of Natural History and the only trail she's really comfortable on is a flat paved 2-lane street with sidewalks and art galleries. Also, she does not like bugs or snakes, and has a strong aversion to dirt.

Alexis and I had a terrific time camping -- even though it rained and thundered throughout the first night. When we awoke, it was a beautiful sunny morning. As we went for a hike, we picked up dozens and dozens of small "red efts" creeping over the wet leaves. Efts are the juvenile stage of newts, a common amphibian. We looked at the wildflowers, even saw a small snake, and visited the Fish Hatchery and fed the baby trout. We went swimming in Mongaup Pond, watched the many newts and frogs in the area, had S'mores, peanut butter sandwiches, hamburgers, and even pancakes and eggs from my small grill, and sang songs together by the campfire at night. That night was so clear we could see a zillion stars, including the Milky Way. Alexis's constant companion, "Froggie", her ever present stuffed animal, came with us, and the three of us agreed it was terrific adventure. Especially with Daddy.

After that wonderful experience, I returned to Mongaup Pond each year, sometimes twice, for a weekend with Alexis. Then I took Erin, when she turned 6 - initially by herself for a weekend with Daddy. I finally took all three of my daughters once our youngest daughter KC was old enough to go camping with Daddy. As the years went by, there were times when my sister-in-law Claire, Jim, their daughter Emily joined us. Some years my other sister-in-law, Lenore, and her daughter Kate also joined us. My supply of camping gear continued to grow as did my collection of good memories. For several years, joining us was a small herd to My Little Ponies which the girls played with among the wildflowers and trees. Sometimes the food became a little more elaborate with chili, yogurt, or Alfredo noodles, but there were always marshmallows, apples, and Doritos (one of my basic food groups).

Each camping trip included hikes, and we all learned a bit more about the trees, frogs, birds, flowers, and the other wildlife that abounds in this most precious gem of nature's beauty. We took hundreds of photos of the wildflowers and animals. We learned each spot around Mongaup Pond where we were certain to catch tadpoles, frogs, salamanders, and newts. As a scientist, I began to buy guidebooks and learned more about native plants, animals, and the impact of mankind on our natural world (which is an oxymoron, since our own species has certainly not been kind to either the environment or our fellow man.)

We learned, and began to truly appreciate, the significance a place such as Mongaup can have and what it represents as a hope for the future. Several years ago, I organized and printed a few copies of a photo book on our experiences at Mongaup Pond and gave one to each daughter as a Christmas present with a special individual note slipped inside: "You are my favorite daughter, but don't let your sisters know."

At Mongaup Pond there was always at least one new animal to see and be amused by each time we camped. Sometimes it was a simple chipmunk which would dart back and forth eating pieces of the marshmallows we'd placed strategically to get a good photo. Another time a young one-eyed deer walked up to many of the campsites for a much needed handout. There were always frogs, and during the late spring evenings near our campsite on the F - Loop, bordering a small swamp, the night was filled with the croaking and mating calls of thousands of Spring Peepers. I knew where we could find tadpoles of gray tree-frogs in a small culvert. On some camping trips we encountered some baby ducklings and their mom nestled on the ground next to our lakeside campsite. One evening, the mommy duck walked them right to our chairs as we sat by the campfire, and had her babies rest safely near us. Once, Alexis and I saw a black bear come out of the woods across the pond and walk down to the water's edge for a drink of water. Yes, we got a photograph, but from a safe distance across the water.

Part of the "adventure" of camping was the actual car ride itself. Radio service sort of peters out as you travel along Route 17 westward from NYS Thruway Exit 16 at Harriman. Knowing my fondness for "The Muppets", the girls would spend time with me singing Muppet hits and listening to a cassette tape of songs from the show. We'd also make a stop at "Memories" a classic, expansive thrift and collectibles store on Route 17 where invariably we'd find something we just "had to have". Sadly, both cassette tapes and Memories are a thing of the past, and more and more of Route 17 has widened and expanded, eliminating the occasional traffic lights, small towns and gas stations where it was good to take a short break and buy ice cream.

For many years, my typical suburban family had a minivan as our primary vehicle. These are the perfect cars for Mongaup Pond camping trips. The rear seats could be left at home, and the back of the van was just wide enough for me to place my double sized air mattress into and sleep comfortably if my snoring woke up the girls in our tent...or it rained. One year, we finally realized we needed a new tent after a hard rain that lasted all night long. The tent was old, and by now, very leaky. The water came "in", but it didn't go "out" since the floor of the tent was a vinyl layer connected to the tent. The rain filled up the floor to the point where our air-mattress was floating, while our knapsacks and spare clothes simply 'gave up the ghost' and submerged.

As the girls matured, each of them developed their own love and interest in continuing nature-related studies. Alexis certainly developed an interest in trees and native plants. After high school she earned a degree from Cornell University and then was awarded a full scholarship from Virginia Tech. earning an MS in Urban Forestry. She became a Certified Arborist and after several years work and publications on native plants, is continuing at Florida International University towards a Landscape Architecture degree.

Meanwhile, Erin- my middle daughter, initially a music major at Ithaca College, received her Bachelor's degree in Photography with a minor in Natural Science. Erin also loved camping with Daddy and shared my interest in seeing birds as well as frogs. She showed me the value of her musically inclined ear when we went for hikes at Mongaup. She could tell me the names of each of the bird species we heard calling in the trees.

She recognized them all since she had studied bird calls. I remember walking with her many times at Mongaup as she repeatedly asked me what the name of this plant or that tree was. I, in turn, would ask her the name of a bird we heard.

Erin eventually left our Long Island home and spent a year or more backpacking and working her way through the West, including a three-month stint on an unoccupied volcano in the Aleutian Islands on a birding assignment. Her favorite book was *"Into the Wild"* a true story about a young man who went to Alaska to live off the land by himself, and his story ended sadly when his starved and frozen body was found. I remember shuddering to myself when she explained she knew what he had done wrong, (he apparently ate some "bad" plants) and she was going to give it a try herself. She did fall off a cliff once and broke her arm, but she's a tough soul in many respects. There are times I worry whether I should have introduced her to camping and hiking…but I figure she could survive, and I could be with her in spirit even if not there physically.

K.C., our youngest, joined the camping trips with the other girls as she grew up, and would even take the bus from Cornell University to meet up with me and one or more of her sisters near Mongaup while she was at college. All the girls were involved with a program at their colleges as hiking guides for incoming freshmen at camping adventures in the Adirondacks.

Back in 2010, Alexis and K.C. joined me at Mongaup to celebrate Father's Day for a "weekend with Daddy". I recall them giving me Mark Twain books (I was slowly morphing into an elderly version of Mark Twain around that time, but that's another series of stories), a huge S'mores maker, and a bag of Doritos. These were the perfectly unique gifts for their dad. We spent a wonderful weekend hiking and visiting Frick Pond and even Hodge Pond and other ponds along the many trails.

375

Time does fly by. Over the years, Alexis and I probably hiked around Mongaup Pond the most. We'd even used our bicycles along the trails, visiting Wagon Wheel Junction, even finding Beech Lake, the remains of a former Boy Scout camp that had closed and become part of Catskill Park in the 1960s. I have a wonderful photo of her by a tree at Mongaup Pond from several years ago, and a near matching one of me in front of her at the same spot. The young girls have all become adults, and have moved on to other, newer adventures far away. Mongaup Pond seemed a place I could go and relax and enjoy knowing it was 'still there'.

A few years ago, I was mentoring a local Boy Scout who was building a small amphibian pond at a local nature sanctuary I'd started in my hometown on Long Island. He needed some frogs and newts to stock it, and I volunteered to use my annual trip to Mongaup Pond to net a few for him. I left for the weekend with my trusty net, plastic tanks, Doritos, a bit of camping gear, 24 Snickers bars and my thermos of coffee. I arrived at Mongaup Pond and pulled into my favorite camping spot by the swamp but was surprised it was completely dry and quiet. The rest of the weekend, I went to each of my normal frog spotting areas, but neither saw, nor heard, any frogs or even newts in the entire body of water. I carefully checked other areas but didn't even see any toads on the trails along the way. The entire Mongaup Pond amphibian population was missing!! I was mystified.

While I eventually found a few tadpoles and newts at another pond on the way back to Long Island, I began some research and made some inquiries. Apparently, the frog population around the world is undergoing a significant decline and extinctions of some species have been reported. Had Mongaup Pond been affected? It seemed so. My initial discussions with US Fish & Wildlife and US Geological Survey were not promising, as I'm known as a geologist, not a herpetologist or an ecological biologist. One reply I received during my first call was that most likely I'd just missed seeing them. The expert then suggested I collect a few specimens, so they conduct laboratory tests just in case. I explained that I'd been at Mongaup for nearly 30 years and certainly knew where to find a frog. There simply weren't any. The scientist then suggested their disappearance might be from a virus. A virus was spreading that kills all frogs, except bullfrogs which are the carriers. He mentioned there had been a report of a similar sudden eradication of frogs in Ulster County and asked if I knew where that was in New York. He seemed a bit more interested in my report when I said Ulster County was adjacent to Sullivan County.

My observations and concerns lead to more research. I learned a few things about bullfrogs. They are big and one of the most aggressive frogs in the Northeast and are also raised specifically for schools and the home pond trade. That means millions have been shipped across the country and overseas. Somehow, a virus was introduced and spread, with bullfrogs as the main carriers. It doesn't kill them, but spreads to other species which kills those species off. That didn't explain why there was such a drop off in the number of newts since the virus wasn't known to transmit to other types of amphibians. I then found reports of an amphibian fungus that has also been spreading worldwide. That would explain the loss of both the bullfrogs in addition to the newts.

One additional lead came up when I found information on a field studies site associated with Montclair University in New Jersey. A professor from the college had published a few recent articles on frogs, and I called her and asked if she'd noticed anything unusual regarding the frog population at the pond at their field site. She replied that they'd also seen that suddenly all the frogs had disappeared but hadn't even had time to report it. A bit of triangulation on a map revealed that all three sites were within 90 miles of each other.

I went back up to Mongaup Pond the next year with my net and containers, even walking to nearby Frick Pond, but also came back empty handed without frogs or newts. Finally, in 2016, I made two reservations at Mongaup, one in May and another in July. My daughter, KC heard of my plans and volunteered to join me in May. Ironically, it was the first time she had the opportunity to camp at Mongaup with me by herself. She'd always been there with one or both of her older sisters, and never had the opportunity to have exclusive "Daddy time". The trip was certainly memorable.

We packed up the old minivan with our equipment and set off on a Friday afternoon. I'd wanted to take our newer, more reliable car, but Suzie said no. Suzie knew from my previous experiences at Mongaup and she didn't want the car to come back home smelling like a swamp. Unfortunately, the old minivan was on its last legs with nearly 200,000 accumulated miles on the engine, no functional heat or air conditioning, a missing rear seat, and enough dents and dings on its fourteen- year- old body that I could leave it running with the keys in it in Brooklyn and no one would bother stealing it. We drove slowly as it had been mysteriously overheating recently and been towed and repaired enough times to tax my wallet and patience.

KC and I arrived in Livingston Manor without incident, and bought a ton of food, some ice, beer and some firewood, then drove the last leg to Mongaup Pond, checked in, and drove to our campsite just before dark. Bingo! Even as we approached, we could hear the mating calls of hundreds of Spring Peepers, a tiny native frog with a big voice, calling from the swamp behind our campsite. I could also detect an occasional "grunt" of another frog species, and when I walked down to the shore of the swamp, saw two newts idly basking in the silty water. Life!

We were also surprised that there was an extensive ten-foot-long pile of cut firewood carefully stacked by the fire pit and learned that the rangers did that as a courtesy over the winter as they trimmed trees and did maintenance. It was still the beginning of camping season, and many campsites had stacks of wood available. We lit a fire, set up the tent, cooked and ate dinner, and relaxed with a beer and some S'mores, looking forward to a fun weekend together.

The next morning, however, when we got in the minivan and turned the ignition key…we got no response. The car was completely dead. It had died in its sleep. There wasn't even any power to open the electric windows or use the electronic door locks. We were stuck. KC used her cell phone and called Mommy to tell her the bad news…and ask that she make plans to drive up to Mongaup and bring us home on Sunday. Fortunately, we had plenty of food, beer and firewood. We couldn't drive anywhere and let the Park Ranger know we'd get the car towed out Sunday after we got to a nearby town. He was very understanding.

KC and I spent the day hiking and searching for frogs and newts. There weren't a lot, and the ones we saw were mainly by the swamp area. We enjoyed the walks and talking to other campers who noticed us with our nets. Every year at Mongaup brings a new discovery. This year, we came across a dead tree that had had part of the trunk physically gouged out six inches deep in a long line by some animal. The width was about the size of a bear's front claw. I was a bit worried whether the bear had found enough insects in the tree…or might still be hungry enough to be tempted to eat us two campers in the woods.

We came across the remains of an old beaver dam along a stream feeding to Mongaup Pond. It had been partially removed by the State as it had blocked water flow towards the swamp area – a reason the swamp area at Mongaup had been drying up over the last several years. We also came across a bog area what seemed filled with gelatinous egg cases – not any toad or frog egg that I recognized, and we wondered if they were salamander spawn or perhaps leeches. We enjoyed our day together as well as that night with another campfire dinner and slept well with the sounds of the Spring Peepers in the background.

379

Suzie arrived Sunday afternoon with our rescue car, and we emptied the minivan completely and drove back to Livingston Manor. Unfortunately, I found out there were no local tow trucks and no repair facilities anywhere. We drove back home to Long Island and on Monday, I was finally able to contact a tow service in a larger town near Mongaup - Roscoe, New York and planned to have the service agency tow the minivan. We donated it to a Roscoe based children's medical fund charity. Goodbye minivan, RIP. They advised to me mail my title and keys to the Mongaup Pond Ranger and they would take care of everything else. Our minivan era of the last 30 years sadly came to an end similar to my youthful days with Ford Mustangs that ended soon after we had our first child. Time rolls on.

In July I returned to Mongaup by myself driving our newer and more reliable car. This time, however, there were no "peeps" from any Spring Peepers near the swamp, and I saw no amphibians at all anywhere at Mongaup Pond. I was more than a bit depressed. I hiked to nearby Frick Pond (about two miles away) and, while I didn't see any frogs, at least I saw some newts swimming in that water. I turned back and then hiked to Hodge Pond another two miles way according to the trail signs.

It was during that second hike when it dawned on me that I was no longer an enthusiastic young Daddy, or even a middle aged man. I am merely...old!?!!! (depending on your perspective) and not in good physical condition anymore...sort of similar to our old minivan which by now has probably been crushed and recycled into 2,000 aluminum cans. I knew I'd been 'sputtering' a few times during that hike, but those last four miles to and from Hodge Pond seemed to be uphill both ways. As a geologist, I started wondering if I was experiencing a sudden shift in the continental plate which caused everything to be uphill. My legs and feet felt as if they weighed 200 pounds...each. Sadly, when I finally reached Hodge Pond, I only saw a few large tadpoles...bloated and floating dead in the otherwise clear water. No newts at all, and only the dried mummified remains of a large toad lying in the nearby field. I did find a few tadpoles in a small tributary feeding Hodge Pond. On the grass, however, was the dried out corpse of a large toad. It was totally desiccated, but in otherwise perfect condition. I felt sad, and wondered why not even one predator, whether a raccoon, bird, or insect had bothered to try to eat it and recycle the nutrients.

Frankly, I don't consider dead toad as one of my own basic food groups. Nope! I'll stick with caffeine, nicotine, and Doritos. Hodge Pond was not at all as alive as I'd remembered it when hiking there with Alexis many years ago. My heart was crushed. I started the long walk back towards my car. As I was leaving a group of young men carrying fishing rods passed me. They were also leaving Hodge Pond. I said hello and asked how the fishing was. The guys complained that they'd caught no fish, and had been at Hodge Pond several times before, with usually much better luck. When I asked if they'd noticed any dead frogs or tadpoles, one of the fishermen mentioned that he'd noticed quite a number of dead tadpoles floating near the shore where they were fishing. They passed me by and headed for Frick Pond. I wished them luck.

I met with other people on the trail more frequently than I expected. One young group passed me as they headed for Hodge Pond. Later, I saw a second group of people headed towards the pond but being followed by what I first thought was a polar bear on the prowl. "No," I thought, "It's a bit smaller than a bear...perhaps it's a white fox?" Still too small. I suddenly realized it was Lambchop, the famous Shari Lewis hand puppet! It was even wearing a bright red ribbon collar and smiling. Wrong again. It was a dog.... sort of, and I think Lambchop was bigger and actually fiercer. The little white dog was about six inches high and valiantly trying to keep up with the hikers. It kept tripping over the grass and appeared to be concerned that it was going to ruin its toenail polish. The dog also apparently had never been outside an apartment in its life. As the little dog passed me, I could see it wasn't actually smiling. Its mouth was wide open in a silent scream! The little dog's eyes looked at me pleadingly, trying to beg me to either step on it and put it out of its misery, or simply pick it up and carry it back indoors where it really belonged-- somewhere, anywhere but outdoors in the wild.

I kept walking. Later, I passed another group of hikers who were simply out for a walk in the woods. They were recent retirees from Michigan. I waved them on and told them to be on the lookout for a white, wild dog that was reported to be stalking hikers. I didn't ask them if they'd walked all the way from Michigan. I assumed it might have been easy for them if the continental plate really had shifted suddenly. Even later, the first group that had passed me going towards Hodge Pond caught up with me again while on their way back to their cars. I asked them if they'd seen a white miniature polar bear or hand puppet following another group. The hikers laughed and said yes, and that the little dog was being carried by one of the hikers in that other group.

After what seemed a three day hike up Mount Kilimanjaro, I made it back to my car and drove to my camping spot at Mongaup. I didn't bother lighting a campfire. I didn't make S'mores. I simply ate a cup of yogurt, an apple and a salad…then looked once more at Mongaup Pond and sighed. It was still. As soon as it was dark, I went into the tent and tried to go to sleep. It was still too quiet. I couldn't get to sleep at all. Around midnight I gave up. I dressed, rolled up my sleeping bag, took down the tent, threw everything into my car and drove the three hour ride home back to Long Island. My wife was surprised but understood and I only had to say one word, "Nothing."

That wasn't actually the last of Mongaup Pond and I hope it's not the last of the frogs and amphibians. In September, I had to drive to Binghamton for a public meeting on a Superfund Site. I found myself on Route 17 and took a short detour at Livingston Manor and drove to Mongaup. I identified myself at the entrance gate and said I wasn't going camping, but merely wanted an opportunity to take a brief look at a couple of places. The attendant called the park supervisor, and both readily approved my request. I drove over to where the tributary from the old beaver dam passed through a culvert at Mongaup Pond and fed into the lake.

I parked on the grass, got out of the car and stood watching carefully at the water as it flowed towards the swamp area. No newts. No frogs. Another vehicle pulled up and the driver asked if I was Mr. Avery. "Close enough, my name's Rob Alvey" I replied. He was the park supervisor, Jesse. We talked for a while, with me explaining I'd been camping at Mongaup Pond for decades and that I was investigating why all the frogs and newts had disappeared. Jessie said he'd been supervisor at Mongaup for the last seven years, and had also noticed the decline, especially the last couple of years. He noted that he doesn't even see any roadkill anymore. I told him about my recent trip to nearby Hodge Pond where I'd seen mostly dead tadpoles, and Jesse commented that he recalled noticing something odd the previous spring when he noticed hundreds of dead newts lining the Hodge Pond shore.

Jesse lives in the area, and even has a couple of ponds on his own property. He said that there were plenty of frogs in his ponds and wondered why they left Mongaup. I told him that there appeared to be a one-two punch of a virus and a fungus spreading and I thought that might be the cause. His first concern was "What about the fish?" which was logical since this region is well- known as a trout fisherman's paradise. If fish were affected, it would really harm the local economy. I thought about that and what little I'd learned about the virus and fungus. I shared my best guess that the virus and fungus were pretty specific and shouldn't transfer to fish or reptiles or mammals. We also agreed I could pass on his name as a contact if I could get in touch with the right agency doing research on the amphibians. Jesse added one more comment. "Rob, I was the person who called you about your old van when you got stuck back in May. When I got the keys that you mailed to Mongaup, I was able to start the minivan up without any problem. I drove it to the gate so the tow truck operator could have an easy time towing it away."

We both laughed. We both agreed there had to be some sort of electrical problem with that van and were glad it was being put to good use for the children's hospital. I thanked him again and drove off to my meeting. As I passed nearby Roscoe, I made one more stop. First, I bought a case of the new Roscoe Trout Town Ale – a new microbrewery that had opened. Then I took a short walk along the shore of a nearby pond adjacent to the road. Within fifteen minutes, I'd seen over nine frogs, and spotted at least two newts hiding amidst the lily pads. I knew I'd return again someday. It's too beautiful a place to ignore. That is why I love the Catskills, and why I enjoy being a Daddy.